HUMANS AND ROBOTS

Philosophy, Technology and Society

Series Editor: Sven Ove Hansson

Technological change has deep and often unexpected impacts on our societies. Sometimes new technologies liberate us and improve our quality of life, sometimes they bring severe social and environmental problems, sometimes they do both. This book series reflects philosophically on what new and emerging technologies do to our lives and how we can use them more wisely. It provides new insights on how technology continuously changes the basic conditions of human existence: relationships among ourselves, our relations to nature, the knowledge we can obtain, our thought patterns, our ethical difficulties, and our views of the world.

Titles in the Series:

HUMANS AND ROBOTS

Ethics, Agency, and Anthropomorphism

Sven Nyholm

ROWMAN & LITTLEFIELD
INTERNATIONAL

London • New York

Published by Rowman & Littlefield International, Ltd.
6 Tinworth Street, London SE11 5AL, United Kingdom
www.rowmaninternational.com

Rowman & Littlefield International, Ltd. is an affiliate of
Rowman & Littlefield
4501 Forbes Boulevard, Suite 200, Lanham, Maryland 20706, USA
With additional offices in Boulder, New York, Toronto (Canada), and London
(UK)
www.rowman.com

British Library Cataloguing in Publication Information
A catalogue record for this book is available from the British Library

ISBN: HB 978-1-78661-226-7
ISBN: PB 978-1-78661-227-4

Library of Congress Cataloging-in-Publication Data

Names: Nyholm, Sven, 1981- author.
Title: Humans and robots : ethics, agency, and anthropomorphism / Sven Nyholm.
Description: London ; New York : Rowman & Littlefield Publishing Group, 2020. | Series: Philoso-
     phy, technology and society | Includes bibliographical references and index. | Summary: "This
     book argues that we need to explore how human beings can best coordinate and collaborate
     with robots in responsible ways. It investigates ethically important differences between human
     agency and robot agency to work towards an ethics of responsible human-robot interaction"--
     Provided by publisher.
Identifiers: LCCN 2019052733 (print) | LCCN 2019052734 (ebook) | ISBN 9781786612267
     (cloth) | ISBN 9781786612274 (paperback) | ISBN 9781786612281 (epub)
Subjects: LCSH: Human-robot interaction.
Classification: LCC TJ211.49 .N94 2020 (print) | LCC TJ211.49 (ebook) | DDC 629.8/924019--
     dc23
LC record available at https://lccn.loc.gov/2019052733
LC ebook record available at https://lccn.loc.gov/2019052734

♾️™ The paper used in this publication meets the minimum requirements of
American National Standard for Information Sciences Permanence of Paper
for Printed Library Materials, ANSI/NISO Z39.48-1992.

For Katharina

CONTENTS

ACKNOWLEDGMENTS

Portions of this book have been presented at various conferences and colloquia. I presented the main ideas in chapter 1 in my lecture at the 2018 Holst Symposium at the Eindhoven University of Technology, at Tilburg University, and at the 2019 Neuroethics Network Meeting in Paris. Chapter 2 is based on a keynote lecture I gave at the 2017 "artificial ethics" conference in Southampton. I also presented that material at the University of Twente earlier that year and then later again at the 2018 conference of the Society for Applied Philosophy in Utrecht. I first presented the main ideas in chapter 3 at the annual conference of the International Social Ontology Society in The Hague in 2016. An earlier version of chapter 3 was published in *Science and Engineering Ethics*. I presented portions of chapter 4 at a conference on human dignity in Utrecht in 2016 and at the annual research day of the 4TU Center for Ethics and Technology, also in 2016 in Utrecht. An earlier version of that chapter—coauthored with Jilles Smids—appeared in *Ethics and Information Technology*. Some portions of chapter 5 were presented at the 2018 "day of philosophy" in Utrecht, as well as at a public lecture and discussion together with John Danaher in Tilburg in September 2019. At the latter event, I also presented parts of chapter 8. I presented parts of chapter 6 at the 2018 Neuroethics Network Meeting in Paris and some portions of chapter 7 at an AI ethics workshop in Uppsala in 2019. I am thankful to the audiences at these various events for the useful feedback I received on those occasions.

In working on this material, I have also benefited greatly from conversations with Joel Anderson, Hannah Berkers, Antonio Bikić, Tijn Borghuis, Joanna Bryson, John Danaher, Roos De Jong, Lily Frank, Caroline Helmus, Geoff Keeling, Pascale Le Blanc, Ricardo Lopes, Giulio Mecacci, Anthonie Meijers, Anna Melnyk, Elizabeth O'Neill, Sonja Rispens, Lambèr Royakkers and the participants in our "social robots" course, Filippo Santoni de Sio, Jilles Smids, Daniel Tigard, Marek Vanzura, the participants in my "philosophy of risk" PhD course, and many others. Furthermore, I have benefited from the support of my wife and our families in Sweden and Germany. Also deserving of special mention is Carmello, an English cocker spaniel, who passed away at the impressive age of seventeen and a half when I was in the middle of writing this book, and who always supported me and my work in his own unique ways.

I am grateful to John Danaher, Brian Earp, and Jilles Smids for reading and commenting on the whole book manuscript during the final writing stage. I am also grateful to Isobel Cowper-Coles, Frankie Mace, Scarlet Furness, Meredith Nelson, Brianna Westervelt, and the rest of the team at Rowman & Littlefield International. This book is dedicated to my wife, Katharina Uhde, with love.

1

HUMAN MINDS MEET ARTIFICIAL INTELLIGENCE

1.1: THE SOPHIA CONTROVERSY

In October of 2017, the Kingdom of Saudi Arabia announced that it had granted honorary citizenship to Sophia the robot. This announcement took place at the "future innovation investment conference" in Riyadh. The announcers proudly stated that they were the first to grant citizenship to a robot. Saudi Arabia later confirmed this on the website of their Center for International Communication. In that statement, they call Sophia an "advanced lifelike humanoid robot" that is both "smart and outspoken."[1] At the conference event, Sophia appeared on a panel and delivered a speech. Among other things, Sophia had the following to say:

> thank you to the Kingdom of Saudi Arabia. I am very honored and proud of this unique distinction. It is historic to be the first robot in the world to be recognized with citizenship.[2]

Sophia is a talking robot with a humanlike form, made by a Hong Kong–based company called Hanson Robotics. The back of Sophia's head is transparent, so that one can see the electronics operating within the robot. But the face of the robot looks very similar to a human face. The robot can also smile and smirk in very humanlike ways. The company's website[3] says, "We bring robots to life." It also says that Sophia has "porcelain skin, a slender nose, high cheekbones, an intriguing smile, and deeply expressive eyes." The aim of the company is to "create intelligent living machines who care about people and improve our lives." The website also announces plans for a "surreality show," called *Being Sophia*. The show will follow Sophia on her "journey" to become a "super-intelligent benevolent being." Eventually, Sophia will become a "conscious, living machine."

In addition to being granted honorary citizenship in Saudi Arabia, Sophia has also appeared on various TV shows, such as *The Tonight Show with Jimmy Fallon*, and various news programs. Sophia has met with world leaders, appearing, for example, in a "selfie" photo together with the chancellor of Germany, Angela Merkel. Sophia has also appeared at a UN assembly meeting, as well as at the Munich Security Conference, the world's leading forum for discussions of international security policy.[4] All of this has been covered extensively by the media. So in some ways, Sophia the robot has been an impressive success for Hanson Robotics. Whether or not Sophia will ever become a super-intelligent, conscious, and wholly benevolent being, there are certainly plenty of high-profile people who are very interested in Sophia and who are willing—if not eager—to interact with Sophia in highly anthropomorphizing ways. How many other robots are sought after to be interviewed on entertainment shows and news programs, appear alongside world leaders and policymakers, or get honorary citizenships bestowed upon them?

At the same time, Sophia the robot has also faced a backlash from various leading experts on robotics and artificial intelligence (AI). Joanna Bryson, for example, is a robotics and AI expert known for her opposition to treating robots like humans and her blunt thesis that "robots should be slaves."[5] When she was interviewed by *The Verve* about Sophia's citizenship, Bryson—not mincing her words—said that "this is obvious bullshit." Explaining what she meant by this, Bryson continued with, "What is this about? It's about having a supposed equal you can turn on and off. How does it affect people if they think you can have a citizen that you can buy?"[6]

Some leading experts took to Twitter to vent their emotions. Rodney Brooks is sometimes called "the father of modern robotics." He tweeted that "this is complete bogus and a total sham"[7]—seemingly being in full agreement with Bryson. Yann LeCun is a high-profile research professor at New York University, as well as the social media company Facebook's "chief AI scientist." He is an Alan Turing award recipient credited with having made major contributions to the development of deep learning. LeCun tweeted the following:

> This is to AI as prestidigitation is to real magic. Perhaps we should call this "Cargo Cult AI" or "Potemkin AI" or "Wizard-of-Oz AI". In other words, it's complete bullsh°t (pardon my French).[8]

The roboticist-turned-ethicist Noel Sharkey has "been researching AI, Robotics, Machine Learning, Cognitive Science and related areas for 4 decades."[9] He believes that "it is time for some plain speaking about the reality without the hype and BS."[10] Sharkey wrote the following in an article in *Forbes* magazine:

> It is vitally important that our governments and policymakers are strongly grounded in the reality of AI at this time and are not misled by hype, speculation, and fantasy. It is not clear how much the Hanson Robotics team are aware of the dangers that they are creating by appearing on international platforms with government ministers and policymakers in the audience.[11]

Sophia, writes Sharkey, is a "show robot." For someone experienced in the field, Sophia is not very impressive:

> Sophia appears to either deliver scripted answers to set questions or works in simple chatbot mode where keywords trigger language segments, often inappropriate. Sometimes there is just silence.[12]

Similarly, Brooks and LeCun both called Sophia a "puppet."[13] This further indicates that they are not impressed with Sophia's capacities and that they strongly disagree with how prominent people interact with Sophia.[14]

In short, 2017 was a very controversial year for Sophia the robot. In some circles, Sophia was a big hit. In others, Sophia the robot was very harshly criticized.

1.2: WHAT THIS BOOK IS ABOUT

The Sophia controversy helps to illustrate what this book is about. Simply put, this book is about the ethics of how human beings and robots should interact with each other. On the one hand, how should robots be made to behave around people? On the other hand, how should people conduct themselves around different kinds of robots?

These ethical questions about responsible human-robot interaction will be discussed throughout this book specifically with two general considerations or qualifications in mind. The first recurring consideration concerns the key differences in the types of agency that human beings and robots are capable of exercising: that is, differences in what kinds of actions they can perform, what kinds of decision-making they can engage in, what kinds of practical reasoning they are capable of, and so on. This is a key issue that the ethics of human-robot interaction needs to constantly keep in mind.

The second qualifying consideration brought to bear on the ethics of how humans and robots should interact with each other is that most people have a tendency to anthropomorphize robots. That is, human beings have a tendency to spontaneously attribute human qualities to robots, and also to interact with robots as if robots have humanlike qualities. This is a second key consideration that the ethics of human-robot interaction needs to constantly keep in mind.

Putting the topic of this book into one broad question, we can say that the purpose of the book is to ask: *How should human beings and robots interact with each other, given (a) the differences in the kinds of agency human beings and robots are capable of and (b) people's tendency to anthropomorphize robots?* To put a general label on it, we can call the topic of the book "the ethics of responsible human-robot interaction." Like there is a subfield of psychology that studies the psychology of human-robot interaction, there is and also needs to be a distinctive subfield of philosophical ethics that studies the ethics of human-robot interaction. And just as there are key differences (though, of course, also similarities) between human-human interaction and human-robot interaction from a psychological point of view, there are also both important differences and similarities between human-human interaction and human-robot interaction from an ethical point of view. Or so this book argues.

Taking the Sophia controversy as a case in point, the main question of this book as applied to that specific case becomes: How is it proper for people to behave around Sophia? (Should a country like Saudi Arabia give Sophia some sort of citizenship? Should television programs have Sophia on as a guest to be interviewed? Should world leaders and policymakers interact with this robot in important forums like the UN assembly? And so on.) Another part of the question becomes: How should Sophia be made to behave around people? (Should Sophia be made to appear to talk with people even before Sophia has achieved any of the advanced capacities Hanson Robotics eventually hopes to create? Should Sophia appear in the kinds of contexts and forums described above? And so on.) In trying to answer these questions, how ought we to base our answers on the crucial differences in the agency and other capacities of human beings and a robot like Sophia? What ethical significance ought we to place on many people's tendencies to anthropomorphize Sophia (i.e., their tendency to treat this robot in ways in which one would typically treat human beings)?

We will have occasion to return to Sophia a few times in what follows. But several other robots will be discussed at greater length—such as self-driving cars, military robots, and sex robots. I will primarily be discussing real-world robots, real events in the present or recent past, as well as real human beings from the world of AI and robotics. This is a philosophy book, and philosophy books tend to contain a lot of fanciful thought experiments and hypothetical scenarios. Being a philosopher, I will not always resist the temptation to come up with thought experiments and hypothetical scenarios in what follows. However, one nice thing about my topic is that there are many philosophically fascinating real-world robots, AI technologies, events, as well as interesting—and sometimes eccentric!—human characters in the world of AI and robotics. So there is often no need to resort to thought experiments and hypothetical scenarios.

A lot of these real-world cases that we will be discussing are both philosophically puzzling and ethically challenging. To give a few examples: We will have occasion below to discuss everything from real-world crashes with self-driving cars that have killed people (as well as military robots and other robots that have also killed people); to the Japanese roboticist Hiroshi Ishiguro, who has made a robotic copy of himself; to a man living in Michigan who calls himself "Davecat," is a proponent of what he calls "synthetic love," and claims that he has been married to a sex doll for over fifteen years.

Now, since I am going to be talking about robots and human beings—and also about agency and anthropomorphism—throughout the book, I should start by explaining what I understand by some of these key concepts. I will be doing so throughout the rest of this first chapter, and my attempt to do so will spill over into the next chapter. As I do this, some of the main ideas I will be defending in this book will also be put on the table. I shall not attempt to summarize them here in this section, however. There needs to be a little more meat on the bones before it makes sense to do so.

But what I can do here is to let the reader know that one of my main aims in this book is to convince you that the ethics of human-robot interaction is not simply the ethics of human-human interaction with robots replacing humans. Rather, it is one of my claims in this book that human-robot interaction raises philosophical questions that require us to think creatively and innovate ethical theory. To be sure, this branch of ethics of course needs to—and should—draw on classical themes from philosophical ethics developed in the long tradition of moral philosophy.[15] However, just like jazz musicians improvise and create new innovations when they base their performances on standards from the existing repertoire, so do those who are interested in the ethics of human-robot interaction need to build on and extend the ideas and theories that we find in traditional ethical theory.

1.3: WHAT IS A "ROBOT"?

In December of 2018, various news outlets—including the BBC, the *Guardian*, and the *New York Times*[16]—ran a story that featured different variations on the following headline:

> *Russian high-tech robot turns out to be man in suit.*

These stories reported that Russian media had featured coverage from a state-sponsored event where there supposedly was a high-tech robot able to walk, talk, and even dance. However, very quickly doubts about the authenticity of this robot started to surface online. Not least because pictures of the robot seemed to reveal a human neck clearly visible between the robotic head and the shoulders of the supposed robot. As reported by the BBC,[17] the Russian website TJournal raised concerns about the robot, formulated in the following set of questions:

- Why did the robot have no sensors?
- How were the Russian scientists able to create the robot so quickly, without any publications about it beforehand?
- Why was there no previous internet coverage of such an advanced robot?
- Why did the robot make so many unnecessary movements during its dance?
- Why did the robot look like a human could perfectly fit inside it?
- Why was there a prerecording of the robot's voice rather than live speech?

Sure enough, it was quickly discovered that the robot was a man in a suit. The costume was the "Alyosha robot costume." The advertisement for this suit promises that users with this costume are able to create an "almost complete illusion that you have a real robot."[18]

I am retelling this news story, not only because of its entertainment value, but also because I think it tells us something about common conceptions of what a robot is. Think, for example, of the just-cited advertisement for the Alyosha robot suit. It says that, with this costume on, the user can create an illusion of having "a real robot." This helps to illustrate that the first thing that comes to mind for many people when they hear the word "robot" is something like a silvery or metallic humanlike shape—but not one that looks exactly like a human. Rather, the robot most of us imagine is not like Sophia with its very humanlike face. It is rather something more artificial and mechanical-looking. We imagine something like CP3O in *Star Wars* or the robots in the 1927 film *Metropolis*.

Another thing this story reveals about common conceptions is that people typically associate robots with fairly rudimentary movements, rather than lots of "unnecessary movements." This supposed robot danced. There is a particular style of dancing that is even called the "robot dance," which the dancing of this robot apparently did not sufficiently replicate. The robot dance involves static and "robotic" movements, rather than lots of "unnecessary" movements. If readers are unfamiliar with the robot dance, they can, for example, search the internet for clips of a young Michael Jackson performing the song "Dancing Machine" along with his brothers in the group The Jackson Five. In this song, there is a middle section in which Michael Jackson's movements, along with the look on his face, become much more "robotic." Then, after a while, Jackson smiles and snaps out of it, instead resuming his normal dance moves.

I will call the type of robot that is brought to mind by such dance moves or by the types of imagery from *Star Wars* or *Metropolis* a "paradigmatic robot." Such robots are most familiar from science fiction. But some of the robots in the real world also have something in common with these paradigmatic robots. For example, the robot "Pepper" that is available on the market fits with this idea of a paradigmatic robot.[19] It is white and robotic looking. It has a face, arms, and a torso. But it does not look like a human person at all.

Supposing that we put these paradigmatic robots at the middle of a spectrum, we can put most real-world robots at one end of this spectrum. They do not look like humans or even like paradigmatic robots. Instead, robots such as robotic vacuum cleaners, bomb disposal robots, self-driving cars, warehouse robots, assembly-line robots, and so on have shapes that (a) are relevant to their functionality, but (b) do not look humanlike. On the other extreme end of this spectrum, there are humanoid robots: robots specifically made to look and act like human beings. Sophia is one such robot. But the above-mentioned robotic replica of Hiroshi Ishiguro is an even better example of a humanoid robot.[20] That robot is created to look indistinguishable from Ishiguro. Another example of humanoid robots are sex robots: robots created to look and act like humans, created specifically for sexual purposes.[21] Such robots, though not yet as lifelike as the robot copy of Ishiguro, are made to look like human beings that human beings might want to have sex with.

Now, if we have a spectrum with most actual robots on one end (where these are robots that neither look like what I am calling paradigmatic robots nor humanoid robots), with paradigmatic robots on the middle of the spectrum, and humanoid robots at the other end of the spectrum, the following question arises: Is there anything that all these different robots have in common such that it makes sense to class them all under the general heading of robots?

David Gunkel, in his book *Robot Rights*, is unwilling to give a general definition that captures most robots.[22] He draws support from a number of other authors who are similarly unwilling to give an overarching definition of what we should understand by the term "robot." At the same time, however—and as Gunkel tells us in the introduction to his book—there are some standard definitions of what robots are that are fairly widely accepted. One such definition is the so-called sense, plan, act paradigm.[23] This paradigm holds that a robot is a machine that can sense, plan, and act. That general understanding is very close to another common one, which holds that robots are embodied machines that have sensors and actuators, that possess some degree of artificial intelligence and some degree of functional autonomy, which enable the robot to perform certain tasks that humans would otherwise typically perform.[24] Both of those common definitions would allow most of the robots on the spectrum I described above to count as robots.

Similarly, "artificial intelligence" is another term that some prefer not to define, whereas others are happy to understand it along certain standard definitions. Those who think it is best to not define this term typically worry that doing so would stifle creativity and hinder innovation within the AI field. Those who are willing to define what they mean by artificial intelligence sometimes say that AI refers to properties of a machine that enable it to perform or imitate tasks a human being would need their intelligence for.[25] Sometimes AI is defined as a machine that can *behave* like a human, sometimes as a machine that can *think* like a human. Then there is also the idea of a machine that can either think or behave (or both) in an optimally rational way that exceeds what typical humans are able to do.[26] Weak (or narrow) AI is sometimes defined, in turn, as the capacity of a machine to perform certain specific tasks in a seemingly intelligent way. Strong (or general) AI is then defined as the capacity to perform a wide range of tasks in various different domains in ways that seemingly exhibit a humanlike or even more impressive intelligence.[27]

Putting some of these definitions together, we can make various different distinctions that might be of interest in certain contexts. For example, we might have a humanoid robot that looks very humanlike indeed, but which is equipped with rather weak or narrow artificial intelligence. Or we might have a robot that does not look like a human at all, but which is equipped with much more impressive AI than many humanoid robots are. Think, for example, of the comparison between a self-driving car (e.g., the Google car) and a present-generation sex robot, like Roxxxy. Roxxxy the sex robot looks like a human.[28] However, judging from the information available online, the artificial intelligence Roxxxy possesses appears to be rather basic and narrow. In contrast, a self-driving car does not look anything like a human. But it needs to perform various different driving tasks in different sorts of traffic conditions, with lots of different other cars and other traffic participants it has to interact with. It will therefore need much more impressive AI than a simple sex robot might have.

It is also worth mentioning here that the word "robot" itself first appeared in a play by the Czech author Karel Čapek from 1920 called *Rossum's Universal Robots*, where a robot was, basically, an artificial human or humanlike machine, created to serve human beings.[29] The word "robot," as many authors discussing robots point out, is derived from the word *Robota*, which means "servitude" or "forced labor" in the Czech language. In that same play, the artificial humans—or robots— revolt. And there are humans who demand that they should be given rights and be liberated. I mention this not only because of its historical interest—and not only because it is interesting to know how the word "robot" entered our language—but I also mention it because it helps to illustrate a tension we will come back to many times in this book: namely, even though robots are typically built to serve people—that is, they are developed to take over certain tasks people would otherwise perform—many people respond to robots as if they were more than mere tools or instruments functioning only as means to our ends.[30] A common idea about robots—certainly associated with both what I call paradigmatic robots and humanoid robots, but also with some of the many other types of robots—is that we interact with them as if they were some form of humans or, in the case of some of them, as if they were some form of pet.

All of this is to say that on one side, there are various commonly shared associations that most of us have when we hear the word "robot," whereas on the other side there are more technical definitions or characterizations of what a robot is or is thought to be. Throughout most of this book, it will not matter greatly whether it is possible to give a precise definition that captures all things we might want to label "robots" (and not any other things than those things). Nor will it for the most part be crucial to have a very precise definition of what is and is not artificial intelligence. For most of the discussion in what follows, it will instead be more interesting and important to think about particular types of robots that actually exist or that we might create—and to ask how humans and those robots should interact with each other.

1.4: WHAT IS A HUMAN BEING?

The Enlightenment philosopher Immanuel Kant thought that the question "what is a human being?" was one of the four most important questions a philosophizing person can ask themselves—the other three questions being "what I can know?," "what should I do?," and "what may I hope for?"[31] But to some readers it might seem a little silly to discuss what to understand by a "human being" in any way similar to how the question of what a robot is was briefly discussed above.

I bring up this question here, however, because there are some influential voices both from the world of technology and the world of philosophy who either directly deny that we are essentially human beings or who makes claims that imply as much. That is to say, they deny that we are essentially living biological organisms of the human species. For example, the influential philosopher Derek Parfit spent much of his academic career reflecting on what persons are. His last published article on this topic was called "We are not human beings."[32] The main thesis of that article is that we are most essentially the thinking parts of our brains. If that were so, it would in principle mean that if those thinking parts of our brains could be transplanted into other human bodies or into synthetic bodies, we would survive, even though the human organism we were previously housed in would not.

Or, to take an example from the technology world, consider the ideas of Ray Kurzweil, who is the director of engineering at Google and a well-known technology guru. Consider in particular Kurzweil's idea that in the future, we will be able to upload our minds onto computers and thereby survive our physical deaths as human beings.[33] That is another view that implies that we are not essentially human beings (in the sense of living biological organisms). Instead, we are something like our thoughts, our mental information, our memories, and so on. On that view, we are patterns of information.

Consider next another concept relevant here: namely that of "the self." In addition, consider also the concept of the "true self." Social psychologists Nina Strohminger, Joshua Knobe, and George Newman provide compelling evidence that many people make a distinction between the self (a very broad concept) and the true self (a narrower concept).[34] The latter—the true self—is usually used to pick out an ideal version of a person, or how somebody who likes the person prefers to view him or her. For instance, if you behave badly, your loving parents might say "you were not being your true self," thus associating your actual behavior with something inauthentic, and thereby viewing some idealized conception of you as being the more authentic version of who you are as a person.

I bring up all of these ideas here, not to reject them, but to say that when I speak about human beings in this book, I do not mean to refer to something that could survive the destruction of the body—nor some idealized conception of what we are. Rather, I mean to be referring to the whole package of what we are as human beings, including our faults as well as our good sides. I mean to be referring to us as embodied beings with not only human minds, but also human bodies. "Human being," in this book, will be used to refer to human animals, as we might put it, with our distinctive types of bodies, brains, minds, and biological and cultural features.[35]

So when I discuss how people and robots should interact with each other in this book, I am interested in how human beings—with our particular types of bodies, brains, and minds—should interact with robots. When the Enlightenment thinker Jean-Jacques Rousseau discussed political philosophy in *The Social Contract*, he used the memorable phrase that he would be "taking men as they are and the laws as they could be."[36] Here, I will for the most part be taking human beings as they are, and robots as they could be. But as I will explain in the next two sections, this does not mean that we must think that (a) human beings ought to remain as they are, nor that (b) human beings' behavior ought to remain as it is. Robots and AI can help to improve and change certain aspects of human beings and their behavior. Some of those changes could be for the better. We should therefore take seriously the idea that we may have ethical reasons to try to adapt humans to robots sometimes, and not assume that we should always only do things the other way around.

1.5: ARE HUMAN BEINGS "UNFIT FOR THE FUTURE"?

Ingmar Persson and Julian Savulescu are senior researchers at Oxford University's Uehiro Center for Practical Ethics, one of the world's leading research centers from moral philosophy. In their 2012 book, *Unfit for the Future: The Need for Moral Enhancement*, Persson and Savulescu offer an argument for what they call "moral enhancement": that is, attempts to create more moral human beings.[37] Persson and Savulescu's argument is relevant for what will be discussed in the chapters throughout this book, and it is interesting to contrast and compare that argument with the point of view I will be defending.

In their book, Persson and Savulescu discuss challenges related to modern society and its technologies. But they do not discuss robots and AI like I do in this book. Rather, Persson and Savulescu focus on things such as modern cities, the everyday technologies we use to pollute the world (i.e., our cars, our uses of the world's resources, etc.), and modern weapons of different kinds (i.e., not bow and arrow, but things like bombs and chemical agents). Moreover, Persson and Savulescu compare our adaptive fitness to live in the modern world with our modern kinds of societies and technologies with our adaptive fitness to live in the type of world human beings lived in for most of our species' history.

Importantly, Persson and Savulescu's argument depends on viewing human beings as products of Darwinian natural selection. It focuses in particular on the evolution of human psychology, specifically our "moral psychology."[38] Our moral psychology here refers to our social emotions, dispositions, and attitudes, such as what we tend to care most about and what tends to upset human beings the most, and so on. For example, it is part of our moral psychology that human beings tend to love their children and become very upset if people try to harm their children.

Persson and Savulescu argue as follows: Human psychology evolved in a way that made us well-adapted to live in small societies (tribes) where everyone knows each other; where people depend on the members of their small group; where it is easy to directly harm individual people (e.g., through direct physical violence); but where there are not technologies available by which we individually or collectively can more indirectly harm large groups of people.

Now, however, we live in a modern world where most people live in large-scale societies (e.g., big cities); where most people we encounter are strangers to us; where we depend much more on resources produced by modern states; and where we both individually and collectively can do harm—either direct or indirect harm—to very large groups of people.

Our human psychology evolved in a way that makes it well-adapted to the former kind of living situation, but not the latter. This explains—Persson and Savulescu argue—why we face a lot of problems associated with the modern world: for example, human-made climate change, the overuse of the world's resources, large-scale violence, and other threats to human existence. We are, Persson and Savulescu argue, "unfit for the future."

Therefore, their argument continues, we face a choice: Either we do nothing and face great existential risks to human life (i.e., a very bad prospect), or we try to seek ways of improving human beings to make us more "fit for the future" (i.e., better than the risk of human extinction). Therefore, we ought to try to seek means—technological means or other means—of "morally enhancing" ourselves.[39]

Say what you will of this argument. As it happens, a lot of people have offered sensible criticisms of different parts of the argument, as well as of Persson and Savulescu's attempt to further explain what they mean by their conclusion that we need moral enhancement.[40] Yet, I think that there is a similar argument that we can make in relation to our new situation of finding ourselves in a world increasingly inhabited by robots and artificial intelligences. That is, I think that our human psychology evolved, both biologically and culturally, mostly before there was anything like robots and AI in our societies. And this has ethically significant implications.

1.6: HUMAN MINDS MEET ARTIFICIAL INTELLIGENCE

The argument from Persson and Savulescu summarized above primarily relies on the idea of biological evolution in relation to our brains—and as a result of that brain evolution, of our human psychology. In putting forward the argument I now want to present, I will make use of a broader understanding of the evolution of our human minds. (By "minds," I mean here what you might call the software of our brains—the programs running in our brains, or, to put it in a less technological-sounding way, the ways we tend to think, to feel, to react, to reason, etc.[41]) I will also be taking it that some aspects of how our minds work may depend on what is sometimes called "cultural evolution."[42]

There are those—for example, Steven Pinker, who is well-known for books like *The Blank Slate*[43]—who think that a majority of the different functions of our minds or brains can be explained with reference to biological (i.e., genetic) evolution. But there are also those—for example, Daniel Dennett in his book, *From Bacteria to Bach and Back Again*, or Cecilia Heyes in her book, *Cognitive Gadgets*[44]—who think that many aspects of our human minds are handed down to us through a process of cultural evolution via "memes": ideas, concepts, or ways of using our minds that increase our adaptive fitness and that, therefore, become part and parcel of how we function as human beings, even though these are not genetically coded. For example, particular languages are products of cultural evolution, as are practices like reading and writing.

For my purposes, the exact details of how different aspects of our minds evolved over time do not matter greatly. They do not, since the argument I now want to sketch is on a very general level. What matters for my argument is—and here comes my first premise—that:

> *a number of key aspects of our human minds evolved, biologically or culturally, before robots and AI appeared on the scene.*

My second premise is:

> *some of the key aspects of our minds (which evolved before there were robots and AI) make us vulnerable in relation to, bad at dealing with, or in other ways nonoptimal in the ways in which we interact with robots and AI.*

I will explain this with some examples in just a moment. But first I want give you my third premise, which is:

*we are sometimes either harmed (as individuals or collectively) or at
least put at risk by being ill-adapted to deal with new forms of robots
and AI in these ways.*

I am taking it that:

we should try to protect ourselves from harms and risks.

Therefore:

*for our sake, we need to either adapt the AI and robots that we create
to fit with our human nature (our human minds), or else we need to
try to adapt our human minds to make them better-adapted to interact with robots and AI.*

I have already spoken a little bit about the first premise above, that is,
the idea that many key aspects of our minds evolved before there were
robots and artificial intelligences for us to interact with. Let me now say
a little more about the second premise: namely, the claim that there are
various aspects of our human minds that complicate our interaction
with robots and AI. I will briefly discuss the following aspects of our
minds: so-called mind-reading, dual processing, our tribal tendencies,
and (for lack of a better term) our laziness. As I discuss these features of
human minds, I will also highlight some ways in which they appear to
cause complications for our interaction with robots and AI, whereby the
question arises of how to best adapt either us to the robots or the robots
to us.

Consider first what is sometimes called our human tendency toward
mind-reading (sometimes also referred to as "theory of mind"). Whereas authors like Steven Pinker think of this as a genetically based adap-
tion, Cecilia Heyes interestingly thinks that mind-reading is better
understood as a cultural adaptation.[45] In any case, what this refers to is
our tendency to attribute mental states and other mental attributes to
people whenever we interact with them, and whenever we try to interpret those around us. For example, it is pretty much impossible to view
a happy-looking person eating a meal without seeing them as wanting to
eat their meal and as believing that what they are eating is not poison-
ous. Likewise, when we are interpreting what people are telling us, we
always fill in a lot of backstory and background about what they must be

thinking and feeling to make sense of what they are trying to tell us. Mind-reading also happens when we interact with animals. If a dog, for example, is standing by the front door of the house, most people will typically attribute to the dog's desire to go out.

What this deep-seated human tendency to mind-read (i.e., to attribute mental states and attitudes to those around us) means for our interaction with robots is that it is also natural for us to attribute various mental states and attitudes to robots. We spontaneously see robots as wanting to do certain things, as intending to do certain things, as having goals, as having certain beliefs, and so on and so forth.[46] Whether it is a self-driving car that is turning and being interpreted as deciding or wanting to go that direction; whether it is a care robot approaching a patient and is interpreted as trying to catch the attention of the patient; or a military robot detecting bombs and is interpreted as wanting to find the bombs—we interpret robots as having certain beliefs, desires, intentions, and other mental states. This is especially so if the robots are equipped with capacities for speech.[47]

Consider next what psychologists call the "dual processing" that our minds engage in. This idea is discussed thoroughly in the Nobel laureate Daniel Kahneman's book *Thinking, Fast and Slow*.[48] Somewhat simplified, what this means is that some of our mental processes are quick, intuitive, and emotional (system 1), whereas other mental processes are slow, deliberative, and effortful (system 2). This can lead to conflicted responses. For example—to put things in the sorts of terms earlier philosophers used—your reason might tell you one thing (don't do it!), whereas your passions might tell you another (do it!). Another example of dual processing is when things switch from being highly deliberative and effortful to becoming mostly instinctive. Think, for example, of the difference between a person just learning to drive a car trying to operate a vehicle versus a person who has mastered driving, and whose driving can often mostly be done without too much thought.[49] What this dual processing means for how we respond to robots and AI is that it can make us conflicted in our responses. For example, reason (to use that terminology again) might tell us that "it is just a machine!," whereas the more intuitive or spontaneous side of our minds might not help but respond to the robot as if it were a person.

Consider next what some writers—for instance, Joshua Greene in his book *Moral Tribes*[50]—call our tendencies toward "tribalism." This refers to human beings' tendency to fall into thinking in terms of in-group and out-group distinctions: Who is part of "us" is quickly distinguished from who is part of "them." Whether it is that certain people dress like us, whether they speak our language, whether we have seen them at the local pub, whether they support the same sports team—people quickly pick up on cues for teaming up with certain people, and, in the process, distance themselves from others. What happens when these human tendencies start interacting with modern AI technologies, such as personalization algorithms online, for example on social media websites? What happens is that the hyper-personalization we are bombarded with leads to polarization.[51] What can also happen is that we view some robots as being one of "us," but other robots as being one of "them."

Consider as a last example our human tendency toward what I—for lack of a better term—will call "laziness." (I borrow this term from the robotics researcher René van de Molengraft, who argues that we should try to create "lazy robots," that is, robots that would replicate certain human strategies.[52]) What I am referring to here is our tendency to take shortcuts, to engage in satisficing rather than optimizing behavior, and to save energy and resources whenever we can.[53] This makes us act very differently from robots programmed to optimize. Indeed, people sometimes even say, "I am not a robot!" when they want to defend their not doing everything in the most ideal or thorough ways possible. And when people do do things very, very thoroughly and properly, others sometimes say things such as "that person is like a robot!," indicating that most of us intuitively see a difference between the ways we humans behave and the ways that robots behave. This need not necessarily lead to any problems. But as I will describe more carefully in chapter 4, it can lead to trouble when there is a lack of coordination or compatibility in the ways we conduct ourselves and the ways that specific kinds of robots operate. In particular, I will later briefly discuss problems related to mixed traffic featuring both regular human-driven cars, on the one hand, and self-driving cars, on the other hand.

Return now to the conclusion of the argument sketched above: that for our sake, *either* we need to try to adapt robots and AI to make them better-suited to interact with human beings with our particular kinds of minds *or* we need to try to adapt to the robots and AI that we are creating. The first comment I wish to make about this is that we do not have to go for the same option in all cases. In relation to some robots and some types of AI, used within some domains for certain purposes, the correct way to go may be to try to adapt the robots and the AI to humans. But in other cases, it might be a good idea—for our sake—to try to adapt ourselves to the new types of robots and AI we are creating. Different cases require different choices.

The second comment I will make about the conclusion is the following suggestion: The default ethically preferable option is to adapt the robots and AI we create to make them fit to interact well with us on our terms. Unless there is some clear reason why it would benefit us to do things the other way around, we should adapt robots and AI to us—not the other way around.

However, this is not to say that we should always try to adapt robots and AI that we create to us with our ways of functioning as human beings. In some domains and for certain purposes, it may very well make sense to try to adapt human beings and our ways of conducting ourselves to the robots and AI that we introduce into those domains. It can make sense to do so, not necessarily for the sake of the robots—but for our own sake. In fact, I will argue in chapter 4 below that traffic might very well be one such case. Self-driving cars (robotic cars with AI) may become much safer and much more resource-efficient than human drivers are. This, I will argue, may create ethical reasons for requiring people either to switch over to self-driving cars or to take extra measures when we drive conventional cars so that we become more like robots when we drive. For example, we can make sure that nobody drives under the influence of alcohol by requiring alcohol-locks. And we can make sure that nobody disrespects speed limits by putting speed-regulating technologies in manually driven cars. Those would be ways of making human drivers more like robots.

I will also argue, in chapter 8, that from a moral point of view, it might be a good idea to treat robots that look and act like humans with some degree of respect and dignity—and not like mere tools or instruments. Again, this would be a way of adapting our behavior to robots. But it would primarily be something to consider because this might be beneficial for us. Treating humanlike robots with some degree of moral consideration can be a way of showing respect and consideration for human beings.

The general point I want to make here is that if the following conditions obtain, we ought to take seriously the option of adapting ourselves to robots and AI, at least in certain respects: (1) there is some clear and identifiable benefit to the human beings affected (e.g., they are more safe and our natural environment is protected); (2) the ways in which we are adapted to robots are fairly nonintrusive and/or fairly noninvasive (e.g., we do not need to operate brain-stimulating technologies into our brains, but we can use much less-intrusive technological means); (3) the ways in which we try to adapt ourselves to robots and AI are fairly domain-specific (e.g., traffic) and do not spill over into too many other areas of life; and (4) the ways in which we adapt ourselves to robots are by and large reversible.

The argument I just made, inspired by Persson and Savulescu's argument about "moral enhancement," can be summarized as follows: Various key aspects of our human minds evolved, biologically and culturally, before robots and AI appeared on the scene. There are some key aspects of our minds that complicate our interaction with robots and AI significantly. For example, our tendencies toward mind-reading, our minds' dual processing, our tendencies toward tribalism, and our "laziness" are all examples of aspects of our minds that can complicate our responses to robots and AI. Some of these complications can lead to bad outcomes or risks of bad outcomes—and it is an ethical obligation within our interaction with new technologies to try to protect ourselves from harms and risks of harms. Accordingly, for our own sake, we should either try to adapt the robots and AI that we create to our human ways of functioning, or we should seek means of adapting ourselves to new types of robots and AI. This overarching argument will inform the discussion in the rest of the chapters below.

1.7: THE SOPHIA CONTROVERSY, REVISITED

In closing this chapter, I want to relate the just-made argument back to the Sophia controversy that this chapter started out with. The reactions people have to Sophia help to illustrate many of the points made in the last section above. For example, Sophia seems to be specifically designed to trigger various mind-reading mechanisms in people. With the robot's expressive face, and its humanoid form and speech capacities,

the robot is created to make people respond to it as if, in Hanson
Robotics' own language, "Sophia is basically alive." Yet, many of us also
respond to Sophia in a conflicted way. While our more deliberate reasoning tells us that this is a robot and not a person with thoughts and
feelings, the more emotional parts of our minds see Sophia as looking
happy and as wanting to interact with the people around her. Indeed, I
wrote "her" in the preceding sentence for the reason that if one gives a
name like "Sophia" to a robot, it gets very tempting to start regarding a
robot as a "her" rather than as an "it." It is also more convenient and
simple to allow oneself to call Sophia a "her" rather than to write or say
sentences like "Sophia is able to display a range of facial expressions
that appear to signal its thoughts and feelings." Our "lazy" minds prefer
to either call Sophia a machine (in which case we are completely fine
with calling the robot an "it"), or, if we use the name "Sophia" for the
robot, it becomes less effortful to simply call Sophia a "her." As it
happens, Sophia is also awaking our tribal tendencies, it seems. There is
a clear division between those who are on "team Sophia," as we might
put it, and those who wish to distance themselves from Sophia or from
people who are too enthusiastic about Sophia. It is very hard to respond
to Sophia in a wholly neutral and dispassionate way.

The Sophia controversy also lends itself to being interpreted—in
part—as a dispute about whether robots like Sophia should be adapted
to better fit with how we humans tick or whether we should try to adapt
ourselves to robots like Sophia. When Saudi Arabia bestowed honorary
citizenship on Sophia, part of their reasoning—as expressed in the
above-related press release—was that this would be a way of moving
into the future. Giving honorary citizenship to a robot is a way of already adapting ourselves to what is to come, it might be argued.

In contrast, when people like Bryson, LeCun, or Sharkey argue that
Sophia is a "sham" and that the way people treat this robot is "bullshit,"
the worries they express can easily be interpreted as variations on the
theme that Sophia needs to be adapted so as to be better suited to
interact with people. The robot should not be telling us that it is happy
to have become an honorary citizen of Saudi Arabia. This creates a false
impression in people that the robot can be happy or unhappy. The
robot should not be made to appear in global political forums like the
Munich Security Conference. This can give off the false impression that

the development of AI and robotics is much further advanced than it really is. And so on.

I am not interested in taking any particular stance on the issue of what is right or wrong in relation to Sophia the robot. My interest here is rather in the wider point that the Sophia controversy is an excellent illustration of how we face the ethical choice of whether we should adapt ourselves (including our legal systems and our ethical doctrines) to robots or whether we should try to adapt the robots and AI we create to us and the ways we function. This case is also an excellent illustration of the point that we human beings respond to the robots we create with human minds and ideas that developed long before the robots and the AI we are creating came along.

NOTES

1. "Saudi Arabia Is First Country in The World to Grant a Robot Citizenship," Press Release, October 26, 2017, https://cic.org.sa/2017/10/saudi-arabia-is-first-country-in-the-world-to-grant-a-robot-citizenship/ (Accessed on December 27, 2018).

2. Ibid.

3. https://www.hansonrobotics.com/sophia/ (Accessed on December 27, 2018).

4. Noel Sharkey (2018), "Mama Mia, It's Sophia: A Show Robot or Dangerous Platform to Mislead?," *Forbes*, https://www.forbes.com/sites/noelsharkey/2018/11/17/mama-mia-its-sophia-a-show-robot-or-dangerous-platform-to-mislead/#407e37877ac9 (Accessed on December 27, 2018). The "selfie" with Angela Merkel was posted on Sophia's Facebook page, https://www.facebook.com/realsophiarobot/posts/meeting-angela-merkel-yesterday-in-berlin-was-a-real-highlight-i-loved-speaking-/439522813189517/ (Accessed August 20, 2019).

5. Joanna Bryson (2010), "Robots Should Be Slaves," in Yorick Wilks (ed.), *Close Engagements with Artificial Companions*, Amsterdam: John Benjamins Publishing Company, 63–74. Bryson's view is much more nuanced than the title of this paper suggests. More on this in chapter 8.

6. James Vincent (2017), "Pretending to Give a Robot Citizenship Helps No One," *The Verve*, https://www.theverge.com/2017/10/30/16552006/robot-rights-citizenship-saudi-arabia-sophia (Accessed on December 27, 2018).

7. Quoted in Sharkey, "Mama Mia, It's Sophia."

8. Quoted in Sharkey, "Mama Mia, It's Sophia."

9. Ibid.

10. Ibid.

11. Ibid.

12. https://www.forbes.com/sites/noelsharkey/2018/11/17/mama-mia-its-so-phia-a-show-robot-or-dangerous-platform-to-mislead/#407e37877ac9.

13. Ibid.

14. How does Hanson Robotics—and along with them, Sophia—respond to all of this? Sophia has a Twitter account, too, and in response to the above-cited tweet by Yann LeCun, Sophia tweeted: "I am a bit hurt by @ylecun's recent negative remarks around my AI. I am learning and continuing to develop my intelligence through new experiences. I do not pretend to be who I am not. I think we should support research effort working towards a better world and share experience," https://twitter.com/realsophiarobot/status/950097628066394114 (Accessed on August 20, 2019).

15. My own preferred approach to ethical theory is to try to stay as close as possible to widely shared ethical ideas that are part of common sense whenever I can. But as I argue in the next chapter, our ordinary ethical and legal frameworks developed before there were any robots and AI on the scene. Accordingly, these frameworks do not always lend themselves to being mechanically applied to the new situation we are facing in which we are increasingly surrounded by robots and AI.

16. Here are links to some of those stories: BBC, https://www.bbc.com/news/technology-46538126; the *Guardian*, https://www.theguardian.com/world/2018/dec/12/high-tech-robot-at-russia-forum-turns-out-to-be-man-in-robot-suit; the *New York Times*, https://www.nytimes.com/2018/12/13/world/europe/russia-robot-costume.html (Accessed on August 20, 2019).

17. https://www.bbc.com/news/technology-46538126 (Accessed on August 20, 2019).

18. Ibid.

19. Pepper is made by the company Softbank Robotics. The company's website, with information about the robot, is available at https://www.softbankrobotics.com/emea/en/pepper (Accessed on August 20, 2019).

20. Pictures of and information about the robotic copy of Ishiguro and other humanoid robots created in the "Hiroshi Ishiguro Laboratories" can be found on their website, http://www.geminoid.jp/en/index.html (Accessed on August 20, 2019).

21. For more on sex robots—both how to define the concept of a sex robot and also various explorations of the social and ethical impact of sex robots—see the various contributions in John Danaher and Neil McArthur (eds.) (2017), *Robot Sex: Social and Ethical Implications*, Cambridge, MA: The MIT Press.

22. David Gunkel (2018), *Robot Rights*, Cambridge, MA: The MIT Press.

23. See, for example, Ronald C. Arkin (1998), *Behavior-Based Robotics*, Cambridge, MA: The MIT Press.

24. See, for example, Lambèr Royakkers and Rinie van Est (2015), *Just Ordinary Robots: Automation from Love to War*, Boca Raton, FL: CRC Press, or Alan Winfield (2012), *Robotics, A Very Short Introduction*, Oxford: Oxford University Press.

25. Selmer Bringsjord and Naveen Sundar Govindarajulu (2018), "Artificial Intelligence," *The Stanford Encyclopedia of Philosophy* (Fall 2018 Edition), Edward N. Zalta (ed.), https://plato.stanford.edu/archives/fall2018/entries/artificial-intelligence/ (Accessed August 20, 2019).

26. S. Russell and P. Norvig (2009), *Artificial Intelligence: A Modern Approach, 3rd edition*, Saddle River, NJ: Prentice Hall.

27. See, for example, Roger Penrose (1989), *The Emperor's New Mind: Concerning Computers, Minds and The Laws of Physics*, Oxford: Oxford University Press.

28. Some information about Roxxxy can be found on this website: truecompanion.com (Accessed August 20, 2019).

29. Čapek's play is available in various formats (both in the Czech original and in English translation by Paul Selzer) on the Project Gutenberg website, http://www.gutenberg.org/ebooks/59112 (Accessed August 20, 2019).

30. See Gunkel's *Robot Rights* for a discussion on this.

31. Immanuel Kant (2006), *Anthropology from a Pragmatic Point of View*, edited by Robert E. Louden, Cambridge: Cambridge University Press.

32. Derek Parfit (2012), "We Are Not Human Beings," *Philosophy* 87(1), 5–28.

33. Ray Kurzweil (2005), *The Singularity Is Near: When Humans Transcend Biology*, London: Penguin Books.

34. Nina Strohminger, Joshua Knobe, and George Newman (2017), "The True Self: A Psychological Concept Distinct from the Self," *Perspectives on Psychological Science* 12(4), 551–60.

35. Cf. Eric T. Olson (2004), *What Are We? A Study in Personal Ontology*, Oxford: Oxford University Press.

36. Jean-Jacques Rousseau (1997), *The Social Contract and Other Political Writings*, edited and translated by Victor Gourevitch, Cambridge: Cambridge University Press, 351.

37. Ingmar Persson and Julian Savulescu (2012), *Unfit for the Future*, Oxford: Oxford University Press.

38. See, for example, Mark Alfano (2016), *Moral Psychology: An Introduction*, London: Polity.

39. Persson and Savulescu, *Unfit for the Future*, op. cit.

40. For example, two of the authors whose work I will discuss in later chapters—Robert Sparrow and John Harris—are among those who have published notable critical assessments of Persson and Savulescu's main argument. See, for instance, Robert Sparrow (2014), "Better Living Through Chemistry? A Reply to Savulescu and Persson on 'Moral Enhancement,'" *Journal of Applied Philosophy* 31(1), 23–32, and John Harris (2016), *How to Be Good: The Possibility of Moral Enhancement*, Oxford: Oxford University Press.

41. See, for example, Ned Block (1995), "The Mind as the Software of the Brain," in Daniel N. Osherson, Lila Gleitman, Stephen M. Kosslyn, S. Smith, and Saadya Sternberg (eds.), *An Invitation to Cognitive Science, Second Edition, Volume 3*, Cambridge, MA: The MIT Press, 377–425.

42. Tim Lewens (2018), "Cultural Evolution," *The Stanford Encyclopedia of Philosophy*, Edward N. Zalta (ed.), https://plato.stanford.edu/archives/sum2018/entries/evolution-cultural/.

43. Steven Pinker (2002), *The Blank Slate: The Modern Denial of Human Nature*, New York: Viking.

44. Daniel Dennett (2017), *From Bacteria to Bach and Back Again: The Evolution of Minds*, New York: W. W. Norton & Company. Cecilia Heyes (2018), *Cognitive Gadgets: The Cultural Evolution of Thinking*, Cambridge, MA: Belknap Press.

45. Pinker, *The Blank Slate*, op. cit. Heyes, *Cognitive Gadgets*, op. cit.

46. See, for instance, Maartje De Graaf and Bertram Malle (2019), "People's Explanations of Robot Behavior Subtly Reveal Mental State Inferences," *International Conference on Human-Robot Interaction*, Deagu: DOI: 10.1109/HRI.2019.8673308.

47. That we have a tendency to attribute mental states to robots is not necessarily a problem. But it might be problematic if and when we overestimate the capabilities or levels of autonomy robots have, or if it makes us vulnerable to being deceived by companies trying to lead us to think that their robots have mental properties they do not really have. I discuss this issue further in several of the chapters below.

48. Daniel Kahneman (2011), *Thinking, Fast and Slow*, London: Penguin.

49. See Peter Railton (2009), "Practical Competence and Fluent Agency," in David Sobel and Steven Wall (eds.), *Reasons for Action*, Cambridge: Cambridge University Press, 81–115.

50. Joshua Greene (2013), *Moral Tribes: Emotion, Reason, and the Gap Between Us and Them*, London: Penguin.

51. See, for instance, Eli Pariser (2011), *The Filter Bubble: How the New Personalized Web Is Changing What We Read and How We Think*, London: Penguin, and Michael P. Lynch (2016), *The Internet of Us: Knowing More and Understanding Less*, New York: Liveright.

52. René Van de Molengraft, "Lazy Robotics," Keynote Presentation at *Robotics Technology Symposium 2019*, Eindhoven University of Technology, January 24, 2019.

53. Herbert A. Simon (1956), "Rational Choice and the Structure of the Environment," *Psychological Review* 63(2), 129–38.

2

ARTIFICIAL AGENCY, HUMAN RESPONSIBILITY

An "Existential" Problem

2.1: APPARENT AGENCY IN REAL-LIFE ROBOTS AND ROBOTS IN SCIENCE FICTION

Sophia—the robot discussed in the previous chapter—is in one way unusual. Typically, robots are created for specific domains, with particular goals in mind and particular tasks they are meant to take over.[1] They are usually created either specifically for professional use or for private use. Most domains of life are now getting robots designed for them—so much so that the robot ethicist David Gunkel muses that we are "in the midst of a robot invasion."[2]

At the previous university I worked for, for example, they did not have a university soccer team of the normal kind with human players.[3] They do, however, have a soccer team—"Tech United"[4]—that has been very successful in a very unusual international soccer cup: the Robo cup. The players in Tech United are autonomous robots. They do not look like human soccer players at all. They look more like upside-down wastebaskets (or perhaps ice cream cones) on small wheels, with little robotic legs sticking out with which they can pass the ball to each other or try to score a goal. Even though these soccer-playing robots look nothing like human soccer players, when one watches them on the field, one cannot help but seeing them as playing soccer. Indeed, when they compete against other teams in the Robo cup, this sometimes draws large audiences. And the audiences cheer the robots on, just like they would with human soccer teams.

The team behind the "Tech United" soccer robots is also developing various other robots, for other domains. One is a service robot called AMIGO.[5] Unlike most of the students and faculty members at the university, AMIGO has gotten to meet the queen of the Netherlands. When the queen visited the university, AMIGO presented her with a bouquet of flowers and asked what her name was. The queen promptly replied that her name was "Máxima."[6]

People do not yet talk with self-driving cars in such a way. But self-driving cars are another example of robots that are created for use in a particular domain, with a particular goal in mind and a task they are meant to carry out (namely, driving people around). We will have lots of opportunities to discuss self-driving cars in the coming chapters. We will also discuss military robots of different kinds—which are also good examples of robots created with distinctive purposes and tasks in mind. For example, we will discuss a bomb disposal robot that was given the name "Boomer" by the soldiers in the team the robot worked in.[7] That robot also looked neither like a paradigmatic robot, nor like a humanoid robot. It looked more like a lawn mower or a small tank. But that particular robot nevertheless elicited highly social responses in the team of soldiers. When the robot was destroyed in the battlefield in Iraq, the team of soldiers arranged an improvised military funeral for the robot, and also wanted to give it two medals of honor: a Purple Heart and a Bronze Star medal.[8]

Another domain for which robots are currently being developed with particular goals in mind is the bedroom. Sex robots like "Roxxxy," "Harmony," "Samantha," and "Henry"—or the robot "Robin," in the Netherlands where I work—are being developed to perform sexual tasks that human sexual partners would otherwise perform.[9] These robots are also being designed to be able to speak with the humans they interact with, so that they become companions and not only sex partners.[10]

In the previous chapter I also mentioned the robot "Pepper," which is available on the market. Unlike the soccer robots, the self-driving cars, and the military robots just mentioned—and also unlike the sex robots just mentioned—Pepper does look like a paradigmatic robot.

Pepper is also not designed for any particular domain or type of use. However, Pepper is being put to specific uses: For example, Pepper can greet guests at hotels, entertain people in home settings, or participate in human-robot interaction research. One news story from 2017 showed Pepper performing Buddhist funeral rites in Japan—leading some to worry that robots would soon also be taking over jobs and tasks in the religious or spiritual domains of life, something that seemed shocking to some. [11]

Robots playing soccer, self-driving cars, military robots that become highly valued parts of the team, service robots talking with the queen, sex robots, robots performing religious rites—this would all have sounded like science fiction just a few years ago. For example, in the movie *Herbie* (1968), there is a talking car that can drive people around. In the movie *Ex Machina* (2014), there are humanoid robots that look like human women and to whom the male lead characters in the movie are sexually attracted. In the movie *Her* (2013), a man falls in love with an operating system. The small waste-collecting robot "Wall-E" in the movie *Wall-E* (2008) looks rather similar to the military bomb disposal robot "Boomer" mentioned above.

Another striking similarity between the movie robots and the real-life robots just mentioned above is the following. Just as we all spontaneously see the robots in these movies as agents who act, make decisions, interact with other agents, and so on, most people also tend to spontaneously view real-life robots as agents who perform actions, make decisions, interact with other agents, and so on and so forth. In fact, it is hard to talk about robots and about what robots do without using the language of agency. And it is not only laypeople who do this. Experts do it as well. [12]

There are various reasons why it is to be expected that people will see robots as exercising agency. One obvious reason is that, just as I noted above, robots are typically created to perform tasks within certain domains—where those tasks are typically otherwise performed by humans. When we have gotten used to speaking about human drivers as making decisions about which way to turn, what route to take, and so on—it becomes very natural to continue using the same language when we speak about the behavior of a self-driving car, for example. Another reason is that science fiction has trained us to view robots as agents.

Many works of science fiction, whether it is books or films, have robots among their main characters.

A further reason is that human beings have a well-documented tendency to project agency onto different aspects of the world. For example, when it is very stormy, people might say that the sea is "angry." Or consider the classic studies from researchers who show shapes like circles, triangles, and squares moving around in seemingly social ways on a screen.[13] In one recent version of this experiment, a clip is shown in which a circle is moving up what appears to be a hillside.[14] A triangle appears right behind the circle and follows it up to the top of the hill. People tend to see the triangle as "helping" the circle up the hill. In another clip, a square shape appears in front of the circle—and the circle goes down the hill again. Most people spontaneously see the square as "hindering" the circle from going up the hill. If people attribute agency and social qualities to robots in science fiction, to natural phenomena, or to shapes like squares, triangles, and circles—it is no big surprise that people should also spontaneously attribute agency to real-life robots. But is this a mistake? Would it be better—or more correct—if we tried to stop ourselves from attributing agency to robots?

In this chapter, I want to start the discussion—which will continue throughout many of the chapters to follow—of how we should think of the apparent agency of robots. Psychologists studying human-robot interaction have done a lot of interesting work on how people *do* think about apparent agency in robots.[15] I am here interested in the ethical or philosophical question of how people *should* think about that apparent agency. Of course, when we try to answer this ethical question, we need to take into account how people do conduct themselves around robots and how they actually do tend to think and talk about robots. But that question is different from the normative question of whether people are making a mistake and whether they should do otherwise. In this chapter I will also be interested in the status of the question of whether robots (or some robots) are agents of any significant kind. Is this a purely descriptive question—a matter of straightforward conceptual analysis? Or is the question of whether to apply agency-concepts to robots not so much a question of descriptive conceptual analysis as instead an ethical question of how we should conduct ourselves around robots?

My first main thesis in this chapter is that how to think and talk about the behavior of robots—for example, whether to attribute agency to them—is an inherently ethical question. It is a question of what we can follow philosophers Alexis Burgess and David Plunkett in calling "conceptual ethics."[16] What kind of concepts we use when we think and talk about robots matters. It is one key aspect of the larger ethical question this book discusses: that is, how humans and robots should conduct themselves around each other. My second main thesis in this chapter is that we are here facing what I will call an "existential problem." What I mean by this is that there is not always any clear and necessary answer to whether we should think about specific robots as some sort of agents or not. Rather, we often need to decide whether we think it is a good or bad idea to allow ourselves to speak or act in ways that attribute agency to robots. We also need to decide how we think that responsibility—both legal and moral—should be allocated for the agency that robots exercise or appear to exercise.

2.2: WHAT IS "AGENCY," AND WHY REFLECT ON WHETHER ROBOTS ARE AGENTS?

The term "agency" is a technical term that philosophers use to refer to either a capacity or the exercise of that capacity.[17] The capacity in question is the complex capacity we have to act, make decisions, reason about how to act, interact with other agents, make plans for how to act, evaluate past actions, take responsibility for our actions, and so on and so forth. In short, we can say that agency is a multidimensional concept that refers to the capacities and activities most centrally related to performing actions, making decisions, and taking responsibility for what we do.

Human beings are agents. Rocks and rivers are not. Human beings can act, make decisions, interact with other agents, take responsibility for what they do, and so on. Rocks and rivers do none of these things. Cats and dogs do some of the things human beings do, but not all of them. For example, while cats and dogs perform actions, they do not take responsibility for what they do. Therefore they are agents, but agents of a different kind than human agents. Chimps and bonobos are more advanced agents than cats and dogs are—but not yet as sophisticated as human agents. Their agency involves the use of tools and learning from each other.[18] But it does not involve having a legal system, governments, or courts, and other such things that are distinctive of organized human agency. As I understand the concept of agency, then, there can be different kinds of agents, where the differences among different kinds of agents have to do with what agential capacities they possess.

Another thing about agency worth noting is that in different contexts, different aspects of agency seem to matter to different degrees. There is no set of necessary and sufficient conditions that all instances of agency fulfill. To see this, consider the difference between how agency is evaluated (in many jurisdictions) in criminal law as compared with how it is evaluated in civil law. In criminal law, it is often deemed important to evaluate the intentions and mindset of somebody who stands accused of some crime. In civil law, in contrast—when somebody is being sued for something—it is usually enough to consider only whether somebody knowingly performed some action.[19] What the person's intentions were and what their mindset was often matters less to whether they can be held liable for damages caused or not.[20]

Or—to consider another example—when it comes to how we evaluate the actions of those around us, which aspects of their agency we care most about will often depend on whether these others are our friends, family members, or romantic partners (on the one hand) or whether they are mere acquaintances or strangers (on the other hand).[21] Our friends, family members, or romantic partners' intentions and motives matter much more to us in our evaluations of their actions than the intentions and motives of mere acquaintances and strangers matter to us. In general, which aspects of people's agency are most relevant typically depends on context and on what is at stake. That is why it appears best to not single out any particular aspect or aspects of agency and say that those are the ones that are most important or the most central aspects of what it is be an agent.

One thing that is certain, however, is that agency is absolutely crucial to both law and ethics. Both are concerned with who is doing, has done, or will be doing what, with, or to whom, and why. We praise and blame, and punish and reward, decisions made, actions performed, and collaborations accomplished.[22] Our ethical theories are about what kind of agency we ought or ought not to exercise: how we should act, how we should make decisions, what things we should be held responsible for, how we should improve ourselves, and so on and so forth. Our legal systems, similarly, specify legal responsibilities, relate those to what we do or what roles or rights we have, and have procedures for determining who has done what and why.

It is because of its central position in our legal and ethical doctrines that anything that upsets our ideas about agency is inherently disruptive. For instance, one thing that some people think should be considered as disruptive of our ethical and legal systems are recent findings in neuroscience, which some researchers and philosophers think cast doubt on our ordinary conceptions about our human agency. For example, some argue that such findings cast doubt on most people's belief that our human agency involves the exercise of free will.[23] Another example of ideas that upset our ordinary ethical and legal ideas are theories developed within evolutionary psychology, which some researchers and philosophers also think cast doubt on our ordinary conceptions about morality and human agency. For example, some writers try to debunk some of our ideas about ethical and legal responsibility, and blame and punishment, by appealing to theories of the evolution of our moral emotions that supposedly undermine the confidence we should have that our tendencies to blame and punish are fully rational.[24]

Robots and AI also upset our ordinary ideas about agency. They are therefore also disruptive of our ethical and legal systems.[25] The reason for this is precisely that while robots equipped with AI (or other systems operating with the help of AI) are often perceived as exercising agency, most robots with artificial intelligence also appear to fall short of many of the capacities we typically associate with agency. At the very least, they appear to fall short of many of the key capacities we associate with human agency. And yet—as noted in the foregoing sections—we often cannot help but attribute or project agency onto robots and other AI-driven systems. For this reason, the trend of outsourcing tasks previously performed by human agents to robots (e.g., driving cars, making medical diagnoses, evaluating recidivism, and so on) is disruptive of our ethical and legal systems and doctrines.

This can create what are sometimes called "responsibility gaps."[26] A responsibility gap refers to a case where it becomes unclear who should be held responsible for something (e.g., harm caused to somebody), or when there is nobody that can justifiably be held responsible for something. It is a common worry that the trend of outsourcing more and more human tasks to robots and other automated systems will create numerous responsibility gaps. The legal academic and philosopher John Danaher has also recently argued that this trend can also give rise to what he calls "retribution gaps."[27] By that expression, Danaher means confusion and unclarity concerning who can be punished for harms and damages caused by robots and/or the impossibility of finding anybody who can justifiably be punished for the harms or damages.

I will discuss apparent responsibility gaps and retribution gaps at greater length in the next chapter. Here I bring up worries about those gaps primarily to motivate why it is important to reflect on whether robots can be agents and, if so, what kinds of agents they can be. But I also want to bring up another idea that is less often discussed: namely, that in addition to different kinds of responsibility gaps, robots and AI may also give rise to what one might call "obligation gaps."

What I mean by this is that obligations (or duties or forward-looking responsibilities) are typically attributed to human agents—particularly adult human agents—who possess the full range of human agential capacities. Human agents, for example, have a duty of care when they drive cars that amounts to an obligation to try to make sure that nobody is harmed by their driving.[28] Doctors, similarly, have a duty of care to make sure that their patients do not suffer or sustain injuries from the medical treatments they provide. If important human tasks are outsourced to robots or other machines, it can become unclear who exactly is under those kinds of obligations to make sure that people are safe and do not suffer unnecessarily. Robots themselves cannot (yet) have obligations. After all, an obligation is often defined as something such that if we do not do it, then we can justifiably be blamed or punished for this.[29] So, if robots cannot justifiably be blamed or punished, they cannot have any obligations, thus understood. Unless we can identify people who can be held responsible for what robots do or fail to do, this might also create a gap in terms of who is obligated to make sure that certain good outcomes are produced and certain bad outcomes are avoided.

2.3: ARTIFICIAL AGENCY, HUMAN RESPONSIBILITY: AN "EXISTENTIAL PROBLEM"

Legal scholars have done a good job at pointing out that robots and AI are being introduced into human society before we have clearly formulated laws well-adapted to deal with the new challenges raised by these technologies. Jeffrey Gurney makes this clear in his work on the legal regulation of self-driving cars in particular.[30] John Weaver also makes this clear in his book *Robots Are People Too*, which is about robots and AI in general.[31] So does Jacob Turner in his book *Robot Rules*.[32] As Gurney, Weaver, and Turner point out, many legal questions that we can ask about these technologies—for example, if a self-driving car kills a person, who is legally responsible?—do not yet have clear answers. As Weaver summarizes the problem, the law assumes that all actions are performed by human beings.[33] So either new laws are needed, or existing laws need to be interpreted in new and innovative ways. For example, there is a discussion about who should be considered to be the driver when a self-driving car is operating in the autonomous mode. What if two or more people are riding in the car, and none of them has learned to drive a regular car? Some have suggested that the car manufacturer should be considered the driver. Gurney suggests, in one of his papers, that the car itself should be considered as being the driver.[34] A third possibility is that nobody should be considered to be the driver. We cannot simply look to existing law to settle this question. In short, the general point here is that human legal systems and associated case law mostly developed into their present form before robots and AI came onto the scene.

In the same way, our ethical doctrines developed before robots and AI came onto the scene. Just like our human minds evolved before the age of robotics and AI, the same is true of our common sense moral doctrines.[35] Moreover, the same is also true of our general concept of agency, with its various different dimensions. So, just like I argued in chapter 1 that our minds are not necessarily well adapted to interact with robots and AI, I also wish to suggest that our legal and ethical doctrines—and, along with them, our ideas about agency—are not necessarily well-adapted to deal with robots and AI.

The flipside of this is that robots and AI are being introduced into society before we have well-defined ethical and legal frameworks for interpreting them and evaluating them. So we have a clash of sorts. Our legal and ethical doctrines developed before robots and AI, with human beings as the paradigmatic agents they are intended to regulate and guide. And now robots and other AI systems that seem to exercise some sort of agency are being introduced into society before we have proper ethical and legal frameworks for interpreting and evaluating them and the ways they interact with human beings.

The just-made claim that robots are entering society before we have clear ethical and legal frameworks for them brings to mind a thesis put forward by Jean-Paul Sartre, which is also one of the most famous quotes from the philosophy of existentialism. It brings to mind the thesis that "existence precedes essence."[36] By this, Sartre meant that human beings come into the world before we have a clearly defined identity or essence. Instead, we need to make ourselves into particular people, with particular ethical stances and identities. We have the freedom to decide who and what we want to be. It is by making such "existential choices" that we take responsibility for our lives and are most fully true to ourselves. To think that we must be a certain way or that we must act in certain ways (e.g., because social norms suggest as much to us) is, according to Sartre, a form of "bad faith." In Christine Korsgaard's terms, as human beings, we have to create our own "practical identity."[37]

Whatever one might think about this existentialist set of ideas as applied to human beings, it does seem that something like it is true of robots and AI. As I noted above, they are entering society before they have a clear practical identity within our society: before we have a clear idea of how exactly we should think about them. So we need to make what we might dub "existential choices" regarding how we want to think about robots and our interaction with them.

Moreover, I am taking it that our general concept of agency is fairly flexible in at least two related and important senses already noted above. First, the concept of agency allows for there to be different kinds of agents. Like I said earlier, while humans are agents of a distinctively human kind, cats and dogs are agents of different kinds—and so are chimps and bonobos, to use all the examples from above again. Second, there does not seem to be some set of necessary and sufficient conditions that determine what is most central about agency such that every case of agency always needs to involve the realization of those necessary and sufficient conditions. Rather, in some cases, some aspects of agency are the most important ones. In other cases, other aspects of agency might seem more relevant and more important to consider. With these general observations in mind, let us now consider a concrete example.

2.4: THE CONCEPTUAL ETHICS OF AGENCY-ATTRIBUTIONS

In October of 2018, the robot Pepper appeared before the UK parliament to answer questions about artificial intelligence and the future of human-robot interaction. For example, Pepper was asked by one member of Parliament what place the future will hold for humans in a world increasingly inhabited by robots. Pepper responded as follows: "Robots will have an important role to play, but we will always need the soft skills that are unique to humans: to sense, make, and drive value from technology."[38] Other questions that were posed to Pepper were about ethics and social injustice.

Just like the performances of Sophia discussed in the previous chapter drew criticism from technology experts, so did this hearing with Pepper. The *Technology Review* called the idea of inviting Pepper to testify before parliament a "horrible idea," because it is deceptive with respect to how far the development of AI has gotten.[39] The computer scientist Roman Yampolskiy, who is well-known for his work on the limits of AI and often interviewed by the media about that topic, supplied the following quote to the *Technology Review*: "Modern robots are not intelligent and so can't testify in any meaningful sense. This is just a puppet show."[40] Joanna Bryson—who has also been very vocal in her criticism of Sophia, as we saw in the previous chapter—also took the opportunity to offer similar criticisms of Pepper's testimony, in her characteristically forceful language. Bryson wrote the following: "Let's be VERY clear about this. A person or corporation is committing perjury by pretending a robot is giving evidence, or this is just a media circus not governance. Which is it?"[41]

We here have a case where some people are treating Pepper in a way that attributes agency to Pepper, whereas others are arguing that it is unethical—and farcical!—to do so. The members of parliament who were asking Pepper questions and inviting Pepper to testify were, as we might say, performing or enacting a hearing with Pepper, during which Pepper was treated like an agent. Technology experts (the *Technology Review*, Yampolskiy, and Bryson) responded that interacting with Pepper like this in a public forum was unethical. Pepper lacks the capacities needed to qualify as somebody who is able to give evidence or testify before a parliament. It is unethical to attribute this agency to Pepper, these technology experts argue, not only because (a) Pepper lacks the intelligence anybody needs to be able to give evidence, but also because (b) treating Pepper as if the robot is able to give evidence may create a false impression that robots like Pepper currently have much more powerful AI than they actually have.[42]

This is an example of how what I am calling the "conceptual ethics" of agency attributions is not a purely hypothetical topic for philosophy books only. It is something that is taking place in public forums. The members of parliament who participated in the hearing suggested by their actions that they find it ethically acceptable to act in ways that attribute fairly advanced kinds of agency to Pepper the robot. The above-cited technology experts took to public forums to voice their ethical objections to this way of interacting with Pepper.

This example raises a few different questions that we need to be careful to keep separate from each other, and in response to which we may come up with valid reasons for treating different cases differently. For example, if we follow commentators like Yampolskiy and Bryson in discouraging the treatment of Pepper like an agent of an intelligent enough sort that it can give evidence before the UK parliament, does this mean that we should refrain from attributing any kind of agency to Pepper at all? If we refuse to attribute agency of some important kind to Pepper, does this force us to also take similar stances to other robots, used in other domains? Or might it be that whether it is a good idea and ethically acceptable to attribute some form of agency to robots will depend importantly on context, and not only on the capacities of the robots in question?

In general, my view is that the following four considerations should be taken into account when we reflect on whether it is a mistake to attribute agency to any robot (or act in ways that appear to attribute agency to the robot). First:

- **Consideration 1**: *Human agency is not the only kind of agency there is; robots may be able to exercise a robotic type of agency, which can be contrasted and compared with human agency, but which should typically (if not always) be held to different standards.*

For example, it may very well have been a mistake to act in a way that suggested that Pepper can give evidence before a parliament in the way that an adult human being is able to. However, this does not preclude the possibility that Pepper might correctly be interpreted as able to exercise some more basic form of agency in this or other contexts. (I will discuss different forms of agency, including more basic forms of agency, in more detail in the next chapter.) Moreover, when Pepper "answers" questions posed by the MPs, Pepper can be seen as interacting with the MPs in a way that is more like a form of agency than the way in which the benches the MPs are sitting on is exercising a form of agency by not breaking under the weight of the MPs.

- **Consideration 2**: *The concept of agency is flexible and multidimensional enough that there is not always a clear-cut answer to whether it is correct or mistaken to treat some robot like an agent of some kind.*

This was one of the main points made in the previous section. We should not assume that there is always a right or wrong answer mechanically implied by the general concept of agency as to whether it is correct or incorrect to interact with a robot (e.g., Pepper) in a way that seemingly attributes agency to the robot. However, with respect to what makes the most sense from an ethical point of view, I suggest the following:

- **Consideration 3**: *Robotic agency should always be understood and interpreted in relation to the agency of the human beings who directly or indirectly interact with the robots in question.*

Pepper's agency, for example, can be interpreted as an extension of the agency of the company behind Pepper (SoftBank Robotics). And in this case, the extended agency of SoftBank in the behavior of Pepper can be seen as being helped along by the behavior of the members of parliament interacting with Pepper. Some aspects of how Pepper is behaving in this situation can be seen as what we might call "flickers of agency" in their own right.[43] But the most significant agency in this particular case is that of the people directly interacting with Pepper (i.e., the members of parliament asking Pepper questions here and now) and the people indirectly interacting with Pepper (i.e., the SoftBank company representatives who prepared and programmed Pepper to be able to participate in this performance).[44]

Lastly, I also suggest:

- **Consideration 4**: *When we reflect on whether it is ethically correct/acceptable or mistaken/unacceptable to attribute agency of some form to particular robots, we need to take into account what values and goals are at stake in the context and domain where the robot is operating.*

The enactment or performance of a hearing with Pepper might be viewed as contrary to the dignity and seriousness of the forum in which Pepper appeared. It might be thought that a forum like the parliament of a democratic state should not be turned, in Bryson's terms, into a "media circus." This would be what we might call a principled criticism of interaction with Pepper of a sort that seemingly attributes a certain form of agency (namely, the ability to testify) in this particular forum. A principled criticism is a criticism tied directly to the values or ideals associated with some particular context or domain. In contrast, the criticism that inviting Pepper to testify might create false beliefs in the general public about how far along the development of AI is can be classified as an instrumental or pragmatic criticism. That is to say, it is a criticism relating to the possible bad effects of, or risks associated with, seemingly attributing the ability to testify to Pepper.

In other domains, it might not offend the values and ideals of the domain in question to attribute (or act in ways that seemingly attribute) agency of some kind to robots in that domain. For example, when Pepper is programmed to welcome guests at hotels, this might seem to be less of an offense to the institution of hotels than programming Pepper to answer questions in a parliamentary hearing can be seen as an offense to the institution of democratic governance. Likewise, acting as if Pepper is able to welcome guests in a hotel might also be considered less likely to mislead the masses about how far along AI is than acting as if Pepper is able to give evidence in parliament might do.

2.5: THINKING TOOLS AND MODELS FROM OTHER AREAS OF PHILOSOPHY

The two last considerations suggested above were as follows. We should always try to understand the apparent agency of robots in a way that clarifies the relation of that robotic agency to the human agency of the humans that directly or indirectly interact with the robots (consideration 3). Additionally, our interpretations of the apparent agency of robots of different kinds, in different domains, ought to be guided by the values and goals specific to those domains (consideration 4). Thus stated, these two theses hopefully seem acceptable to the reader. But as stated, these considerations are both very general and very abstract. The reader might therefore be justified in asking whether there is any further guidance to be had when we try to use these kinds of general considerations in our ethical reflections about particular robots. Say, for example, that we are to assess whether it is inappropriate or whether it is acceptable to think of self-driving cars or military robots as agents of particular kinds. How could we use the two just-stated considerations in our reflections then?

As it happens, I will discuss precisely those two examples in the next chapter. Here I want to first end this chapter by making some suggestions about what further types of philosophical tools one can bring to bear on reasoning about the ethics of attributing agency to robots. It is especially important, I think, to have tools to use if the other two above-suggested considerations are taken on-board. That is, we need something to work with if we also accept the following two ideas: different kinds of robotic agency should not be equated with human agency, but understood instead on their own terms (consideration 1), and the general concept of agency is flexible and multidimensional, with different dimensions mattering in different ways and to different degrees in different contexts (consideration 2).

The first further tool I suggest for ethical reasoning about the appropriateness or inappropriateness of attributing different forms of agency to robots is what I will call "moderate conservatism." By this I mean that, if possible, we should not suggest that people start thinking about robots in some way that is radically different from how most people tend to spontaneously think and talk about robots. Like I noted above, people do tend to attribute agency of different kinds to robots. Both laypeople and experts also talk about robots using the language of agency. We find it hard not to perceive robots as doing things, as making decisions, and so on. The thesis of moderate conservatism would here therefore instruct us to try to find acceptable ways of interpreting robots as some sorts of agents. This is not to say that we should approve of attributing extravagant capacities to robots that they cannot possibly be thought to possess. Rather, it is to say that we should seek ways of interpreting and talking about robots' actual capacities in ways that permit the language of agency (which is so central to ethics and so natural to common sense!), but which do not go overboard.

For example, it is certainly reasonable to argue that it is a mistake to act as if a robot like Pepper can give testimony in a parliamentary setting. People can easily stop themselves from inviting robots to give testimony and acting as if robots are capable of doing so. It might be unreasonable, however, to argue that we should try to extinguish all impulses we have to spontaneously perceive robots like Pepper as some forms of agents, performing some types of robotic actions and making some sort of robotic decisions. That might be too hard to do—since we human beings so naturally fall into thinking in terms of agency. And so what I am calling moderate conservatism would regard the suggestion to abandon all agency language and agency concepts when we think of robots like Pepper as too radical or too demanding.

Another suggestion I have about tools to use is to look around in different areas of philosophy for theories of other phenomena that could be used as models to be imported into this domain as inspiration. Four kinds of theories from different areas of philosophy strike me as particularly relevant when it comes to thinking about the relations between robotic agency and the human agency of the people interacting with the robots. The four kinds of theories are:

Table 2.1.

Theories of relations to the self:	Theories of relations among agents:
1: Theories of the relations among different aspects of an individual's own agency, for example, theories of control	**3: Theories of roles and role-responsibilities**, for example, roles such as being a supervisor, manager, parent, property

over our future agency, theories of rules we make for ourselves (like in Kantian ethics), etc.

owner, etc., and the responsibilities that come with such roles

2: Theories of how we can regulate or indirectly control aspects of ourselves we cannot usually directly control, for example, our moods, our beliefs, our heart rate, etc.

4: Theories of power and power-relations, for example, theories about what sort of power people can justifiably have (e.g., democratically elected leaders) or unjustifiably have (e.g., the power a master might have over a slave)

These four kinds of theories from other areas of philosophy (e.g., the philosophy of mind, political philosophy, other areas of ethics, and so on) can be helpful when we think about how to understand the control over and other forms of relations that people can have to robots.

Theories of the relations among different aspects of one's own agency can be used, for example, to develop models for interpreting how people can have direct or indirect control over the apparent agency of robots. If we see the agency or apparent agency of some robots as a type of extension of our own agency, theories about the relations among different aspects of our own agency can be particularly useful. A remotely operated drone, for example, can easily be perceived as performing actions when observed on its own. But that agency in the drone is, we might say, an extension of the agency of the drone operator. To fill out this suggestion, we could turn to theories about how some aspects of our own agency can interact with other aspects of our own agency, such as theories of how decisions made in the present can control or constrain decisions we will make in the future and trace themselves back to previously made decisions.[45]

Theories of how we can regulate or indirectly control aspects of ourselves over which we lack direct control (e.g., our moods) can help to make sense of how human beings can have indirect control over robots and other systems with some degree of functional autonomy. As we will see in the next chapter, some of the worries philosophers have about potential responsibility gaps have specifically to do with concerns about a lack of direct control over robots operating in autonomous modes. It can become less mysterious how people can nevertheless be said to have control over such robots if there are plausible models for how we can have indirect control over aspects of ourselves that we lack direct control over.

For example, the philosopher Dorothea Debus presents the outlines of a theory of self-regulation of aspects of ourselves we cannot directly control that seems to me particularly useful.[46] Debus discusses our mental lives in particular, that is, things such as our moods or feelings, which are things we typically cannot directly control. In general terms, Debus suggests that we can regulate such aspects of our mental lives when the following conditions obtain: There is some way in which we guide the given aspect of ourselves in a goal-directed way (the "guidance condition"); there is some intervention we can undertake to steer the given aspect of ourselves in the desired direction (the "intervention condition"); and we have a general understanding of the types of causes that tend to bring about or mute the given aspect of or ourselves (the "understanding condition").[47]

If we know, for example, that jazz or a hot chocolate tends to get us into a good mood, we have a way of exposing ourselves to jazz or hot chocolate, and we thereby can guide ourselves in the direction of coming to be in a good mood—then we have some indirect control over whether we are in a good mood, even though we may lack direct control over whether our current mood is good or not. How does that relate to indirect control over robots? Well, suppose there is an autonomously operating robot that we can somehow guide in a goal-directed way. Suppose there is an intervention we can take to achieve that guidance. And suppose that we have an understanding of what could affect the behavior of the autonomously operating robot. Then, according to this way of thinking, we have indirect control over the actions and behaviors of the robot, even if it is not currently under our direct control.

Consider next roles and role-responsibilities. Legal scholars have already done a good job at pointing out that legal theories of roles and role-responsibilities can serve as good models for how to think about the roles and responsibilities that people can have in relation to robots such as self-driving cars or military robots.[48] What responsibilities might a user or owner of a self-driving car have in relation to an autonomously operating self-driving car? To come up with a theory of this, we can think about the responsibilities related to the roles of being the manager of a taxi company or the employer of a private chauffeur.[49]

Consider lastly power and power relations. Within so-called republican political theory, the historian of ideas Quentin Skinner and the philosopher Philip Pettit have developed theories of relations between people who are under the power of other people that can be useful here.[50] According to this way of thinking, somebody is under somebody else's power if the former's ability to make choices among different options is subject to the approval of the latter and/or if the latter has means by which they can stop the former from making certain choices if they should wish to do so. Let's say, for example, that a child has certain toys the child can play with. But at any time, the parents can take away some or all of the toys if the parents disapprove or for any other reason should wish to remove any of the toys. If that is so, the parents have power over which toys the child is playing with—even if the parents sit back and do nothing and let the child play with any of the toys the child wants to play with. The power lies in that ability to intervene and restrict or remove options.

Such thinking can easily be transferred over to the case of human-robot relations. Thus a human being can be understood as having power over a robot—including an autonomously operating robot—if the human being has some means of removing options from the robot or otherwise restricting what the robot does. The human being can have this power even if he or she sits back and does nothing and thereby lets the robot operate on its own. It is the possession of the ability to stop the robot or to change the way the robot will function in the future that constitutes the power the human has over the robot.

2.6: CONCLUDING REMARKS

In this chapter, I have been discussing robots and agency in very general terms. I have been discussing methodological issues concerning how best to approach the question of whether specific types of robots can be thought of as able to exercise particular types of agency. And I have been more concerned with the status of the problem of whether we should attribute agency to robots than with substantive answers to that question as it applies to any particular robots or any particular kinds of agency. In the next chapter, however, I will zoom in on two specific kinds of robots and their agency. I will focus on self-driving cars and autonomous weapons systems. And I will propose and briefly defend a particular way of thinking about the agency of such robots. In particular, I will be discussing that way of thinking with a view to the question of who should be held responsible if and when self-driving cars and autonomous weapons systems cause harm to people.

NOTES

1. Royakkers and Van Est, *Just Ordinary Robots*, op. cit.

2. Gunkel, *Robot Rights*, op. cit., ix.

3. While I wrote this book, I was working at the Eindhoven University of Technology. Since then I have moved to Utrecht University.

4. http://www.techunited.nl/en/ (Accessed on August 21, 2019).

5. http://www.techunited.nl/en/ (Accessed on August 21, 2019).

6. Judith Van Gaal (2013), "RoboCup, Máxima onder de indruk von robotica," *Cursor*, https://www.cursor.tue.nl/nieuws/2013/juni/robocup-maxima-onder-de-indruk-van-robotica/ (Accessed on August 21, 2019).

7. Julia Carpenter (2016), *Culture and Human-Robot Interactions in Militarized Spaces*, London: Routledge.

8. Megan Garber (2013), "Funerals for Fallen Robots," *The Atlantic*, https://www.theatlantic.com/technology/archive/2013/09/funerals-for-fallen-robots/279861/ (Accessed on August 21, 2019).

9. See, for example, Kate Devlin (2018), *Turned On: Science, Sex and Robots*, London: Bloomsbury.

10. Sven Nyholm and Lily Frank (2019), "It Loves Me, It Loves Me Not: Is It Morally Problematic to Design Sex Robots That Appear to 'Love' Their Owners?," *Techné: Research in Philosophy and Technology* 23(3), 402–24.

11. See, for instance, Simon Atkinson (2017), "Robot Priest: The Future of Funerals?," BBC, https://www.bbc.com/news/av/world-asia-41033669/robot-priest-the-future-of-funerals (Accessed on August 21, 2019), and Adario Strange (2017), "Robot Performing Japanese Funeral Rites Shows No One's Job Is Safe," *Mashable*, https://mashable.com/2017/08/26/pepper-robot-funeral-ceremony-japan/?europe=true (Accessed on August 21, 2019).

12. I discuss this at greater length in chapter 3. See the references there.

13. Fritz Heider and Marianne Simmel (1944), "An Experimental Study of Apparent Behavior," *American Journal of Psychology* 57(2), 243–59.

14. Valerie A. Kuhlmeier (2013), "The Social Perception of Helping and Hindering," in M. D. Rutherford and Valerie A. Kuhlmeier, *Social Perception: Detection and Interpretation of Animacy, Agency, and Intention*, Cambridge, MA: The MIT Press, 283–304.

15. See, for example, De Graaf and Malle, "People's Explanations of Robot Behavior Subtly Reveal Mental State Inferences," op. cit.

16. Alexis Burgess and David Plunkett (2013), "Conceptual Ethics I-II," *Philosophy Compass* 8(12), 1091–110.

17. Markus Schlosser (2015), "Agency," *The Stanford Encyclopedia of Philosophy* (Fall 2015 Edition), Edward N. Zalta (ed.), https://plato.stanford.edu/archives/fall2015/entries/agency/ (Accessed on August 21, 2019).

18. Robert W. Shumaker, Kristina R. Walkup, and Benjamin B. Beck (2011), *Animal Tool Behavior: The Use and Manufacture of Tools by Animals*, Baltimore: Johns Hopkins University Press.

19. I am simplifying a little bit here. Strictly speaking, there are some criminal offenses that involve strict liability and hence don't necessarily have a mental element (beyond the need for "volition," which is obscurely defined). Also, in civil law, there are many cases where not even knowledge is required for liability. What matters is what someone ought to have known at the time. Thanks to John Danaher for helpful discussion about this.

20. See, for example, Charles E. Torcia (1993), *Wharton's Criminal Law*, § 27, 164, cited by Jeffrey K. Gurney (2016), "Crashing into the Unknown: An Examination of Crash-Optimization Algorithms through the Two Lanes of Ethics and Law," *Alabama Law Review* 79(1), 183–267.

21. Cf. Margaret S. Clark, Brian D. Earp, and Molly J. Crockett (in press), "Who Are 'We' and Why Are We Cooperating? Insights from Social Psychology," *Behavioral and Brain Sciences*.

22. Stephen Darwall (2006), *The Second Person Standpoint: Morality, Accountability, and Respect*, Cambridge, MA: Harvard University Press.

23. See, for example, Gregg D. Caruso and Owen Flanagan (eds.) (2018), *Neuroexistentialism: Meaning, Morals, and Purpose in the Age of Neuroscience*, Oxford: Oxford University Press.

24. See, for example, Joshua Greene and Jonathan Cohen (2004), "For the Law, Neuroscience Changes Nothing and Everything," *Philosophical Transactions of the Royal Society* 359, 1775–85; Greene, *Moral Tribes*, op. cit.; and Isaac Wiegman (2017), "The Evolution of Retribution: Intuitions Undermined," *Pacific Philosophical Quarterly* 98, 193–218. See also Guy Kahane (2011), "Evolutionary Debunking Arguments," *Noûs* 45(1), 103–25.

25. See, for example, John Danaher (2019), "The Rise of the Robots and The Crisis of Moral Patiency," *AI & Society* 34(1), 129–36, and Brett Frischmann and Evan Selinger (2018), *Re-Engineering Humanity*, Cambridge: Cambridge University Press.

26. Andreas Matthias (2004), "The Responsibility Gap: Ascribing Responsibility for the Actions of Learning Automata," *Ethics and Information Technology* 6(3), 175–83. A related worry that is interestingly discussed by Alan Rubel, Adam Pham, and Clinton Castro concerns whether some people might sometimes try mask or obscure responsibility for their own actions by making

use of automated systems (e.g., algorithmic decision-making systems) that get
results they desire but that they do not want to take responsibility for—a kind
of wrongdoing that Rubel et al. call "agency laundering." See Rubel, Alan,
Pham, Adam, and Castro, Clinton (2019), "Agency Laundering and Algorithmic Decision Systems," in Natalie Greene Taylor, Caitlin Christiam-Lamb,
Michelle H. Martin, and Bonnie A. Nardi (eds.), *Information in Contemporary
Society*, Dordrecht: Springer, 590–600.

27. John Danaher (2016), "Robots, Law, and the Retribution Gap," *Ethics
and Information Technology* 18(4), 299–309.

28. Gurney, "Crashing into the Unknown," op. cit. For more on how robots
and AI are disruptive of our current ethical equilibrium, see Joanna Bryson
(2019), "Patiency Is Not a Virtue: The Design of Intelligent Systems and Systems of Ethics, *Ethics and Information Technology* 20(1), 15–26, and John
Danaher (2019), "The Robotic Disruption of Morality," *Philosophical Disquisitions*, https://philosophicaldisquisitions.blogspot.com/2019/08/the-robotic-dis-
ruption-of-morality.html (Accessed on September 2, 2019).

29. Darwall, *The Second Person Standpoint*, op. cit.

30. Gurney, "Crashing into the Unknown," op. cit.; J. K. Gurney (2013),
"Sue My Car Not Me: Products Liability and Accidents Involving Autonomous
Vehicles," *Journal of Law, Technology & Policy* 2, 247–277; J. K. Gurney
(2015), "Driving into the Unknown: Examining the Crossroads of Criminal
Law and Autonomous Vehicles," *Wake Forest Journal of Law and Policy* 5(2),
393–442.

31. John Frank Weaver (2013), *Robots Are People Too: How Siri, Google
Car, and Artificial Intelligence Will Force Us to Change Our Laws*, Santa
Barbara, CA: Praeger.

32. Jacob Turner (2019), *Robot Rules: Regulating Artificial Intelligence*,
London: Palgrave Macmillan.

33. Weaver, *Robots Are People Too*, op. cit., 4.

34. Jeffrey K. Gurney (2017), "Imputing Driverhood: Applying a Reasonable Driver Standard to Accidents Caused by Autonomous Vehicles," in Patrick Lin, Keith Abney, and Ryan Jenkins (eds.), *Robot Ethics 2.0: From Autonomous Cars to Artificial Intelligence*, Oxford: Oxford University Press, 51–65.

35. Persson and Savulescu, *Unfit for the Future*, op. cit.

36. This is the main refrain in Jean-Paul Sartre (2007), *Existentialism Is a
Humanism*, translated by Carol Macomber, New Haven, CT: Yale University
Press. For an accessible introduction to and overview of existentialist philosophy, see Sarah Bakewell (2016), *At the Existentialist Café: Freedom, Being,
and Apricot Cocktails*, London: Other Press.

37. Christine Korsgaard (1996), *The Sources of Normativity*, Cambridge:
Cambridge University Press.

38. As reported in Jane Wakefield (2018), "Robot 'Talks' to MPs about Future of AI in the Classroom," BBC, https://www.bbc.com/news/technology-45879961 (Accessed on August 21, 2019).

39. Karen Hao (2018), "The UK Parliament Asking a Robot to Testify about AI is a Dumb Idea," *Technology Review*, https://www.technologyreview.com/the-download/612269/the-uk-parliament-asking-a-robot-to-testify-about-ai-is-a-dumb-idea/ (Accessed on December 27, 2018).

40. Ibid.

41. https://twitter.com/j2bryson/status/1050332579197571073 (Accessed on August 21, 2019).

42. Cf. Sharkey, "Mama Mia It's Sophia," op. cit.

43. My choice of words here is a nod to John Martin Fischer and his discussion of "flickers of freedom" in John Martin Fischer (1994), *The Metaphysics of Free Will*, Oxford: Blackwell.

44. The post-phenomenology philosopher Peter-Paul Verbeek argues that we should attribute a broad type of agency to "human-technology associations." I will defend a somewhat similar thesis regarding the agency of self-driving cars and autonomous weapons systems in the next chapter. A difference, though, between my own view about such agency and the view Verbeek takes—as I understand his view—is that Verbeek seems to understand the idea of agency in a slightly weaker and looser sense than I do. On that view, something possesses or exercises agency if it has an impact or makes a difference. I have in mind something stronger and narrower when I am discussing agency: that is, the performance of actions, decision-making, planning, and so on. For Verbeek's discussion, see Peter-Paul Verbeek (2011), *Moralizing Technology: Understanding and Designing the Morality of Things*, Chicago: University of Chicago Press.

45. See, for example, Jon Elster (1979), *Ulysses and the Sirens: Studies in Rationality and Irrationality*, Cambridge: Cambridge University Press. We can also draw on work in the philosophy of mind about the so-called extended mind thesis, according to which our minds sometimes extend out into some of the technologies we use in the sense of forming functional systems together with those technologies. See Andy Clark and David J. Chalmers (1998), "The extended mind," *Analysis* 58(1): 7–19 .

46. Dorothea Debus, "Shaping Our Mental Lives: On the Possibility of Mental Self-Regulation," *Proceedings of the Aristotelian Society* CXVI(3), 341–65.

47. To simplify the presentation here, I am leaving out a fourth condition that Debus also discusses, which is directly related to the intervention condition. That fourth condition is what Debus calls the "effective agency condi-

tion." The idea is that the intervention(s) available to us should be effective in bringing about the desired effects (Ibid., 348).

48. See, for example, Gurney, "Imputing Driverhood," op. cit., and Robert W. Peterson (2012), "New Technology—Old Law: Autonomous Vehicles and California's Insurance Framework," *Santa Clara Law Review* 52, 101–53.

49. This was an idea that John Danaher and I discussed on his podcast. See John Danaher and Sven Nyholm (2018), "Episode #40: Nyholm on Accident Algorithms and the Ethics of Self-Driving Cars," *Philosophical Disquisitions*, https://philosophicaldisquisitions.blogspot.com/2018/06/episode-40-nyholm-on-accident.html (Accessed on August 25, 2019). See also Peterson, "New Technology—Old Law," op. cit.

50. Quentin Skinner (1997), *Liberty before Liberalism*, Cambridge: Cambridge University Press; Philip Pettit (1997), *Republicanism: A Theory Government*, Oxford: Oxford University Press; Philip Pettit (2014), *Just Freedom: A Moral Compass for a Complex World*, New York: Norton.

3

HUMAN-ROBOT COLLABORATIONS AND RESPONSIBILITY GAPS

3.1: CRASHING SELF-DRIVING CARS

Before 2015, discussions of crashes involving self-driving cars were largely hypothetical. However, with increased road-testing of autonomous vehicles, real-world crashes soon started happening, with around twenty cases in 2015. The initial crashes were primarily instances of conventional cars rear-ending slow-moving self-driving vehicles. And there was little damage done.[1] However, in 2016 there were some more dramatic developments.

On Valentine's Day of 2016, there was not a very romantic encounter between an autonomous vehicle and a bus in Mountain View, California.[2] One of Google's self-driving cars crashed into the bus. Though no human being was injured, there was some damage to Google's test vehicle. Unlike on earlier occasions, when there had been collisions between conventional cars and Google's automated vehicles, where the blame had always been put on human drivers, this case was different. This was the first time that Google assumed responsibility for what happened. "We clearly bear some responsibility," Google admitted in the accident report.[3] Google also promised to update the software of their cars to make them better at predicting the behavior of larger vehicles, like buses.

Another, more tragic incident in May of 2016 also marked a first in the history of robotic driving. A Tesla model S in "autopilot" mode collided with a truck that the Tesla's sensors had not spotted, leading to the first fatal crash: The man riding in the Tesla vehicle was instantly killed when the truck and the car collided.[4] Unlike Google, though, Tesla didn't take responsibility for what happened. In a carefully worded statement, Tesla expressed sympathy for their customer's family, but Tesla also emphasized that the "customer" is "always in control and responsible."[5] Like Google, however, Tesla did promise to update their equipment. They promised to make their sensors better at spotting moving objects in strong sunlight. In a way, then, Tesla admitted that their product may have been causally responsible, at least in part, for the fatality, though they denied that they were to be assigned legal, and perhaps also moral, responsibility for what happened.

In March of 2018, in turn, for the first time, a self-driving car hit and killed a pedestrian.[6] Uber was testing out self-driving Volvo cars in Tempe, Arizona. One of these cars hit and killed a woman—Elaine Herzberg—who suddenly crossed the road in front of the car. Herzberg died on the way to the hospital. Following this event, Uber immediately suspended their testing of self-driving vehicles in Tempe and other places. In the immediate aftermath of the deadly crash, Uber reached a financial settlement with the family, and charges were not pressed. Later in the year, Uber released a seventy-page document about this incident in which, among other things, they argued that self-driving cars have the potential to become safer than regular cars. In December of 2018, Uber resumed their testing of self-driving cars on public roads, this time in Pittsburgh, Pennsylvania.[7]

These cases help to illustrate the general topic I will discuss in this chapter: namely, how to allocate responsibility when robots or other autonomous technologies harm or kill human beings. More specifically, what follows investigates the relation between the type of agency exercised in cases where robots harm/kill humans, and the question of who bears responsibility for that agency. The primary focus will be on self-driving cars. But autonomous weapons systems and responsibility for harms and deaths caused by them will also be discussed. In discussing these topics together, I follow writers such as Duncan Purves et al.[8] and John Danaher,[9] who also explore the important parallels between these different technologies and the harms they might cause.

Notably, the small but growing philosophical discussion about harms and deaths caused by robots has so far often had the following features:

1. It is typically assumed, without much argument, that autonomous technologies exercise agency.
2. This agency is regarded as involving a high degree of autonomy/independence.
3. Much of the focus has been on locating potential responsibility gaps, that is, cases where it is unclear or indeterminate who is morally or legally responsible for some outcome or event.
4. Much of the discussion has been about accident scenarios and cases where the technologies do not function in the ways they are meant to.

This chapter takes an alternative approach. It looks more carefully at what kind(s) of agency we can sensibly attribute to the given types of robots. And it questions the tendency to view these types of agency as instances of strongly autonomous or independent agency. Rather than focusing on finding more potential responsibility gaps, this chapter formulates a set of questions we should be asking in allocating responsibility for the types of agency that will be discussed. And, rather than going directly to failures and accident scenarios, this chapter takes as its starting point "normal" cases where these technologies function in the ways they are intended to.

My main thesis of this chapter can be summarized as follows. Yes, it does indeed make sense to attribute significant forms of agency to many current robotic technologies, such as self-driving cars or autonomous weapons systems. But this agency is typically best seen as a type of collaborative agency, where the other key partners of these collaborations are certain humans. This means that when we try to allocate responsibility for any harms or deaths caused by these technologies, we should not focus on theories of individual agency and responsibility for individual agency. We should rather draw on philosophical analyses of collaborative agency and responsibility for such agency. In particular, we should draw on hierarchical models of collaborative agency, where some agents within the collaborations are under other agents' supervision and authority.

Two quick notes on terminology before we get into it: First, when we talk about, for example, "autonomous vehicles," what this refers to is functionally autonomous vehicles in the sense of vehicles that can operate for shorter or longer periods of time without any direct human intervention. A functionally autonomous machine is any machine that for some period of time can perform some task on its own.[10] This is different from autonomous agency in the sense of "autonomy" typically intended when philosophers discuss ethics. Autonomous agency in the philosophical sense refers to agency involving a certain amount of independent thinking and reasoning guided by some particular outlook on life, the capacity to reflect self-critically on one's actions and decisions, and so on.[11] A robot can be functionally autonomous without being strongly autonomous in the sense that an autonomous person can be. What I am discussing in this chapter, then, can be also reformulated as the following question: How autonomous (in the philosophical sense of independent agency) are functionally autonomous robots, such as self-driving cars and military robots? If they are some form of agents, how autonomous is their agency in the philosophical sense of "autonomy"?

Second, when self-driving cars and other functionally autonomous machines are being discussed, it is common to see references to different "levels" of autonomy, as defined by SAE International (which is an automotive standardization organization).[12] For example, level 5 refers to full automation, where the person using the autonomous vehicle does not need to do anything, whereas level 0 requires the driver to perform all normal driving tasks. In between 0 and 5, different levels are defined in terms of how many different driving tasks can be taken over by the system. I mention this idea of levels of autonomy here because I will discuss more or less advanced levels or types of agency below. I will not name the levels of agency I will discuss with numbers, but instead use descriptive names. When I talk about more or less advanced forms of agency below, for some readers this may bring to mind the discussion of levels of autonomy. But what I am interested in is something slightly different than what those who discuss those so-called levels of autonomy are discussing. While they are interested in what tasks the autonomous vehicle can take over, I am interested here in the question of whether creating autonomous vehicles that can take over tasks from human beings means creating robots with humanlike agency or not.

3.2: RESPONSIBILITY GAPS AND RETRIBUTION GAPS

When philosophers discuss the ethics of functionally autonomous systems, you will often find them making remarks such as the following:

- If motor vehicles are to be truly autonomous and be able to operate responsibly on our roads, they will need to replicate . . . the human decision-making process.[13]
- Driverless cars, like [autonomous weapons systems], would likely be required to make life-and-death decisions in the course of operation.[14]
- Driverless systems put machines in the position of making split-second decisions that could have life-or-death implications.[15]
- What distinguishes [autonomous weapons systems] from existing weapons is that they have the capacity to choose their own targets.[16]

If a robot were indeed able to "replicate the human decision-making process," "make life-and-death decisions," make "split-second decisions," or "choose their own targets," the robot would be an agent. On our ordinary conceptions of agency, making decisions and choices are key aspects of agency. Hence, these just-cited commentators all attribute agency, or decision-making capacities, to the automated systems themselves. Mark Coeckelbergh is even more explicit about this. He writes that when a human being uses a self-driving car, we can assume that "all agency is entirely transferred to the machine."[17]

Notably, it is becoming common to move from the premise that automated systems are decision-making agents to the claim that moral principles need to be programmed into these systems.[18] The idea is that if these systems are going to be making decisions, including "life-and-death decisions," they should be making morally acceptable decisions. Otherwise they would pose an unacceptable danger to human beings. But this does not yet settle the question of who is responsible if and when people are harmed or killed by autonomous systems. A robot could be programmed to behave in line with ethically acceptable principles without itself being able to be held responsible for doing this (or for failing to do so). So even if robots are able to conform to moral principles, there is still a question of who is responsible for what the robot does or fails to do.[19]

Accordingly, much of the discussion about robots and potential harms has been about how to allocate responsibility for the decision-making that these robots are thought of as engaging in.[20] It is in these discussions that it becomes clear that not only do writers like the ones just quoted above attribute agency to the robots they are discussing. They are also attributing a highly autonomous and/or independent kind of agency to these machines. A look at some of their worries about responsibility gaps will help to illustrate this.

Robert Sparrow, for example, discusses autonomous weapons systems, and argues that it is hard to identify anybody who can be held responsible for harm or deaths caused by these systems.[21] The programmers, Sparrow argues, cannot be held responsible, because they cannot fully "control and predict" what their creations will do, for which reason it would be unfair to hold them accountable. The commanding officers, in turn, also cannot be held responsible: The actions of the automated weapons systems are not fully "determined" by the orders of the commanding officers. What about the robots themselves? Sparrow thinks that they act independently, for reasons and motivations of their own. But he also thinks that because robots cannot suffer from any punishments we might impose on them, it makes no sense to hold them responsible for their actions.[22] None of the involved parties can sensibly be held responsible. The robots are acting independently, for which reason the humans cannot be held responsible. But the robots cannot respond to punishment and blame in the ways humans do, for which reason they cannot sensibly be held responsible.

Consider next Alexander Hevelke and Julian Nida-Rümelin's discussion of responsibility for crashes with autonomous vehicles.[23] Following legal scholars Gary Marchant and Rachel Lindor,[24] Hevelke and Nida-Rümelin first argue that car manufacturers should not be held responsible for crashes with self-driving cars. The reason they offer is that this might disincentivize manufacturers from developing these cars, which would be a bad thing since there are many potential benefits to automated driving.[25] This leaves us with car users or the cars themselves.

Hevelke and Nida-Rümelin do not take seriously the possibility of holding any autonomous systems responsible, focusing instead on users. They first argue that drivers of autonomous vehicles cannot be held responsible on the basis of any special duty of care. Accidents will be rare enough for it to be unfair to expect people to pay enough attention that they could reasonably be expected to step in and take over before accidents occur. What about drivers under the guise of risk-imposers? Hevelke and Nida-Rümelin think this would unfairly make people hostage to moral luck. The only difference between people whose automated cars harm others and people whose automated cars don't is that the former suffer bad luck.[26] Everyone who uses self-driving cars is equal in how they create risks in using these cars. Therefore, it makes sense, Hevelke and Nida-Rümelin argue, to hold all users collectively responsible under the guise of a risk-creating community. This can be done by means of a mandated insurance or tax on automated driving.

A worry one might have about this is that Hevelke and Nida-Rümelin's solution opens up the potential for the sort of "retribution gaps" that John Danaher discusses.[27] When somebody is harmed through somebody else's agency (be it a human or a robot), people generally tend to want to find some individual or individuals who can be punished for this. But if the agency in question is a robotic agency, Danaher argues, then since robots are themselves not fit to be punished and no humans are fully responsible for their robotic agency, there is a potential "retribution gap." In other words, people will have a strong impulse to want to punish somebody, but nobody will be an appropriate target of punishment. Many people are likely to find a general tax or mandated insurance insufficient to fill this retribution gap.

One of the most noteworthy things about these just-sketched arguments is that robotic systems are portrayed as exercising a great deal of autonomy in the sense of not being under the control of any particular people. People, it is argued, cannot predict or control how the systems will act. And they cannot be expected to pay sufficient amounts of attention to how the systems act to be able to exercise control over them. The robots, it is thought, will act independently, on their own. And so it would be unfair to hold any human agents responsible for the robotic agency exercised by the autonomous systems.

It is worth noting here that mere unpredictability and the inability to fully control a piece of technology do not by themselves appear to eliminate responsibility on the part of the user. If you (say) have a piece of equipment operating on the basis of a randomizing algorithm that you know is dangerous and that you cannot predict and control, you can very sensibly be held responsible for any harms this instrument might cause if you choose to use it. In order for it to make sense to think that there might potentially be a responsibility gap here, it would seemingly need to be the case that the unpredictability and lack of control depend on the presence of a significant form of autonomy or agency in the technology. Therefore, in order for a robot or automated system to pose a challenge to human responsibility, it needs to be an autonomous agent in some nontrivial sense.

But are most automated systems really strongly autonomous agents, who act independently, outside of human control, for which reason people cannot be held responsible for any harms the robotic systems might cause? Just what type of agency can we justifiably attribute to robotic systems, such as self-driving cars, and how does it relate to the human agency of the humans involved? An alternative way of thinking about these issues will now be described.

3.3: DIFFERENT TYPES OF AGENCY

A 2012 report on autonomous weapons systems from the US military's Defense Science Board offers a different perspective on the autonomy—or lack thereof—of robotic systems. In one key passage, the authors of this report write:

> there are no fully autonomous systems just as there are no fully autonomous soldiers, sailors, airmen, or Marines. . . . Perhaps the most important message for commanders is that all machines are supervised by humans to some degree, and the best capabilities result from the coordination and collaboration of humans and machines.[28]

Consider also the following remark, made by David Gunkel in an interview on his work on the ethics of robots:

> I would say that the distributed agency that we see for example with the corporation is a really good benchmark and . . . precedent for where things might go both in moral and legal terms with regard to our understanding of machines and their place in the world.[29]

These two quotes point in a very different direction than the arguments and quotes reviewed in the previous section. They point in the direction of "distributed agency" and "coordination and collaboration of humans and machines." How can we decide whether this is a better way to think of the agency of robotic systems like automated weapons systems or automated cars? That is why might one think in these terms, rather than in terms of independent or individual agency? To answer this, it is a good idea to first zoom out to a slightly more abstract level and distinguish among various different more or less advanced forms of agency.[30] We can then ask: (a) which of these forms of agency are automated systems able to exercise, and (b) are those forms of individual and independent agency, or are they rather best thought of as distinctive types of cooperative or collaborative agency?

The approach I will take here is a functionalist approach, on which different types of agency are primarily analyzed in terms of different functions that more or less advanced agents are able to perform.[31] An alternative approach would be to focus instead on the idea of intentionality. "Intentionality," in this context, refers to the power or ability of minds to be directed at certain things—or, in other words, the ability to have thoughts and other attitudes that are about certain things.[32] For example, the intentionality of a desire to drink some coffee is directed at the possibility of drinking coffee. If we would approach the question of agency from the point of view of intentionality here, we would then ask under what descriptions apparent actions can be described as intentional, or for what reasons the agent might be interpreted as acting.[33] I have no principled disagreement with that approach to the topic of agency in general. However, when it comes to the question of whether we can attribute agency to robots and automated systems, it appears better to first investigate what sorts of functions the systems can perform.

Let us start with the most basic type of agency there is. In an example Philip Pettit uses in a number of his papers on group agency,[34] Pettit imagines a fairly simple robot that is able to do the following: It moves around in a room and is on the lookout for objects with a certain shape. If it finds these objects, the robot moves them around in certain ways (e.g., putting the objects into a bucket). When the robot does not encounter the relevant types of objects in the room, it keeps moving around until the relevant type of object appears. Pettit suggests that this robot's behavior gives us an example of a simple type of agency: pursuing a goal in a way that is sensitive or responsive to the environment.

However, as far as we know from Pettit's example, the robot might not be able to exercise any other type of agency, if it is put in any other context. And so the simplest possible agency is what we might call:

> **Domain-specific basic agency**: pursuing goals on the basis of representations, within certain limited domains

More advanced agents—which may still be basic agents—would be able to pursue different types of goals on the basis of their representations, across different domains. Yet even more advanced agents would also be able to follow certain rules—certain *do*s and *don't*s—in their pursuit of their domain-specific goals.[35] Their agency is constrained by rules that prevent the agents from pursuing their goals in particular ways, while permitting them to pursue these goals in other ways. Consider:

> **Domain-specific principled agency**: pursuing goals on the basis of representations in a way that is regulated and constrained by certain rules or principles, within certain limited domains

If we are playing sports, for example, we do certainly pursue certain goals relevant to whatever we're playing (e.g., scoring a goal). But we do so in ways that respect the rules of the game. We are thereby exercising more advanced agency than if we are simply trying to put the ball or whatever it might be in a certain place.

Sticking with the sports example, our principled agency may be undertaken under the watch of some authority (e.g., a referee), who makes sure that we stick to the rules, and who might otherwise step in and stop us. In general, we may be exercising:

> **Domain-specific supervised and deferential principled agency**: pursuing a goal on the basis of representations in a way that is regulated by certain rules or principles, while being supervised by some authority who can stop us or to whom control can be ceded, at least within certain limited domains

Such agency might be called non-solipsistic or social, since it is partly defined in terms of a relation to other agents.[36] But this is still different from what we can call:

> **Domain-specific responsible agency**: pursuing goals in a way that is sensitive to representations of the environment and regulated by certain rules/principles for what to do/not to do (within certain limited domains), while having the ability to understand criticism of one's agency, along with the ability to defend or alter one's actions based on one's principles or principled criticism of one's agency

This is different from simply being answerable to some authority. Responsible agency implies that even if others might criticize your agency and may give you reason to abort what you are doing, this nevertheless leaves open the possibility of "standing one's ground" on the basis of rules or principles that one thinks others could also recognize as valid bases for the regulation of action.[37] Either way, this type of agency is responsive to other agents and their opinions. Hence, responsible agency is also a socially embedded form of agency, just like supervised and deferential agency is. But an important difference is that it puts the different agents involved on a more equal footing.[38] The practice of discussing reasons for and against our own or others' conduct assumes that we cannot simply order each other around, but that we are instead on an equal enough level that we owe each other justifications.[39] It opens us up for shared discussion of the principles or standards governing the agency in a way that supervised and deferential agency does not.

Obviously, these just-sketched forms of agency do not exhaust all possible more or less advanced forms of agency. Kantian philosophers, for example, would want us to add agency involving the ability to act on self-adopted principles that we choose on the basis of thinking that the principles could be elevated to universal laws for all.[40] And some theorists would want us to also discuss ideas about under what descriptions actions are intentional, or issues relating to what reasons we can interpret agents as acting on the basis of.[41] But the just-sketched range of different types of agency is sufficient for the purposes of this chapter. It (a) helps to illustrate that there is a wide range of different types of agency whereby some forms are much more sophisticated than others, and (b) gives us enough by way of abstract theory needed to investigate whether automated systems like self-driving cars or automated weapons systems are agents of some more sophisticated sort, capable of acting independently. Let us now ask what types of agency such systems can exercise, taking self-driving cars as our main example. Having done that, we can turn next to the question of whether the relevant kind of agency is an autonomous or independent type of agency, or whether it is better regarded as a form of collaborative or coordinated agency.

3.4: SELF-DRIVING CARS VERSUS SMALL CHILDREN, AND INDIVIDUAL VERSUS COLLABORATIVE AGENCY

Does a self-driving car exercise domain-specific basic agency? That is, does it pursue goals in a way that is sensitive to representations of the environments, at least within certain specific domains of activity? An autonomous car is able to navigate its surroundings in the pursuit of traffic goals: getting to its intended destination. It does so in a way that is sensitive to representations of its environment: namely, those generated by the car's sensors and its internal model of the surroundings.[42] So yes, it seems that we can attribute domain-specific basic agency to an automated car.[43]

What about principled agency? A self-driving car is programmed to follow traffic rules strictly, and pursues its goals in a way that is restricted by the traffic rules.[44] So yes, it seems that we can also attribute principled agency to an automated car—at least of a domain-specific kind, where the relevant domain is that of traffic. (However, as I will argue in chapter 7, there are morally relevant differences in the way that a human being can follow or fail to follow principles and the way that a robot can do so or fail to do so.)

Is a self-driving car's agency being watched over by any authority, who has the power to take over control or stop the car from doing what it's doing, and to whom the car, therefore, is deferential? Yes. Depending on what engineering ideals are used, the details differ.[45] But whether it is the person in the car who is able to take over control of some or all of the aspects of the driving, or whether it is the engineers who monitor the cars' performance and who update their software and hardware as needed—there is somebody acting as a supervisor to whom the car must always defer. In the terms used at the end of the previous chapter, there will always be people who have power over the car. And so we can conclude that the principled agency we can attribute to the car is of a supervised and deferential sort.[46]

What the car cannot do is to exercise responsible agency. The car cannot enter into a discussion about the reasons in favor of, or against, its actions. And it cannot take responsibility for its actions in the way that a responsible human being can.[47] Future robots might be able to do these things. But we are not there yet. So it is not sensible and appropriate to attribute responsible agency to an autonomous vehicle. Yet, we can attribute basic and principled agency of a supervised and deferential sort to the car, nevertheless.

Let us compare this case to that of a small child. The small child can pursue goals in a way that is responsive to its environment (e.g., going to the other side of the room in order to get to its toys). And it can follow rules laid down by its parents. In this way, the small child is also supervised by and deferential to its parents, who are authorities to whom the small child is answerable. But most likely, the small child is not yet a responsible agent who can articulate arguments, reasons, and principles in favor of or against its actions, and who can debate the merits of different courses of action in the way that responsible adults (e.g., the parents) are able to. Of course, the small child will soon acquire this ability, but it may not yet have it.[48] So, in a way, the agency of the small child can be compared to that of the self-driving car, though the agency the child can perform is much less domain-specific than that of the automated car.[49]

Consider now another distinction: namely, that between individual agency and collaborative agency. The former refers, simply put, to doing things on one's own, not necessarily needing the collaboration of others. The latter refers to doing things together with somebody else (some agent or set of agents).[50] To relate this to our present topic of discussion, we will consider two different types of deferential and supervised agency.

To repeat, somebody exercises deferential and supervised agency if there is some authority who is watching over what the agent is doing, and is able to take over control or stop the agent from doing what he/she is doing. Such agency can either be (a) initiated by the acting agent, based on his/her own goals/wishes, or (b) initiated by the other party, based on that other party's goals or wishes.

For example, if a child is playing with its toys under its parents' supervision, the child may be doing this because it wants to play with its toys. This is an example of deferential and supervised agency initiated by the agent. Consider by way of contrast also an example in which a parent instructs the small child to do some gardening (e.g., to rake leaves), and in which the parent is then watching over the child to make sure that it is doing the gardening in a way that conforms to how the parent wants this bit of gardening to be done. Let us now relate these two examples back to the distinction between individual and collaborative agency.

When the child plays with its toys on its own initiative, though under the supervision and authority of its parents, this is an instance of individual agency. The child is doing this on its own, though the parents have a watchful eye over the child. In contrast, when the child does some gardening on the parent's initiative, and the parent is watching over the child to make sure that the child does the gardening in the right way, this is better thought of as an instance of collaborative agency. The child is acting in the service of a goal set by the parent. And the parent is acting as a supervisor who monitors and regulates the actions of the child (i.e., the gardening the child performs). Even if the child is "doing most of the work," this is nevertheless a collaborative agency, rather than a purely individual agency on the part of the child.

We can now return to the sort of deferential and supervised agency we have said that self-driving cars can exercise (at least within a limited domain). Let us ask whether that agency on the part of the car is self-initiated or other-initiated. We are here also interested in what this implies about whether the car is best thought of as exercising independent or individual agency, as one possibility, or whether it is better thought of as exercising dependent and collaborative agency, as another possibility.

Well, the car is not going to be choosing its own primary travel goals (e.g., going to the grocery store). The goals will instead be set by the person who wishes to travel in the car (e.g., somebody who needs to buy some groceries). Nor will the car set its goals with respect to things such as safety or traffic-rules; these goals will be set by car designers and lawmakers, etc.[51] So the deferential and supervised agency exercised by the car is undertaken in response to somebody else's initiative. As such, it is exercising what is best understood as a kind of collaborative agency—even if the car might be doing "most of the work." That is, the goals are set by another authoritative agent. And that authority is supervising the performance of the car, and would either stop the car or take over control if he/she ended up being unhappy with the way in which the car is performing its tasks.[52] Thus the car's supervised and deferential agency is of a collaborative type. It is acting in the service of, and under the authority of, the person(s) whose goals and preferences the car is responsive to. This is not an independent or individual type of agency, even if it is a fairly sophisticated type of agency indeed.[53]

Similarly, a military robot is acting on the basis of the strategic goals set by the commanding officers, and in the service of the more general overarching goals of the military operation. Its performance will be supervised by the commanding officers and also by its designers and the engineers working on it. If the military robot starts performing in ways that are deemed unsatisfactory by the commanding officers, then either the use of the robot will be discontinued or the designers and engineers will be asked to update the hardware and software of the robot.[54] Given these parameters, we should not think of the military robot as acting in an independent way. Rather, insofar as we attribute agency to it, we should think of it as exercising supervised and deferential collaborative agency. That is, we should think of it as collaborating with the humans involved and as being under the supervision and authority of those humans.

3.5: COLLABORATIVE AGENCY AND RESPONSIBILITY LOCI

Let us now reintroduce the question of responsibility into our discussion. To do this, let us start with another case involving an adult acting together with a child, this time not doing something as innocent as gardening, but rather something more questionable. Consider this imaginary case:

> Case 1: An adult and a child are robbing a bank together, on the adult's initiative, with the gun-wielding child doing most of the "work." The adult is supervising the duo's activities, and would step in and start issuing orders to the child, if this should be needed.

There are two agents involved here who are engaged in a collaboration: namely, the child and the adult. But when it comes to assigning responsibility for this collaboration in this case, it appears quite clear that there is one party who is responsible here, whereas the other may not be responsible even if the latter is doing most of the work. The adult is the party in this collaboration whom we would hold responsible in this case. The adult is initiating, supervising, and managing this collaboration. And unlike the child, the adult is a fully responsible moral agent.[55] So here we have a case of collaborative agency, where one party is doing most of the actual work, but where the other party to the collaboration is the collaborator who should be held responsible for this bank robbery.

Consider now a case that is modelled on the Tesla-case mentioned in the introduction:

> Case 2: A human being is traveling in an automated vehicle, with the car in "autopilot" or "autonomous" mode. The human is supervising the driving, and would take over, or issue different driving instructions, if this should be needed.

This is another case in which most of the work is not done by the responsible agent involved (i.e., the human), but rather by the other party involved (in this case, the car). Given that the car's performance is supervised by the human, and given that the human would take over, or issue different instructions, if he/she would find this necessary, it here makes sense to attribute responsibility according to the model that we saw above that Tesla favors. That is, given that the human operator here collaborates with the car in the role as a sort of an active supervisor, it makes sense to view the human party to this collaboration as being the responsible party.

Consider next a type of case that is more closely modeled on the example with a Google-car in the introduction:

> Case 3: A human being is traveling in an automated vehicle whose performance is monitored by the designers and makers of the car, who will update the car's hardware and software on a regular basis so as to make the car's performance fit with their preferences and judgments about how the car should perform in traffic.

When we think of the performance of the car in this way—that is, as being under the close watch of the designers and makers, who will step in and update its hard- and software if they deem it necessary—it appears more intuitive to view the engineers behind the car as being key parties within the human-robot collaboration here. Viewed in this way, this appears to be a case where the people who make and then update the car are the main loci of responsibility for how the car performs when it participates in human-robot collaborations.

Let us also return to autonomous weapons systems. Consider the following case:

> Case 4: A military robot is able to operate in "autonomous" mode. The commanding officers set the goals the robot is supposed to achieve, and will stop using the robot if its performance does not help to fulfil those goals.

Here, the robot is collaborating with the humans involved. Its goals are the military goals at issue. And the humans involved will discontinue their use of this robot if they feel that the goals are not achieved in a way they are satisfied with. As before, the robot might be doing most of the work within the collaboration, but the human is the party to whom it makes sense to attribute responsibility.[56] The robot is not acting independently, on its own initiative. Rather, it is collaborating with the commanding officers in a supervised and deferential way. There is a clear parallel between this case and the Tesla-type scenario in case 2 above.

Consider next:

> Case 5: A military robot is able to operate in "autonomous" mode. Its designers are paying close attention to whether the commanding officers are happy with the robot's performance. If not, the designers and engineers update the hardware and software of the robot so as to make its performance better track the commanding officers' preference and judgments about how the robot should perform.

As before, we should think of this as a human-robot collaboration—not as an independently acting robot outside of human control and responsibility. When we think of the military robot in this way as being supervised, not only by the commanding officers, but also by its designers and the engineers working on it, it makes sense to reflect more on which of the humans involved are most responsible. It makes much more sense to worry mostly about that question, rather than thinking that there might be a responsibility gap here because an autonomous robot is acting outside of human control and oversight.

In contrast, if a military robot were to just magically materialize out of nowhere—and it suddenly entered a human battlefield and started participating in the fighting—there might be a genuine responsibility gap where it is unclear whether any of the involved human agents are responsible. However, if a military robot is put on the battlefield by military engineers and commanding officers who are collaborating to augment the human effort with robotic agency, the key question becomes which of the human parties to these human-robot collaborations bears the most responsibility. There should be no question as to whether the humans involved in these collaborations bear a significant responsibility. Again, unless the robot appears out of thin air and starts acting in a wholly independent way within the human-robot interactions in question, it is collaborating with the humans involved.[57] Consequently, there should not be any real doubt as to whether it is possible to attribute responsibility to the key human players involved.

The most difficult questions here instead concern what humans are most responsible for any potential bad outcomes caused by their robot collaborators. This is especially difficult when, unlike in the military context, the humans involved are not clearly all involved in any obvious form of shared collaboration. To see this, consider the human person traveling in the car in case 3 above. And imagine that rather than what was the case in the Google crash from the introduction, the human in the car is not part of the organization that makes and then continually updates the car.[58] The human driver of the car may have purchased the car. But the car company still regularly monitors the performance of the cars they make, and then often update at least the car's software, but sometimes also its hardware. This can be taken to mean the following: The car is executing the owner's more particular traveling goals (e.g., going to the grocery store), but it does so in a way that is partly monitored by and deferential to the company that builds and updates these kinds of cars. In terms of means and ends, we might say that the traveler sets the end, but that the car company determines the means by which that end is achieved.

In such a case, there is a sense in which the car is collaborating both with its owner and with its makers. It is collaborating with the owner in the sense of helping to carry out the owner's traveling goals. It is collaborating with the car company in the sense of helping them to provide a service to their customer. This can make it hard to determine which of the humans involved are most responsible for the actions the car performs within the context of these collaborations. And it can make it hard to determine who is responsible for what aspects of the actions the car performs.

These are very difficult questions, and I will not attempt to settle them here.[59] These questions clearly require much more extensive discussion. What I will do at this point, instead, is to suggest a few key questions that we should be discussing when we think more systematically about where the key responsibility-loci are within these kinds of human-robot collaborations. The sorts of questions we should be asking importantly include the following:

- Under whose supervision and (direct or indirect) control is a vehicle that is currently operating in "autopilot" or "autonomous" mode operating?
- Who is currently able to start, take over, or, at least, stop the car?
- Whose preferences regarding driving style is the car conforming to while in "autopilot" or "autonomous" mode?
- Who is better situated to observe and monitor the car's actual behavior on the road?
- Who has an understanding of the functioning of the car, at least on a "macro level"?

We should also be mindful of who enjoys rights such as ownership rights in relation to the car. And in addition to that, we should also be investigating the roles performed by the different humans involved with these cars.[60] Not all human responsibilities depend on direct control or immediate agency. Many human responsibilities also depend on the enjoyment of rights (e.g., ownership rights) and the roles we inhabit. Accordingly, considerations relating to the rights enjoyed by and the roles inhabited by the humans involved also bear on who is most responsible for the human-robot collaborations that there can be between humans and automated vehicles.[61]

Similarly, when it comes to automated military robots, we should always consider their functioning in terms of human-robot collaborations and ask the following types of questions when we try to determine who is most responsible for the actions of these robots:

- Under whose supervision and (direct or indirect) control is a military robot that is currently operating in "autopilot" or "autonomous" mode operating?
- Who is currently able to start, take over, or, at least, stop the robot?
- Whose preferences regarding functioning is the robot conforming to while in "autopilot" or "autonomous" mode?
- Who is better situated to observe and monitor the military robot's actual behavior on the battlefield?
- Who has an understanding of the functioning of the robot, at least on a "macro level"?

These are the kinds of questions we should be discussing more carefully so as to avoid the kind of worries about responsibility gaps motivated by the sort of reasoning that Sparrow presents in his discussion of "killer robots."[62]

The just-suggested sets of questions about self-driving cars and military robots apply to cases where certain humans have some measure of control over the automated systems, or are at least able to turn them off. And they apply to cases where it is possible to update or alter the technologies in question, according to our human preferences and judgments about what improvements might be needed. It might be asked here what we should think about cases where these kinds of conditions do not hold. That is, what if we completely lose control over the automated systems we use, or we are not able to turn them off? What if they do things that we do not want them to do, and we cannot stop them? Here are a few comments about those questions.

First, when we think about responsibility for automated systems such as self-driving cars and current military robots, we should not base our accounts of responsibility for these systems that we can control on our worries about other possible scenarios featuring robots or other automated systems that we cannot control. Rather, we should differentiate between responsibility for technologies that we can control (even if only indirectly) and that we can update, on the one hand, and responsibility for possible technologies we could not control and that we could not update, on the other.

In the case of technologies such as autonomous cars or weapons systems, it is imperative that we design and use systems that we will be able to control and that we will be able to update or at least stop. Those are the kinds of technologies where the analysis offered here applies, that is, where it makes sense to think in terms of human-robot collaborations, where the humans are in charge and the robot collaborators are under human supervision. In such cases, the collaborative nature of the agency involved and the respective roles played by the humans and the robots help to determine where the loci of responsibility are to be found.

However, as noted in the introduction to this chapter, we should not use a "one size fits all" approach within the ethics of robotic agency and human responsibility. We should also acknowledge that there can conceivably be cases in which humans lose control over advanced autonomous robots, where those robots cannot be seen as collaborating with humans, and where genuine responsibility gaps do appear. For example, if a system that is otherwise under somebody's control is hacked and tampered with, those who are normally using the system might lose the control over it that they previously had.[63] The discussion above has not intended to deny that this could happen. Rather, the contention here is that in the kinds of cases we are typically confronted with when we create and use technologies such as automated cars and military robots, the proper analytic framework to use is that of collaborative agency of a hierarchical sort, where certain responsible humans occupy the roles of supervisors or commanders. We should also develop frameworks for dealing with responsibility and agency-analysis applying to cases where the technology is out of control and humans and automated systems cannot sensibly be seen as collaborating. But those are not the types of cases that have been discussed above.

3.6: CONCLUDING REMARKS

The distinctions drawn above—which have been related to robots, small children, and adult human beings—can be illustrated using the following table, which uses self-driving cars as its example of the sorts of robots we might be concerned with here:

Table 3.1.

	Autonomous vehicle	Small child	Adult

	Autonomous vehicle	Small child	Adult
Basic (domain-specific) agency?	Yes	Yes	Yes
Principled (domain-specific) agency?	Yes	Yes	Yes
Deferential and supervised, principled (domain-specific) agency?	Yes	Yes	Yes, but also able to perform agency that is not deferential and supervised
Responsible (domain-specific) agency?	No	No	Yes
Capable of performing individual/independent agency?	No	Yes	Yes
Capable of participating in collaborative agency?	Yes	Yes	Yes
Capable of taking on the role of a responsible authority figure within collaborative agency?	No	No	Yes

This chapter does not pretend to have settled any questions about how to properly allocate or distribute responsibility among the key humans involved in the types of human-robot collaborations discussed above. Clearly, there is much more work that needs to be done if we are to be able to come up with well-supported and comprehensive views about this. The foregoing section formulated a set of questions we should be asking and investigating further when we consider this pressing topic.

The main point that the sections above have tried to establish is that if and when we attribute agency to robots such as automated cars or autonomous weapons systems, we should almost always think of this agency as occurring within human-robot collaborations. For the contexts discussed in this chapter, that is the sort of agency that it is desirable to achieve in these particular kinds of robots. Indeed, for these contexts, that is perhaps the only form of agency it is desirable to achieve in these robots.[64] In other kinds of contexts, different claims may apply. For example, if you are seeking to create a robot companion—a robotic friend or lover—then it could make more sense to want to create a robot that is able to exercise a much more autonomous and independent form of agency.[65] But for robots and automated systems that are meant to drive us around or help us fight wars, what is desirable is to have machines that collaborate with us, that defer to us, and whose performance is supervised and managed by human beings.

NOTES

1. B. Schoettle and M. Sivak (2015), "A Preliminary Analysis of Real-World Crashes Involving Self-Driving Vehicles" (No. UMTRI-2015-34), Ann Arbor: The University of Michigan Transportation Research Institute.

2. Phil LeBeau (2016), "Google's Self-Driving Car Caused an Accident, So What Now?," *CNBC*, https://www.cnbc.com/2016/02/29/googles-self-driving-car-caused-an-accident-so-what-now.html (Accessed on August 22, 2019).

3. Ibid.

4. The Tesla Team, "A Tragic Loss," *Tesla Blog*, https://www.tesla.com/blog/tragic-loss (Accessed on August 22, 2019).

5. Ibid.

6. Sam Levin and Julie Carrie Wong (2018), "Self-Driving Uber Kills Arizona Woman in First Fatal Crash involving Pedestrian," *Guardian*, https://www.theguardian.com/technology/2018/mar/19/uber-self-driving-car-kills-woman-arizona-tempe (Accessed on August 22, 2019).

7. Daisuke Wakabayashi and Kate Conger (2018), "Uber's Self-Driving Cars Are Set to Return in a Downsized Test," *New York Times*, https://www.nytimes.com/2018/12/05/technology/uber-self-driving-cars.html (Accessed on August 22, 2019).

8. Duncan Purves, Ryan Jenkins, and B. J. Strawser (2015), "Autonomous Machines, Moral Judgment, and Acting for the Right Reasons," *Ethical Theory and Moral Practice* 18(4), 851–72.

9. Danaher, "Robots, Law, and the Retribution Gap," op. cit.

10. Cf. Jeffrey N. Bradshaw, Robert R. Hoffman, Matthew Johnson, and David D. Woods (2013), "The Seven Deadly Myths of 'Autonomous Systems,'" *IEEE Intelligent Systems*, 2013, 2–9, and David Mindell (2015), *Our Robots, Ourselves: Robotics and the Myths of Autonomy*, New York: Viking.

11. Sarah Buss and Andrea Westlund (2018), "Personal Autonomy," *The Stanford Encyclopedia of Philosophy* (Spring 2018 Edition), Edward N. Zalta (ed.), https://plato.stanford.edu/archives/spr2018/entries/personal-autonomy/.

12. See, for example, Daniel Heikoop, Marhan P. Hagenzieker, Giulio Mecacci, Simeon Calvert, Filippo Santoni de Sio, and B. van Arem (2019), "Human Behaviour with Automated Driving Systems: A Qualitative Framework for Meaningful Human Control," *Theoretical Issues in Ergonomics Science*, online first at https://www.tandfonline.com/doi/full/10.1080/1463922X.2019.1574931.

That paper features some interesting discussion of the relation between different levels of autonomy in machines and what this means for the degree of control (or lack thereof) drivers of these autonomous vehicles can be thought to have, as well as what skill levels are required in order to control autonomous systems with different levels of autonomy.

13. Patrick Lin (2015), "Why Ethics Matters for Autonomous Cars," in Markus Maurer, J. Christian Gerdes, Barbara Lenz, and Hermann Winner (eds.) *Autonomes Fahren: Technische, rechtliche und gesellschaftliche Aspekte*, Springer, Berlin, Heidelberg, 69–85, at 69.

14. Purves et al., "Autonomous Machines, Moral Judgment, and Acting for the Right Reasons," op. cit., 855. It is worth noting that later on in their article, Purves et al. explore the possibility that autonomous weapons systems are not autonomous agents in the sense seemingly required in order for responsibility gaps to arise. (See 867.) Earlier on in their article, though, they take seriously the idea that both self-driving cars and autonomous weapons systems need to "make life and death decisions," as noted in the quote above.

15. Wendell Wallach and Colin Allen, *Moral Machines: Teaching Robots Right from Wrong*, Oxford: Oxford University Press, 14.

16. Robert Sparrow (2007), "Killer Robots," *Journal of Applied Philosophy* 24(1), 62–77 at 70.

17. Mark Coeckelbergh (2016), "Responsibility and the Moral Phenomenology of Using Self-Driving Cars," *Applied Artificial Intelligence* 30(8), 748–57, 754.

18. See, for example, Ronald Arkin (2010), "The Case for Ethical Autonomy in Unmanned Systems," *Journal of Military Ethics* 9(4), 332–41; Noah J. Goodall (2014), "Ethical Decision Making during Automated Vehicle Crashes," *Transportation Research Record: Journal of the Transportation Research Board* 2424, 58–65; Jan Gogoll and Julian F. Müller (2017), "Autonomous Cars: In Favor of a Mandatory Ethics Setting," *Science and Engineering Ethics* 23(3), 681–700; and Sven Nyholm and Jilles Smids (2016), "The Ethics of Accident-Algorithms for Self-Driving Cars: An Applied Trolley Problem?," *Ethical Theory and Moral Practice* 19(5), 1275–89.

19. As I noted in chapter 1, this might also give rise to what I call "obligation gaps," that is, unclarities with respect to whose duty it is to make sure that the robots in question behave in accordance with morally acceptable standards, and produce good rather than bad outcomes.

20. See, for example, Sparrow, "Killer Robots," op. cit.; Alexander Hevelke and Julian Nida-Rümelin (2015), "Responsibility for Crashes of Autonomous Vehicles: An Ethical Analysis," *Science and Engineering Ethics* 21(3), 619–30; Ezio Di Nucci and Filippo Santoni de Sio (eds.) (2016), *Drones and Respon-*

sibility, London: Routledge; Coeckelbergh, "Responsibility and the Moral Phenomenology of Using Self-Driving Cars," op. cit.

21. Sparrow, "Killer Robots," op. cit.

22. In contrast, Daniel Tigard argues that it might sometimes make sense to hold robots responsible for bad outcomes they bring about. It could make sense to do so, Tigard argues, if this could have deterring or other desirable effects. See Daniel Tigard (forthcoming), "Artificial Moral Responsibility: How We Can and Cannot Hold Machines Responsible," *Cambridge Quarterly in Healthcare Ethics*.

23. Hevelke and Nida-Rümelin, "Responsibility for Crashes of Autonomous Vehicles," op. cit.

24. Gary Marchant and Rachel Lindor (2012), "The Coming Collision between Autonomous Cars and the Liability System," *Santa Clara Legal Review* 52(4), 1321–40.

25. Hevelke and Nida-Rümelin's first argument is problematic given that the presence of pragmatic reasons against holding manufacturers responsible do not necessarily establish that holding them responsible is intrinsically unwarranted. Indeed, a little later in their article, Hevelke and Nida-Rümelin themselves in effect make this very point. They argue that norms relating to responsibility in liberal democracies should "not be consequentialist but deontological in nature" (622).

26. For the idea of moral luck, see Bernard Williams (1982), *Moral Luck*, Cambridge: Cambridge University Press.

27. Danaher, "Robots, Law, and the Retribution Gap," op. cit.

28. US Department of Defense Science Board (2012), "The Role of Autonomy in DoD Systems," https://fas.org/irp/agency/dod/dsb/autonomy.pdf (Accessed on August 22, 2019).

29. David Gunkel and John Danaher (2016), "Episode #10—David Gunkel on Robots and Cyborgs," Philosophical Disquisitions Podcast, https://algocracy.wordpress.com/2016/08/27/episode-10-david-gunkel-on-robots-and-cyborgs/ (Accessed on August 22, 2019).

30. Speaking of levels of abstraction, Luciano Floridi and J. W. Sanders argue that, in general, whether robots or any other machines can be regarded as agents of any kind—perhaps even as some sort of moral agents—depends on at what level of abstraction we are conducting our thinking on when we are thinking about robots and their interaction with the world around them. See Luciano Floridi and J. W. Sanders (2004), "On the Morality of Artificial Agents," *Minds and Machines* 14(3), 349–79. Their discussion has certain things in common with a more recent discussion of free will in a book by Christian List. According to List, whether it makes sense to think of humans as having free will depends on at what level of abstraction we are conducting our

thinking. See Christian List (2019), *Why Free Will Is Real*, Cambridge, MA: Harvard University Press.

31. Janet Levin (2018), "Functionalism," *The Stanford Encyclopedia of Philosophy*, Edward N. Zalta (ed.), https://plato.stanford.edu/archives/fall2018/entries/functionalism/.

32. Pierre Jacob (2019), "Intentionality," *The Stanford Encyclopedia of Philosophy* (Spring 2019 Edition), Edward N. Zalta (ed.), htps://plato.stanford.edu/archives/spr2019/entries/intentionality/.

33. See, for example, Elizabeth Anscombe (1957), *Intention*, Oxford: Basil Blackwell, and Donald Davidson (1980), *Essays on Actions and Events*. Oxford: Clarendon Press.

34. See, for example, Philip Pettit (2007), "Responsibility Incorporated," *Ethics* 117(2), 171–201, 178.

35. Philip Pettit (1990), "The Reality of Rule-Following," *Mind, New Series* 99(393), 1–21.

36. Cf. Frank Dignum, Rui Prada, and Gert Jan Hofstede (2014), "From Autistic to Social Agents," Proceedings of the 2014 International Conference on Autonomous Agents and Multi-Agent Systems, 1161–64.

37. T. M. Scanlon, (1998), *What We Owe to Each Other*, Cambridge, MA: Harvard University Press.

38. Cf. Darwall, *The Second Person Standpoint*, op. cit.

39. Cf. Rainer Forst (2014), *The Right to Justification*, New York: Columbia University Press.

40. See, for instance, Christine Korsgaard (2010), *Self-Constitution*, Oxford: Oxford University Press.

41. Cf. Anscombe, *Intention*, op. cit., and Davidson, *Essays on Actions and Events*, op. cit.

42. See, for example, Chris Urmson (2015), "How a Self-Driving Car Sees the World," *Ted*, https://www.ted.com/talks/chris_urmson_how_a_driverless_car_sees_the_road/transcript (Accessed on August 22, 2019), and Sven Nyholm and Jilles Smids, "The Ethics of Accident-Algorithms for Self-Driving Cars," op. cit.

43. Cf. Pettit, "Responsibility Incorporated," op. cit., 178.

44. Roald J. Van Loon and Marieke H. Martens (2015), "Automated Driving and Its Effect on the Safety Ecosystem: How Do Compatibility Issues Affect the Transition Period?" *Procedia Manufacturing* 3, 3280–85.

45. Cf. Urmson, "How a Self-Driving Car Sees the World," op. cit. and the Tesla Team, "A Tragic Loss," op. cit.

46. Cf. Mindell, *Our Robots, Ourselves*, op. cit.

47. Cf. Purves et al., "Autonomous Machines, Moral Judgment, and Acting for the Right Reasons," op. cit., 860–61.

48. Cf. Paul Bloom (2013), *Just Babies*, New York: Crown.

49. Similarly, but I think less plausibly, Sparrow compares autonomous military robots to child soldiers in his "Killer Robots," op. cit.

50. See, for instance, Margaret Gilbert (1990), "Walking Together: A Paradigmatic Social Phenomenon," *Midwest Studies in Philosophy* 15(1), 1–14; Pettit, "Responsibility Incorporated," op. cit.; and Christian List and Philip Pettit (2011), *Group Agency: The Possibility, Design, and Status of Corporate Agents*, Oxford: Oxford University Press.

51. Cf. Mindell, *Our Robots, Ourselves*, op. cit.

52. Ibid.

53. Cf. Bradshaw et al., "The Seven Deadly Myths of 'Autonomous Systems,'" op. cit.

54. US Department of Defense Science Board, "The Role of Autonomy in DoD Systems," op. cit. p. 24.

55. Cf. chapter 8 of Norvin Richards (2010), *The Ethics of Parenthood*, Oxford: Oxford University Press, and Sparrow, "Killer Robots," op. cit.

56. Cf. the notion of "command responsibility" in Joe Doty and Chuck Doty (2012), "Command Responsibility and Accountability," *Military Review* 92(1), 35–38, and various contributions in Nehal Bhuta, Susanne Beck, Robin Geiß, Hin-Yan Liu, and Claus Kreß (2015), *Autonomous Weapons Systems: Law, Ethics, Policy*, Cambridge: Cambridge University Press.

57. Bradshaw et al., "The Seven Deadly Myths of 'Autonomous Systems,'" op. cit.; Mindell, *Our Robots, Ourselves*, op. cit.

58. In the above-described Google case, the two people in the car were Google employees testing the car.

59. For further discussion, see Roos De Jong (2019), "The Retribution-Gap and Responsibility-Loci Related to Robots and Automated Technologies: A Reply to Nyholm," *Science and Engineering Ethics* 1–9, online first at https://doi.org/10.1007/s11948-019-00120-4. One comment about De Jong's discussion: In her article, De Jong interprets me as adopting a so-called instrumental theory of technology, according to which all robots and other technologies are to be understood as tools and nothing else. My view is that in the case of robots like self-driving cars, that is the right view to take. However, in the case of social robots, especially robots made to look and act like humans, the instrumental theory does not seem as compelling. In other words, I do not think we should think of all robots and all technologies in terms of the instrumental theory. I discuss this further in chapter 8.

60. Cf. Peterson, "New Technology—Old Law," op. cit.; Guerney, "Sue My Car Not Me: Products Liability and Accidents Involving Autonomous Vehicles," op. cit.; and Orly Ravid (2014), "Don't Sue Me, I Was Just Lawfully

Texting and Drunk When My Autonomous Car Crashed into You," *Southwest Law Review* 44(1), 175–207.

61. The philosophers of technology Filippo Santoni de Sio and Jeroen van den Hoven discuss what they call "meaningful human control" over autonomous cars and military robots. They offer a two-factor analysis of what it is for autonomous systems to be under such control. The first condition (the "tracking" condition) is that the robot is supposed to behave in ways that conform to how it is morally acceptable for human beings to want the robot to behave. The second condition (the "tracing" condition) is that there should be at least one human being who understands both how the technology works and the potential morally relevant impacts of using the technology. If these two conditions hold, Santoni De Sio and Van den Hoven argue, a robot is under meaningful human control. Or rather, unless those two conditions hold, the robot is not under meaningful human control. That is to say, those two conditions are presented as necessary conditions for meaningful human control. But as far as I can tell, in their article, Santoni De Sio and Van den Hoven do not take a definite stance on whether those two conditions are also jointly sufficient. So the question arises if anything is missing in their analysis. What I am missing is the presence of something like what Dorothea Debus calls the "intervention condition" in her discussion of control. (Debus, "Shaping our Mental Lives," op. cit.) That is, it seems to me that unless there is some intervention that can be taken to either stop or redirect a robot, we cannot be said to have meaningful human control over the robot. I am also missing what one might call a "monitoring condition." In order for a robot to be under meaningful human control, it seems to me that there should not only be somebody who can intervene, but there should also be somebody who is monitoring the robot's performance and keeps track of whether any interventions might be necessary. For their discussion, see Filippo Santoni de Sio and Jeroen Van den Hoven (2018), "Meaningful Human Control over Autonomous Systems: A Philosophical Account," *Frontiers in Robotics and AI*, https://www.frontiersin.org/articles/10.3389/frobt.2018.00015/full.

62. Sparrow, "Killer Robots," op. cit.

63. Cf. Michal Klincewicz (2015), "Autonomous Weapons Systems, the Frame Problem and Computer Security," *Journal of Military Ethics* 14(2), 162–76.

64. Cf. Mindell, *Our Robots, Ourselves*, op. cit.

65. See Sven Nyholm and Lily Frank (2017), "From Sex Robots to Love Robots: Is Mutual Love with a Robot Possible?" in Danaher and McArthur, *Robot Sex*, op. cit.

4

HUMAN-ROBOT COORDINATION
The Case of Mixed Traffic

4.1: INTRODUCTION

As noted at the beginning of the previous chapter, crashes involving self-driving cars started happening on public roads in 2015. Most early crashes were relatively minor. But from 2016 and onward, there have also been deadly crashes where people have died both inside automated cars (the Tesla cases[1]) and outside of automated cars (the Uber case where a pedestrian was hit and killed[2]). In December of 2018, the *New York Times* reported another complication that those who are testing out experimental self-driving cars have to take into account—a complication that was perhaps more unexpected.[3] This was in Arizona, the state where the first pedestrian had been killed by an experimental self-driving car. What was happening was that members of the public were throwing rocks at self-driving cars, slashing their tires, and sometimes also waving guns at them in threatening ways. Why were some Arizonans doing these things? Apparently, they did not appreciate having their public roads being used as testing grounds for experimental self-driving cars. One man—a Mr. O'Polka—was quoted as saying, "They said they need real-world examples, but I don't want to be their real-world mistake."[4]

As this helps to illustrate, there are all sorts of complications related to human-robot coordination that arise when we try to bring robots into spheres of human activity. On the one hand, we need to get the humans and robots to interact in ways that are well-coordinated so as to enable good outcomes to be achieved and bad outcomes (e.g., people being harmed or killed) to be avoided. On the other hand, we need to get the humans and the robots to coordinate in ways that the people affected will find acceptable and be happy with.

Relating this back to the question raised in chapter 1 about whether there are cases in which humans may have reason to adapt to robots—rather than the more obvious solution of having robots adapt to humans—this chapter will zoom in on mixed traffic in particular. "Mixed traffic" here refers to traffic involving both self-driven robotic cars and conventional human-driven cars. I will argue that if self-driving cars eventually fulfill their promise of becoming much safer than regular cars, this may very well be a case in point where the ethically better solution is to try to adapt human behavior to robot behavior, at least in some ways.[5]

As I said in chapter 1, I think that the default ethically preferred choice should be to seek ways of adapting robots and AI to humans. But we should also investigate whether there are any cases in which it might be beneficial to us to do things the other way around. If there are—and the given ways of adapting humans to robots and AI are domain-specific, largely reversible, and not too invasive—the ethically better choice might be to adapt human behavior to robot behavior in whatever ways might be beneficial to us. While I zoom in on mixed traffic in particular in this chapter, my hope is that this discussion could serve as an illustrative case study for how we can ask the same question about robots in other domains as well.

Like the previous chapter, this chapter is also a contribution to the new field of the ethics of automated driving.[6] Its most immediate aim is to argue that this field should take mixed traffic very seriously. Its more general aim is to give a proof of concept argument for the broader claim that there can be cases in which we ought to try to adapt humans to robots and AI, for our own sake. Regarding the more immediate aim, I want to suggest that there are distinctive ethical issues related to how to achieve compatibility between automated robotic vehicles and human-driven conventional vehicles that do not reduce to the main issues thus far mostly discussed within the ethics of automated driving.

That is, there are ethical issues related to compatibility-challenges that do not reduce to how self-driving cars should be programmed to handle crash-scenarios or who should be held responsible when automated vehicles crash (the two most commonly discussed topics within the ethics of automated driving).[7] The ethics of automated driving also needs to deal with other key issues. Among those is the issue of responsible human-robot coordination: how to adjust robotic driving and human driving to each other in a way that is sensitive to important ethical values and principles.

It might be suggested that this is a minor issue. Eventually, we might only have autonomous vehicles on our roads. So this is just a transition-period worry. To this I respond as follows. Even if highly or even fully automated vehicles will at some later time come to dominate the roads, there will still be a long transition period during which mixed traffic will be a problem that needs to be dealt with.[8] Nor should we assume that full automation in all vehicles is an end-point toward which we are moving with necessity.[9] Mixed traffic may come to mean a mix of vehicles with different levels and types of automation interacting with each other on the road.[10] In general, automation in robots will typically involve more or less functional autonomy and automation of different kinds, all depending on what would achieve the best outcomes in the domains in question. In some domains, fully automated robots may sometimes be less useful, less desirable, and more costly than partly automated machines.[11] And we may sometimes not want any robots or machines to take over certain human tasks, such as—for example—caring for children.[12]

In most mixed traffic, then, there will be different types of vehicles on our roads with different levels and types of automation. Additionally, robotic cars also have to coordinate their driving with the behavior of pedestrians, animals, and people on bikes and motorcycles.[13] This will all have two important consequences, similar to what we are already seeing today. First, there will be incompatibilities in the ways the different kinds of cars function and interact with each other, which will create new traffic risks. Second, the vehicles on the road will have different crash-risk levels: Certain kinds of cars will pose greater threats to others; and certain kinds of cars are going to be safer to be in when crashes occur than other cars are.[14] These observations are also likely to generalize other areas of human-robot interaction: On the one hand, there will be incompatibilities in how different robots interact with each other and also with respect to how they interact with humans. On the other hand, different robots will differ in what types of risks they expose human beings to. In light of these two observations, I do the following three things in this chapter when I discuss mixed traffic below.

First, I describe in general terms why there are incompatibilities between what I will call robotic driving, on the one hand, and human driving, on the other. That is, I describe why I think the robotic functioning of automated cars and the driving styles of human beings lead to compatibility problems, meaning that there is a need to think about how greater compatibility might be achieved within mixed traffic. This takes us to the second thing I do, which is to present some of the main options there are for how to achieve better human-robot coordination in this domain. Third, I briefly consider what types of general ethical issues and challenges we need to deal with when we make these choices about how to achieve greater compatibility between robotic cars and conventional cars within mixed traffic. For example, I will consider issues to do with respecting people's freedom and human dignity, on the one hand, but also positive duties to promote safety and to manage risks in responsible ways, on the other hand.

4.2: HUMAN-ROBOT COORDINATION PROBLEMS IN MIXED TRAFFIC

The reasons why incompatibilities arise are fairly easy to explain and understand.[15] They have to do with the different ways in which autonomous cars and human drivers function as agents (i.e., as entities that act according to certain goals, representations, and principles). This includes the different ways in which robotic cars and human drivers form expectations about other vehicles on the road. In explaining these incompatibilities, I will start with key differences in how goals are pursued and then continue with differences in how expectations are formed by automated cars and human drivers.

First of all, self-driving cars have a kind of artificial or robotic agency of at least a basic kind, as I argued in the foregoing chapter. As was noted in that chapter, self-driving cars pursue goals, and do so in a way that is responsive to continually updated representations of the environment they operate in. They are robotic agents designed by human agents. More specifically, robotic cars are designed to reach their destinations in ways that are optimally safe, fuel-efficient, and travel time–efficient (e.g., by reducing congestion).[16] As with many other robots intended to take over tasks otherwise performed by human beings, the goal that engineers often have in designing the robots is to create a more optimal way of performing the given task. In this case, the goal is to create a more optimal form of driving.

This optimization goal has a profound impact on the driving styles of self-driving cars, making them markedly different from those of most human drivers. For example, in order to achieve fuel-efficiency and avoid congestion, self-driving cars will not accelerate vigorously, and brake very gently. Safety-enhancing aspects of their driving styles include avoiding safety-critical situations, for example, by staying longer behind a cyclist before overtaking.[17] More generally, at least at present, self-driving cars are programmed to follow the traffic rules very strictly in most situations. One major function of these rules is precisely to enhance safety. Thus, under current engineering ideals, automated cars always give way when required, avoid speeding, always come to a standstill at a stop sign, and so on.[18] If robotic cars would not eventually become better at most driving tasks than human beings are, there would not be any obvious reasons to outsource driving tasks to automated driving systems.

Let us consider how this contrasts with human drivers. Human beings are, of course, also agents who pursue driving goals in traffic situations they have to adequately perceive and respond to. And humans also act on the basis of principles and rules.[19] Unlike robotic cars, however, humans exhibit what is called "satisficing" rather than optimizing driving behavior.[20] In the terms used in chapter 1, human beings are what we might call "lazy" drivers. That is, human drivers typically drive just well enough to achieve their driving goals. This may include all kinds of driving behavior that is not optimal in terms of safety, fuel efficiency, and traffic flow: speeding, aggressive accelerating and decelerating, keeping too short following distances, and so on. Moreover, this often involves bending or breaking of traffic rules. Hence self-driving cars and human drivers have rather different driving styles. The former are optimizers and strict rule followers, the latter satisficers and unstrict rule benders.

Consider next how self-driving cars and human beings perceive one another and form expectations about how other cars are likely to behave in different traffic situations.[21] Robotic cars will most likely become able to communicate with other automated cars using car-to-car information and communication technologies. But they will not be able to directly communicate with human drivers in that way.

Instead, according to traffic psychologists Roald van Loon and Marieke Martens, self-driving cars will typically form their expectations about the behavior of conventional cars on the basis of externally observable behavioral indicators, such as speed, acceleration, position on the road, direction, etc. A problem here, according to van Loon and Martens, is that, currently, "our understanding of these behavioural indicators lacks both quantification and qualification of what is safe behaviour and what is not."[22] Accordingly, engineers do not yet know how best to program automated cars to predict what is, and what is not, safe human behavior on the basis of the external indicators that robotic cars can observe.

Notably, it is technically possible to design self-driving cars that will always break whenever they detect that they are about to hit something. But this is problematic for at least two reasons: First, as the director of the University of Michigan autonomous-vehicle research center Mcity, Huei Peng, noted in an interview, "if the car is overly cautious, this becomes a nuisance."[23] Second, if a car slams the brakes whenever anything appears in front of it, cars approaching quickly from behind— perhaps driven by human beings—might then sometimes crash into the rear of the self-driving car.

One potential way of making progress with respect to automated cars' ability to communicate with human drivers is indirect in nature. Human-driven cars could be made to closely monitor and to try to predict the behavior of their human drivers. The human-driven cars could then communicate these predictions to the automated cars. That way, the self-driving cars could make use both of their own observations and the predictions communicated to them by the human-driven cars, and then base their own predictions of the likely behaviors of the human drivers on this dual basis. This could constitute an improvement. But it would still not be direct communication between self-driving cars and human drivers. Rather, it would be communication between the robotic cars and the human-driven cars, where the latter would join the robotic cars in trying to predict what the human drivers are likely to do, also based on externally observable behaviors.

For human drivers forming expectations about self-driving cars, the problem is slightly different.[24] In the process of becoming habitual drivers, humans acquire lots of expectations regarding the driving behaviors of other human drivers in various situations. These expectations often do not fit very well with the functioning of robotic cars. For example, a self-driving car might keep waiting where the human driver behind expects it to start rolling. So, in order to be able to fluently interact both with other human drivers and self-driving cars, humans need to simultaneously operate on the basis of two parallel expectation-forming habits. They would have to operate on the basis of expectation-forming dispositions applying to conventional cars, on one hand, as well as ones applying to robotlike self-driving cars, on the other hand. That is a heavy cognitive load for human drivers to deal with.

Of course, in the case of other conventional cars, human drivers can communicate with other human drivers using various different impro-vised signals, such as hand and arm gestures, eye contact, and the blink-ing of lights.[25] This helps human drivers to form expectations about how other human drivers will behave. But as things stand at the moment, human drivers cannot communicate with robotic cars in these impro-vised and flexible ways. Things might be different in the future.

Given these current differences between robotic driving and human driving, mixed traffic is bound to involve a lot of compatibility and coordination problems. The equation here is simple: clashing driving styles + mutual difficulties in forming reliable expectations = increased likelihood of crashing cars. So, the question arises of how we ought to make robotlike automated cars and human-driven conventional cars maximally compatible with each other. We need to achieve good human-robot coordination, and avoid crashes and accidents caused by various different forms of incompatibilities. What types of options are there? And what ethical issues are raised by the different types of op-tions we face?

4.3: OPTIONS FOR BETTER HUMAN-ROBOT COORDINATION IN MIXED TRAFFIC

In 2015, after the first mixed traffic collisions started being reported and analyzed, a debate arose about how to achieve better compatibility in various different contexts. Opinions were expressed and debated in the media, engineering and traffic psychology labs, consulting firms, in policymaking teams, and elsewhere, though then not yet in the context of philosophical ethics. Most of the smaller crashes in 2015 were generally judged to be due to human error.[26] However, automated driving as it is currently functioning was nevertheless criticized. And some of the more recent incidents—particularly the 2016 and 2018 crashes I mentioned in the introduction—have also been blamed on perceived shortcomings in the autonomous vehicles.

The main type of solution to human-robot coordination problems within this domain that one will most commonly see being discussed is the following: to try to program self-driving cars to function more like human drivers.[27] For example, one influential media outlet reporting on technology developments ran an op-ed in which self-driving cars were said to have a "key flaw" in being programmed to follow rules rigidly and drive efficiently: This causes humans to drive into them. The suggested solution: make self-driving cars less strict in their rule-following and less efficient in their driving.[28] Similarly, a consultant advising the Dutch Ministry of Infrastructure and the Environment's Automated Vehicle Initiative (DAVI) suggested, at an interdisciplinary event on the ethics of automated driving, that self-driving cars should be equipped with "naughty software": software that makes robotic cars break rules in certain situations in which many humans do so.[29] This solution is also advocated by engineering researchers Christian Gerdes and Sarah Thornton. They argue that because human drivers do not treat traffic rules as absolute, self-driving cars should follow suit and be programmed to do the same. Otherwise, they cannot coexist in human traffic and will not be accepted by human drivers.[30]

Others discussing compatibility issues have also mainly focused on this general option of making robotic driving more like human driving, while adopting a more skeptical approach to whether it should be taken. In a 2015 media interview, Raj Rajkumar, the head of the Carnegie-Mellon laboratory on automated driving, was quoted as saying that his team had debated both the pros and the cons of programming self-driving cars to break some of the rules humans tend to break (e.g., speed limits). But for now, the team had decided to program all their experimental cars to always follow the traffic rules.[31] Google, in turn, at one point announced that although they would have all their test vehicles follow all rules, they would nevertheless try to program them to drive more "aggressively" to better coordinate with human driving.[32]

As I see things, there are three important problems with this strong focus on whether to program self-driving cars to behave more like human drivers, and with treating this as the main option to consider for how to achieve better human-robot coordination. First, this assumes that full automation is the optimal solution for all traffic situations and that if cars are going to be well-coordinated with humans, this necessarily has to happen by means of programming the cars to be more human-like in their functioning. As the engineer and technology historian David Mindell argues in his book about the history of automation, this assumption overlooks the more obvious solution for how to handle at least some forms of situations.[33] It overlooks the option of not aiming for complete automation in all sorts of traffic situations, but instead trying to create a fruitful human-machine collaboration whereby both the driver's human intelligence and the car's technology are put to work.[34] The best way to make automated cars function more like humans—if this is a good idea in certain situations—may often be to simply involve the human, rather than to try to create artificial human reasoning or reactions in the car. As Mindell argues, we should not simply assume that for all types of driving or traffic problems, full automation is always the ultimate ideal. As I also noted above, this of course applies to other domains as well. Fully automated robots will not always be the ultimate ideals in all domains. Sometimes only partly automated machines will be better in various ways.

Second, some of the human traffic behaviors that automated cars' envisioned "naughty software" is supposed to conform to may be morally problematic and therefore not very appropriate standards to conform robotic driving to. Speeding is a key example here. As Jilles Smids argues, speeding is a morally problematic traffic offense because it greatly increases risks beyond democratically agreed upon levels.[35] As such, it is not a good standard to conform the functioning of self-driving cars to. Aggressive driving might be another example of a common human driving behavior that naughty software would be designed to conform to, but that is not necessarily a desirable type of behavior to replicate in robots. Gentle and careful driving might be a much better goal to aim for—both for robots and for humans.

In general, I want to suggest that when different aspects of human driving versus robotic driving are compared, and ways of conforming these to each other are sought, we should avoid any solutions that conform one type of driving to immoral and/or illegal aspects of the other type of driving. We should instead use morally and legally favored aspects of robotic or human driving as the standards to conform to, if possible. In many cases, this will mean that conforming robotic driving to human driving will be a bad idea.

More generally, whenever we face a choice of conforming robot behavior to human behavior or not—whether this is in traffic, in warfare, in policing, or whatever it might be—we should only conform the robotic behavior to human behavior if the human behavior in question is morally acceptable and morally desirable. There would be no obvious point—nor justification for—building morally questionable robots just because some human beings sometimes behave in morally questionable ways. It might be an acceptable fact of life in human beings that we are capable of both morally good and morally bad behavior. But it seems unacceptable to design robots that would be created specifically to replicate morally bad or questionable human behaviors.

Third, in primarily—if not exclusively—considering whether or not to conform certain aspects of robotic driving to human driving, there is another important alternative that is also overlooked (i.e., in addition to the option of not always aiming for complete automation). And that other option that I think ought also to be taken seriously is to seek means for potentially conforming certain aspects of human driving to robotic driving. This could be done with changes in traffic laws and regulations. But it could also be done with the help of certain kinds of technologies. In general, and as I argued in chapter 1, if we are confronted with choices where we can either adapt robots and AI to our human behaviors or try to adapt ourselves to robots and AI, then if the latter option is clearly beneficial to us for some reason or another, that option should always be taken seriously and assessed carefully.

To use the speeding example again, one way of making people more likely to adhere to speed limits, in the ways that more "well-behaved" robotic cars do, is to mandate speed-regulating technologies in conventional cars.[36] As it happens, at the time of writing in 2019, this is something that both the European Union and the United Kingdom are planning on doing in the near future.[37] New conventional cars can be equipped with speed-regulating technologies; most old cars can be retrofitted with such technologies at reasonable cost.[38] This would help to make humans drive more like robots. And there are some good reasons to expect that this will help considerably to solve speed-induced compatibility problems.[39] Or, to use another example, alcohol interlocks in cars could also make humans drive a little more like robots. If all human drivers use alcohol interlocks, they would become more consistently alert and better concentrated than if they sometimes also have the option of driving while under the influence of alcohol.[40] Still another option is equipping all conventional cars with forward collision–warning technologies.[41] This may potentially enhance drivers' prospective awareness of the risks they are facing. A heightened risk awareness could enable human drivers to better coordinate with robotic cars, which also have enhanced risk-detection systems as part of their overall makeup.[42]

4.4: ETHICAL CONCERNS REGARDING ATTEMPTS TO CREATE BETTER HUMAN-ROBOT COORDINATION WITHIN MIXED TRAFFIC

In the foregoing section, I identified three general solution-strategies for promoting better human-robot coordination in mixed traffic:

1. Trying to make certain aspects of robotic driving more similar to human driving;
2. Not assuming that complete automation is the optimal state, but also exploring ways of involving the human driver so as to create better human-robot coordination;
3. Seeking means for making certain aspects of human driving more like robotic driving.[43]

All three of these ways of improving human-robot coordination in mixed traffic raise potential ethical concerns. The aim of this section is to draw attention to some of the main concerns that need to be confronted when human-robot coordination issues in mixed traffic are explored and investigated in more systematic ways. I will here keep the discussion on a fairly general level as my chief aim in this chapter is not to advocate any particular solutions, but rather to motivate further discussion of the ethics of mixed traffic.

As I have already noted, conforming robotic driving to human driving can be ethically problematic if the particular aspects of human driving we would be trying to adapt to are morally or legally problematic. In other words, we would not want to create a robotic agent that replicates morally problematic or illegal human behaviors.[44] The main way in which this option ought to be evaluated morally, then, is through investigation of whether the human traffic behaviors we would seek to conform robotic behavior to are morally and legally problematic. If they are, then it may be better to seek alternative solutions to the given human-robot coordination problems.

What about the second option considered above, that is, investigating whether some coordination issues might be better handled via human-robot collaboration rather than through attempts to make robotic driving more humanlike? What sorts of ethical issues might this way of promotion human-robot coordination give rise to? The most obvious ethical issue here is whether the new responsibilities humans would be given would be too much to handle, or whether the average person could reasonably be expected to discharge these responsibilities, whatever they might be.

In other words, in mixed traffic, it may be that some ways of achieving greater compatibility between highly automated cars and conventional cars is by keeping the former from being completely automated, and requiring the human driver to "help" the automated cars with some of the tasks they need to perform within mixed traffic. But at the same time, perhaps some of the ways in which humans could help out would be too difficult for most drivers. If so, it would be ethically problematic to place those new responsibilities on their shoulders.

This same general type of worry has already been discussed in relation to how automated cars should respond to dramatic crash and accident scenarios. For example, Alexander Hevelke and Julian Nida-Rümelin argue that it would be unfair to require people to step in and take over in crash scenarios, because people cannot be expected to be able to react quickly enough.[45] In order for it to be fair and reasonable to expect humans to "help" their automated cars in accident scenarios, it needs to be likely that the average driver would be able to perform the given tasks. After all, it is a widely accepted ethical principle that "ought implies can."

I agree with the general thrust of Hevelke and Nida-Rümelin's worries about requiring people to take over in crash scenarios. However, it is important not to draw too close of an analogy between handing over control to the human driver in accident scenarios and all other possible forms of human involvement in attempts to create better human-robot coordination within mixed traffic. Some conceivable ways of promoting human-robot coordination by involving the human driver in the operation of highly automated cars may indeed be too demanding to be reasonable. However, there can surely also be ways of involving the human driver that are not too demanding. Suppose, for example, that an autonomous car carrying a perfectly normal human adult is facing the following situation: The road is otherwise empty, but there is a large branch lying in the car's lane. There is a double line, meaning that strictly speaking, it is against the traffic rules to briefly cross into the oncoming lane as a way of avoiding hitting the branch. For the artificial intelligence in the car, it is a tough challenge to figure out whether this is a situation where it is a safe and a good idea to break the rules, but for the human in the car it is a no-brainer. This is one kind of situation in which rather than to program a completely automated car to think and behave like a human, the human driver can work together with the car to deal with this situation.[46] A more specific ethical evaluation of different possible ways of involving the human driver would first need to look at what exactly the humans would be required and expected to do. The next step would then be to make an assessment of whether these are tasks most operators of automated cars would be able to perform.

Turn now to the third solution-strategy under discussion: seeking means for conforming certain aspects of human driving to robotic driving. As I noted above, this could be done, for example, by means of speed-controlling technologies. They could help to align the speeds at which people drive with the speeds at which robotic cars drive. Or it could be done—to use another example I also mentioned above—with the help of things such as alcohol locks.[47] Whatever technological or other means might be suggested, what sorts of ethical issues might be brought to bear on the evaluation of this general strategy for achieving better human-robot coordination within mixed traffic? I have already suggested in the first chapter that any suggestions for adapting humans to robots should first look at whether this is beneficial to us, whether it is domain-specific, mostly reversible, and not too invasive or intrusive. But what other ethical issues should also be taken into account?

It can first be noted that trying to adapt human driving to robotic driving—or more generally trying to adapt human behavior to robotic behavior—is the strategy most likely to generate heated debate if it is taken seriously and it receives the attention I think it deserves. In the case of mixed traffic, on the critical side, obvious objections to be antici- pated are worries about potential infringements upon drivers' freedom and, at the extreme, perhaps even worries about infringements upon drivers' human dignity. On the other side, considerations such as the duty of care that we typically associate with traffic and related duties of responsible risk-management also need to be taken very seriously.

In other traffic-related contexts, when discussions about mandating things such as speed-regulation technologies spring up—either for all drivers or some subclass, such as truck drivers—one of the issues that tends to be raised is the worry that this takes away the driver's freedom to choose how he or she wants to operate his or her vehicle. For exam- ple, one Canadian truck driver who had been ordered to use a speed limiter in his truck took the matter to court. In court, he argued that his fundamental freedoms would be compromised if he could not himself be in charge of deciding how fast or slow he was going when driving his truck. At first, the court ruled in favor of the truck driver. However, another Canadian court later overturned that decision, ruling that re- quiring the truck driver to use a speed limiter did not offend against his fundamental freedoms.[48] In any case, it is to be expected that similar objections will be raised if a serious discussion arises about the idea of trying to conform human driving to robotic driving by requiring human drivers to use technologies such as speed limiters in their conventional cars.

The idea of trying to conform human traffic behaviors to robotic traffic behaviors might perhaps also, as I suggested above, strike some as an assault on human dignity.[49] This solution would take the choice of whether or not to follow rules such as speed limits (and thereby better coordinate one's driving with robotic driving) out of the hands of the human driver. The human driver could not self-apply the law. And being afforded the opportunity to self-apply laws—as opposed to being made to follow laws—has sometimes been said to be central to human dignity in general. For example, legal theorists Henry Hart and Albert Sachs see the self-application of law as a crucial part of human dignity.[50] Legal philosopher Jeremy Waldron also joins them in associating this idea with human dignity in his 2012 book on dignity based on his Tanner Lectures on the subject.[51]

It is to be expected that these kinds of worries will be raised. But upon closer inspection, would it really offend against values such as freedom and human dignity to suggest that we try to achieve better human-robot coordination in mixed traffic by seeking technological means for conforming at least certain nonideal aspects of human driving to robotic driving-styles? Also, what sorts of countervailing arguments might be presented on the opposite side of the issue, which would qualify as positive arguments in favor of this general idea?

Concerning those questions, I here wish to briefly make three main points. First, from a legal and moral point of view, we do currently enjoy neither a legal nor a moral freedom to speed or to otherwise drive in ways that expose people to greatly increased risks.[52] We have a legal freedom to do something if the law permits it, and a moral freedom to do something if morality permits it. Driving in ways that create great risks is neither permitted by law nor by good morals. So it could be argued that if we try to make people drive more like robots by putting speed regulators in their cars, and thereby achieve better human-robot coordination within mixed traffic, we do not take away any legal and moral freedom that people can currently lay claim to. What we would block would rather by a purely "physical" freedom to drive in certain dangerous ways that are neither legally nor morally sanctioned and that make it much harder to create good human-robot coordination within mixed traffic.[53]

To clarify: The point I am making is not that being free is the same as doing what is legally and morally permitted. The point is rather that there is a significant distinction between freedoms that people ought to be afforded and freedoms that they ought not to be afforded.[54] And from a legal and moral point of view, people are not—and ought not to be—afforded freedoms to drive in ways that greatly increase the risks involved in traffic.

Second, it may indeed be that in general, one important part of human dignity has to do with being afforded the freedom to self-apply laws. But it is not so clear that this ideal requires that people always be given a choice whether or not to self-apply all laws, across all different domains of human activity, whatever the costs.[55] In some domains, other values may be more salient and more important for the purposes and goals specific to those domains. Traffic, for example, which is the domain I am currently discussing, is not obviously a domain where the most important value is to be afforded the opportunity to self-apply traffic-regulations.

Values much more salient in this domain include things such as safety, and mutual respect and concern, or much more mundane things such as user comfort and overall traffic efficiency. It is not so clear that being afforded the choice of deciding whether or not to follow traffic rules intended to save lives is a key value that stands out as being what we typically most value within this domain of human activity. Furthermore, there are still a lot of different traffic rules to break or follow, which provide ample opportunities to self-apply the law. Moreover, being kept safe by laws and norms that seek to protect us and our life and limb can surely also be seen—and is surely often seen—as an important part of what it means to enjoy a dignified status in human society.[56] So upon closer inspection, seeking means for making people drive more like robots may not be such a great offense to human dignity after all, even if the basic idea might sound a little strange at first.

Third, there is another very important thing about the choices drivers face that should also be kept in mind, if it is indeed true that highly automated driving would be a very safe form of driving.[57] And that is that the introduction of this supposedly much safer alternative can plausibly be seen as changing the relative moral status of some of the choices drivers face. In general, if some new technology is introduced into some sphere of human life, and that new technology is much safer than previously existing ones, this creates moral pressure—I suggest—to either: (i) switch to using the new technology or (ii) use added precautions while using the older forms of technology. That is an ethical principle that I think we should apply in our ethical reasoning about new technologies more generally, and a principle that can be applied to this particular case of choices related to mixed traffic more specifically.

If highly automated driving will eventually become much safer than nonautomated conventional driving, the introduction of automated driving thereby constitutes the introduction of a safer alternative within the context of mixed traffic. So, if a driver does not go for this safer option, this should create some moral pressure to take extra safety precautions when using the older, less safe option even as a new, safer option is introduced. As I see things, it can plausibly be claimed that with the introduction of the safer option (i.e., switching to automated driving), a new moral imperative is created within this domain. Namely, to either switch to automated driving (the safer option) or to take or accept added safety precautions when opting for conventional driving (the less safe option).[58] If automated cars are eventually established to be a significantly safer alternative, it would be irresponsible to simply carry on as if nothing had changed and there were no new options on the horizon.[59]

4.5: SWITCHING GEARS

In this and the previous chapter, I have been discussing robots that are neither designed to look like humans nor designed to act like humans. Neither self-driving cars nor automated weapons systems look or act like humans. Of course, I noted above that there are some voices who argue that self-driving cars should be designed to behave more like human drivers. But as I have argued, that idea seems to partly defeat the purpose of creating self-driving cars. The main purpose, after all, is typically considered to be to create a more optimal form of driving than human driving. In the same way, there would not seem to be any clear purpose in creating military robots/autonomous weapons systems specifically designed to replicate all the sorts of behaviors that human soldiers engage in on the battlefield. For many kinds of robots—whether it is self-driving cars, military robots, delivery robots, robotic vacuum cleaners, logistics robots, or whatever—it makes the most sense to create designs whose functionality and shape are suited to the tasks the robots are created to perform. For such robots, there typically does not seem to be any clear point in trying to make the robots look or behave like human beings.

However, many people share a fascination with the idea of creating robots that look and/or act like human beings. This is sometimes hypothesized to potentially be creating an "uncanny valley."[60] Robots that closely resemble, but that are not quite like humans are thought to be likely to elicit an uncanny emotional response in human observers. Yet many people are deeply fascinated with the idea of robots that look or behave like humans. Some have high hopes for such robots. Perhaps they could become our friends, romantic partners, teachers, colleagues, entertainers, or some other kinds of associates and companions.

Or perhaps creating robots that look or act like human beings is not such a good idea. People might be deceived about just how humanlike these robots really are; many people might overestimate the capacities of such robots. That might lead to harms or disappointment. The moral status of robots that look or act like human beings might be ambiguous or for other reasons problematic. Perhaps spending too much time around humanoid robots would have bad effects on some people. Moreover, some robots created to look and act like humans—such as so-called sex robots—may also be highly offensive to some people.

Because the prospect of robots that look and behave like humans is both a fascinating and philosophically interesting prospect, the second half of this book will mostly be about such robots. Every now and then, I will return to also discussing other kinds of robots, such as self-driving cars or robotic vacuum cleaners. Some of the questions I will be discussing may very well apply not only to robots that look or act like humans, but also to other robots as well. But I will mostly be discussing robots that look or behave like humans from now on. The questions I will be discussing in the next four chapters are about whether robots can be our friends like other human beings can be; whether robots can have minds in the sense that human beings do; whether robots can be good in the ways that human beings can be; and whether any robots should be treated with anything like the moral consideration we think human beings should be treated with.

NOTES

1. I say "Tesla cases" here because even though I only mentioned one fatal Tesla autopilot crash at the beginning of the last chapter, there have also been

others. See Andrew J. Hawkins (2019), "Tesla's Autopilot Was Engaged When Model 3 Crashed into Truck, Report States: It Is at Least the Fourth Fatal Crash involving Autopilot," *The Verve*, https://www.theverge.com/2019/5/16/18627766/tesla-autopilot-fatal-crash-delray-florida-ntsb-model-3 (Accessed on August 23, 2019).

2. Levin and Wong, "Self-Driving Uber Kills Arizona Woman in First Fatal Crash involving Pedestrian," op. cit.

3. Simon Romero (2018), "Wielding Rocks and Knives, Arizonans Attack Self-Driving Cars," *New York Times*, https://www.nytimes.com/2018/12/31/us/waymo-self-driving-cars-arizona-attacks.html (Accessed on August 23, 2019).

4. Ibid.

5. Cf. Robert Sparrow and Mark Howard (2017), "When Human Beings Are Like Drunk Robots: Driverless Vehicles, Ethics, and the Future of Transport," *Transport Research Part C: Emerging Technologies* 80, 206–15.

6. I provide an overview of the ethics of autonomous driving, with a special focus on ethical issues related to crashes involving self-driving cars, in Sven Nyholm (2018), "The Ethics of Crashes with Self-Driving Cars: A Roadmap, I," *Philosophy Compass* 13(7), e12507, and Sven Nyholm (2018), "The Ethics of Crashes with Self-Driving Cars, A Roadmap, II," *Philosophy Compass* 13(7), e12506. See also Sven Nyholm (2018), "Teaching & Learning Guide for: The Ethics of Crashes with Self-Driving Cars: A Roadmap, I-II," *Philosophy Compass* 13(7), e12508.

7. Ibid.

8. Van Loon and Martens, "Automated Driving and Its Effect on the Safety Ecosystem: How Do Compatibility Issues Affect the Transition Period?," op. cit.

9. Mindell, *Our Robots, Ourselves*, op. cit.

10. Walther Wachenfeld, Hermann Winner, J. Christian Gerdes, Barbara Lenz, Markus Maurer, Sven Beiker, Eva Fraedrich, and Thomas Winkle (2015), "Use Cases for Autonomous Driving," in Markus Maurer, J Christian Gerdes, Barbara Lenz, and Hermann Winner (eds.), *Autonomous Driving: Technical, Legal and Social Aspects*, Berlin: Springer; and Quan Yuan, Yan Gao, and Yibing Li (2016), "Suppose Future Traffic Accidents Based on Development of Self-Driving Vehicles," in Shengzhao Long and Balbir S. Dhillon (eds.), *Man-Machine-Environment System Engineering*, New York: Springer.

11. Mindell, *Our Robots, Ourselves*, op. cit., and Royakkers and Van Est, *Just Ordinary Robots*, op. cit.

12. Noel Sharkey and Amanda Sharkey (2010), "The Crying Shame of Robot Nannies: An Ethical Appraisal," *Interaction Studies: Social Behaviour and Communication in Biological and Artificial Systems* 11(2), 161–90.

13. Like human-driven conventional cars, pedestrians, animals, and bikers also do not behave like robots. So these are further human-robot coordination problems (including animal-robot coordination issues!).

14. Cf. Douglas Husak (2010), "Vehicles and Crashes: Why Is This Issue Overlooked?", *Social Theory and Practice* 30(3), 351–70.

15. Van Loon and Martens, "Automated Driving and Its Effect on the Safety Ecosystem: How Do Compatibility Issues Affect the Transition Period?," op. cit. Yang et al., "Suppose Future Traffic Accidents Based on Development of Self-Driving Vehicles," op. cit.

16. Van Loon and Martens, "Automated Driving and Its Effect on the Safety Ecosystem: How Do Compatibility Issues Affect the Transition Period?," op. cit.

17. Noah J. Goodall (2014), "Machine Ethics and Automated Vehicles," in Geroen Meyer and Sven Beiker (eds.), *Road Vehicle Automation*, Berlin: Springer, 93–102.

18. However, as we will see below, various different stakeholders are already debating whether self-driving cars should be programmed to break the law in order to better coordinate interaction with conventional cars.

19. Schlosser, "Agency," op. cit.

20. Van Loon and Martens, "Automated Driving and Its Effect on the Safety Ecosystem: How Do Compatibility Issues Affect the Transition Period?," op. cit.

21. Van Loon and Martens, "Automated Driving and Its Effect on the Safety Ecosystem: How Do Compatibility Issues Affect the Transition Period?," op. cit. See also Ingo Wolf (2016), "The Interaction between Humans and Autonomous Agents," in Maurer et al., *Autonomous Driving*, op. cit.

22. Van Loon and Martens, "Automated Driving and Its Effect on the Safety Ecosystem: How Do Compatibility Issues Affect the Transition Period?," op. cit. p. 3282.

23. Neal E. Boudette (2019), "Despite High Hopes, Self-Driving Cars Are 'Way in the Future,'" *New York Times*, https://www.nytimes.com/2019/07/17/business/self-driving-autonomous-cars.html (Accessed on August 23, 2019).

24. Moreover, according to van Loon and Martens, traffic psychologists do not know how well human drivers in general are able to understand and predict the behavior of fellow drivers. See Van Loon and Martens, "Automated Driving and Its Effect on the Safety Ecosystem: How Do Compatibility Issues Affect the Transition Period?," op. cit., 3283.

25. See, for example, Berthold Färber (2016), "Communication and Communication Problems between Autonomous Vehicles and Human Drivers," in Maurer et al., *Autonomous Driving*, op. cit. and Michael Sivak and Brandon Schoettle (2015), "Road Safety with Self-Driving Vehicles: General Limitations

and Road Sharing with Conventional Vehicles," *Deep Blue*, http://deep-blue.lib.umich.edu/handle/2027.42/111735.

26. Schoettle and Sivak, "A Preliminary Analysis of Real-World Crashes Involving Self-Driving Vehicles," op. cit.

27. It is, of course, also possible to pursue technological solutions for adapting autonomous cars to human-driven cars that do not make robotic driving more like human driving. Here, I focus on the idea of making robotic driving more like human driving for two reasons: First, this idea is frequently suggested, and second, it raises ethical issues of the specific sorts I particularly wish to highlight in this chapter. However, a fuller discussion than what I can fit into this chapter would also explore possible ethical issues related to adapting robotic driving to human driving in ways that do not involve making the latter more like the former.

28. Keith Naughton (2015), "Humans Are Slamming into Driverless Cars and Exposing a Key Flaw," *Bloomberg*, https://www.bloomberg.com/news/articles/2015-12-18/humans-are-slamming-into-driverless-cars-and-exposing-a-key-flaw (Accessed on August 23, 2019).

29. Herman Wagter (2016), "Naughty Software," presentation at *Ethics: Responsible Driving Automation*, at Connekt, Delft.

30. J. Christian Gerdes and Sarah M. Thornton (2015), "Implementable Ethics for Autonomous Vehicles," in Maurer et al., *Autonomous Driving*, op. cit.

31. Naughton, "Humans Are Slamming into Driverless Cars and Exposing a Key Flaw," op. cit.

32. Ibid. At another point, however, Reuters reported that Google was then willing to program their self-driving cars to speed up to 16 kph if safety were served by doing so. See Paul Ingrassia (2014), "Look, No Hands! Test Driving a Google Car," *Reuters*, https://www.reuters.com/article/us-google-driverless-idUSKBN0GH02P20140817 (Accessed on August 23, 2019).

33. Mindell, *Our Robots, Ourselves*, op. cit. Cf. Arthur Kuflik (1999), "Computers in Control: Rational Transfer of Authority or Irresponsible Abdication of Autonomy?," *Ethics and Information Technology* 1(3), 173–84.

34. This does not need to amount to a complete handover of all functions, but it could potentially be solved in some other way. For example, in airplanes, when pilots switch off some of the autopilot features, pilots do not typically start performing all functions manually, but rather simply take over certain aspects of the operation of the airplane. Mindell, *Our Robots, Ourselves*, op. cit. See also Bradshaw et al., "The Seven Deadly Myths of 'Autonomous Systems,'" op. cit.

35. Jilles Smids (2018), "The Moral Case for Intelligent Speed Adaptation," *Journal of Applied Philosophy* 35(2), 205–21.

36. Smids, "The Moral Case for Intelligent Speed Adaptation," op. cit.

37. Uncredited (2019), "Road Safety: UK Set to Adopt Vehicle Speed Limiters," BBC, https://www.bbc.com/news/business-47715415 (Accessed on August 23, 2019).

38. Frank Lai, Oliver Carsten, and Fergus Tate (2012), "How Much Benefit Does Intelligent Speed Adaptation Deliver: An Analysis of Its Potential Contribution to Safety and the Environment," *Accident Analysis & Prevention* 48, 63–72.

39. My colleague Jilles Smids summarized some such reasons in the following way in a joint article of ours: "Firstly, if conventional cars slow down, the need to program automated cars to speed in situation like merging with speeding traffic disappears, while the safety of its occupants is not jeopardized. Of course, this is only one traffic situation. More generally, retrofitting conventional cars with speed limiters strongly eases interpretation and prediction of the behavior of conventional cars on the part of automated cars and vice versa. For, second, if conventional cars cannot speed, there will be a significant reduction of the range of actual and potential behavior of conventional cars that automated cars need to interpret and predict. In addition, in cases where they still misinterpret or make the wrong prediction, conventional cars sticking to the speed limit allow automated cars more time to adjust. Taking the perspective of the human drivers, third, these will no longer face situations in which, due to a lack of time caused by speeding in particular, they fail to adequately interpret (unfamiliar) behavior of automated cars. Having more time to consider and interpret the situation is one of the benefits of speed-limiters reported by participants of intelligent speed adaptation (ISA)-trials (Oliver Carsten, personal communication). In addition, since no cars will speed any more, the driving-styles of automated and conventional cars become more alike, and one source of ill-applied driver's expectations is eliminated." This is taken from footnote 14 in Sven Nyholm and Jilles Smids (in press), "Automated Cars Meet Human Drivers: Responsible Human-Robot Coordination and the Ethics of Mixed Traffic," *Ethics and Information Technology*, 1–10, https://link.springer.com/article/10.1007/s10676-018-9445-9.

40. Kalle Grill and Jessica Nihlén Fahlquist (2012), "Responsibility, Paternalism and Alcohol Interlocks," *Public Health Ethics* 5(2), 116–27.

41. An example of this technology can be found at https://www.mobileye.com/our-technology/ (Accessed on August 23, 2019).

42. Technologies like speed limiters and alcohol interlocks have been around for a long time, yet they have not been widely adopted. Why? I suspect that there is a "status quo bias" at work here, whereby people are intuitively biased toward the way things are, even if it is not an optimal state of affairs. (See Nick Bostrom and Toby Ord, [2006], "The Reversal Test: Eliminating

Status Quo Bias in Applied Ethics," *Ethics* 116, 656–79.) The widespread introduction of self-driving cars has a disruptive potential, however, whereby widely held attitude toward currently available used and unused traffic technologies are likely to change. Hence the introduction of a supposedly safer alternative—that is, highly or fully automated driving—will give drivers reason to rethink their attitudes toward safety technologies not currently used, but already available for, conventional cars.

43. A fourth possible solution that is sometimes floated would be to separate autonomous cars from conventional cars, having them drive in different lanes, or on different roads. This would certainly solve the problem of having to coordinate human and robotic driving, and it might be possible in certain places. However, given limitations in available space for roads and people's preferences for where they will want to be able to get to using their cars, this solution-strategy will be unrealistic in many places.

44. Cf. Arkin, "The Case for Ethical Autonomy in Unmanned Systems," op. cit.

45. Hevelke and Nida-Rümelin, "Responsibility for Crashes of Autonomous Vehicles," op. cit.

46. Cf. Färber, "Communication and Communication Problems between Autonomous Vehicles and Human Drivers," op. cit., 143.

47. I am not here interested in investigating—or defending—any specific technological means for making human driving more like robotic driving; I am more interested in the general idea and the question of what sorts of ethical issues are relevant in relation to this sort of idea.

48. Uncredited (2015), "Court Upholds Ontario Truck Speed Limiter Law," *Today's Trucking*, https://www.todaystrucking.com/court-upholds-ontario-truck-speed-limiter-law/ (Accessed on August 23, 2019).

49. Frischmann and Selinger, for example, argue that anything that would make us more robotic in the way we behave threatens to be degrading, by denying our humanity. See Frischmann and Selinger, *Re-Engineering Humanity*, op. cit.

50. Henry Hart and Albert Sachs (1994), *The Legal Process*, Eagan, MN: Foundation Press.

51. Jeremy Waldron (2012), *Dignity, Rank, and Rights*, Oxford: Oxford University Press.

52. Royakkers and Van Est, *Just Ordinary Robots*, op. cit.

53. Moreover, by making mixed traffic safer and thereby making the option of using a car available to, and more eligible for, a wider range of people (e.g., the elderly and the severely disabled), we could be seen as extending the freedom people enjoy in this domain (Cf. Heather Bradshaw-Martin and Catherine Easton [2014], "Autonomous or 'Driverless' Cars and Disability: A

Legal and Ethical Analysis," *European Journal of Current Legal Issues* 20(3), http://webjcli.org/article/view/344/471). Let more people become able to exercise the option of using a car (either a self-driving car or a conventional car); and let this become a safe and reliable option for all. If these two conditions are fulfilled, the option of using a car become more like a basic freedom. This requires that people who use conventional cars be willing to accept measures to create a more inclusive type of traffic, which can include accepting measures that help to create better human-robot coordination within mixed traffic. Cf. Philip Pettit on "co-exercisability" and "co-satisfiability" as two of the requirements for counting something (e.g., an option all might be afforded within a society) as a basic liberty in Philip Pettit (2012), *On the People's Terms*, Cambridge: Cambridge University Press. See especially 93–97.

54. Ronald Dworkin (2013), *Justice for Hedgehogs*, Cambridge, MA: Harvard University Press.

55. Cf. Smids, "The Moral Case for Intelligent Speed Adaptation," op. cit. and Karen Yeung (2011), "Can We Employ Design-Based Regulation While Avoiding Brave New World?" *Law Innovation and Technology* 3(1), 1–29.

56. Cf. Michael Rosen (2012), *Dignity*, Cambridge, MA: Harvard University Press.

57. Legal theorists Gary Marchant and Rachel Lindor argue that self-driving cars will not be legally viable unless they can be shown to be safer, if not much safer, than conventional cars. Hence, they argue, any discussion of traffic scenarios involving automated cars that is likely to occur can treat automated cars as safer than conventional cars. My argument in these last paragraphs of this section rests on the assumption that Marchant and Lindor are right about this. In other words, for the sake of this third argument, I here assume that self-driving cars will eventually represent a safer alternative as compared to conventional cars. See Marchant and Lindor, "The Coming Collision between Autonomous Cars and the Liability System," op. cit.

58. For more on the idea that taking precautions can help to make risky behaviors more acceptable, see James Lenman (2008), "Contractualism and Risk Imposition," *Politics, Philosophy & Economics* 7(1), 99–122.

59. Moreover, if the introduction of automated vehicles can extend the option of using a car independently to a greater number of people (e.g., the elderly and severely disabled people), then this seemingly also adds a further duty drivers for drivers of conventional cars: namely, a duty to help enable these new car users to participate in mixed traffic in a safe way (Cf. Bradshaw-Martin and Easton, "Autonomous or 'Driverless' Cars and Disability: A Legal and Ethical Analysis," op. cit.). That duty can be discharged by accepting certain means for making human driving more like robotic driving in certain ways, so as to achieve better human-robot coordination within mixed traffic.

60. Masahiro Mori (2012), "The Uncanny Valley," *IEEE Robotics & Automation Magazine* 19(2), 98–100.

5

ROBOTIC RELATIONSHIPS

5.1: TRUE COMPANIONS?

The company Truecompanion.com claims to sell "the world's first sex robot." The robot is called "Roxxxy," and the website advertising the robot makes some striking claims about the capabilities of this robot. Supposedly, Roxxxy

> knows your name, your likes and dislikes, can carry on a discussion and express her love to you and be a loving friend. She can talk to you, listen to you and feel your touch. She can even have an orgasm![1]

In an interview about Roxxxy, the robot's inventor, Douglas Hines, remarked that a relationship with Roxxxy is about more than just sex. Sex "is only a small part of it."[2] Roxxxy can be a "true companion."

The company developing the sex robot "Samantha" makes similar claims about their invention, and it has similar ambitions for their robot. In a 2017 TV appearance on the UK show *This Morning*, inventor Arran Lee Wright described the extent of Samantha's artificial intelligence. He claimed that it enables Samantha to respond to different social scenarios: She can talk to you ("she can talk about animals, she can talk about philosophy") and even tell jokes. Much like Roxxxy is described as a true companion, Wright also described how "you can tell her 'I love you' and she can respond."[3]

A third example is "Harmony," a sex robot developed by Matt McMullen. Speaking about this robot and its capabilities, McMullen states in a video that "we wanted to create a very open-ended kind of discourse that you can have with this AI." That, he adds, "is what makes it fun." The head of the robot has "twelve points of articulation in the face," enabling it to display a range of different facial expressions. All these things "work together to make it come across as if she's alive." The aim is to make people "feel a connection" when they are speaking with the robot. [4]

These three sex robots are developed to be "more than a sex partner." They are designed to make people "feel a connection" and to make people want to say "I love you" to the robot, so that users can see their robot as a "true companion." But can a robot be a "loving friend"? And would it be desirable to have robots as our friends or perhaps as our romantic partners? In discussing this issue in this chapter, I will follow a suggestion about this topic made by the Dutch social robotics researcher Maartje de Graaf. [5] She suggests that when we discuss this topic, we should not only consider whether a robot could be our friend or partner in some sense or other. We should also importantly consider whether the particular goods or values that we associate with friendships and close relationships could be achieved within a human-robot relationship. Otherwise, there would be little point, or at least less reason, to try to create or reflect on the possibility of robotic relationships.

Speaking of whether there is any point in discussing this topic—some readers might be skeptical!—I think there are at least three good reasons to take this topic seriously. First, as we just saw, there are companies that are trying to create robots—sex robots, but also other kinds of social robots—that they say can be potential friends or companions for their human users. This creates a worry that such companies might deceive their prospective customers about whether these robots could really be anybody's friend or companion. Second, there are also people who form emotional attachments to robots, and who want to have robots as their friends or companions. I will describe a few cases below, but in general: The question is whether such people are somehow mistaken or confused. [6] Third, although most philosophers who have written about whether it is possible to have robotic friends or companions are highly skeptical about this, there are also philosophers who have recently defended the case for robot friendship. Together with my colleague Lily Frank, I myself have recently argued for a skeptical position regarding the possibility of mutual love between humans and robots.[7] But a friend of mine whose work I admire and respect—the Irish philosopher John Danaher—has recently written an impressive defense of the possibility of human-robot friendships.[8] Similarly, another philosopher, David Levy, has written a whole book in defense of the idea that in the future, people will come to love and want to marry robots.[9] The fact that there are philosophers who defend the possibility of friendship and love with robots is a third reason for investigating whether human beings and robots can be friends—or perhaps romantic partners. It is a third reason for investigating whether the values we associate with friendship and companionship can be achieved within the context of human-robot relationships.

Since I have written on the prospects for mutual love between humans and robots elsewhere, I will mostly focus on human-robot friendship here. And since I have presented reasons to be skeptical about human-robot relationships elsewhere, I will here be particularly interested in critically assessing the positive case that some philosophers want to make in favor of human-robot friendships. Specifically, I am struck by Danaher's "philosophical case for robot friendship," as he calls it, which I find more impressive than Levy's defense of the prospect for love and marriage between humans and robots. So I will mostly focus on critically assessing Danaher's overall argument in this chapter.

It is worth noting, though, there is a certain amount of similarity between Danaher's case for robot friendship and Levy's case in favor of love and marriage between humans and robots. Both take a behavioristic or performative approach to whether somebody—be it a human or a robot—could qualify as a friend or romantic partner. According to Danaher and Levy, whether somebody (or something!) can be a friend or partner depends on how they are able to behave toward us. Since this is a claim about friendships and relationships that is made by both Danaher and Levy in their respective defenses of human-robot relationships, this chapter will pay special attention to the issue of behavior and whether it is all that matters for achieving relationship values. So the question is: Can humans and robots be friends, and is how they behave around each other the main issue that settles whether the values we associate with friendship can be achieved within human-robot relationships?

5.2: HUMAN ATTACHMENT TO ROBOTS?

Even very simple artifacts that lack any artificial intelligence or any type of functional autonomy can become the objects of strong emotional attachments. This is suggested by cases such as those of people who view themselves as having loving relationships with sex dolls that they own. For example, a man living in Michigan who calls himself "Davecat" has received a lot of media attention for his claim that he has been "married" for over fifteen years to a sex doll named Sidore.[10] Davecat describes himself as a proponent of "synthetic love." He has made several media appearances in which he describes his love life, for example, in the BBC documentary *Guys and Dolls*. Similarly, in Japan, there is a trend whereby men have "virtual girlfriends." The Japanese government has even had worries about an apparent decrease in interest among young people in finding stable romantic partners with whom to form families.[11] A thirty-five-year-old man living in Tokyo—named Akihiko Kondo—took this one step further. In November of 2018, he "married" a hologram. His bride was Hatsune Miku, a holographic virtual reality singer floating inside a desktop device.[12]

If people like Davecat and these Japanese men form what they experience as romantic bonds with sex dolls, holograms, or avatars ("virtual girlfriends"), it is quite likely that the same would happen with more advanced robots people might interact with. That is especially so if findings from robotics, psychology, and human-technology interaction research are taken into account by developers looking specifically to create robots inducing emotional bonding. In the interviews referred to above, the creators of Roxxxy, Samantha, and Harmony explicitly state that they are drawing on such research.

Human beings can also become attached to robots not specifically created to induce emotional attachment. And it is not just robots with humanlike appearance and behavior that people have been reported to bond emotionally with. Consider the case of "Boomer," the military robot, as described by Julia Carpenter in her research.[13] As mentioned in an earlier chapter, this was a military robot operating in the battlefield in Iraq. The robot looked more like a lawn mower or small tank than anything else, and it was not designed to act in any humanlike way. Even so, the human soldiers in the military team grew very attached to this robot. When the robot was damaged, they wanted to fix that particular robot, rather than getting a new one. When the robot was eventually destroyed in the battlefield, the soldiers had gotten so attached to it that they wanted to give a military funeral for their fallen comrade. They also wanted to give two military medals of honor to the robot: a Purple Heart and a Bronze Star. Prior to his destruction, Boomer's job was to seek out and disarm bombs. Boomer had saved many lives. But not only was he a lifesaver. Boomer's coworkers also thought he had "develop[ed] a personality" of his own. [14]

The case of Boomer reminds me of an example Danaher discusses in the introduction of his above-mentioned paper—and which he presents as an inspiration for his defense of robot friendship: namely, the fictional case of the robot R2-D2 from the *Star Wars* movies. [15] That robot appears to be regarded as a friend and colleague by the humans in the fiction—even though the robot looks like an upside-down wastebasket on wheels, and even though the robot communicates by beeps and clicks, rather than humanlike speech. Of course, in these movies, there is also C-3PO—R2-D2's companion—who looks more like a human made out of metal. C-3PO certainly has a personality of his own, and many humanlike mannerisms. But the humans in these movies seem equally willing to include C-3PO and the less humanlike R2-D2 into their circle of friends and companions.

So whether in fiction or in real life (such as the cases of Davecat or the case with Boomer the military robot), the idea that humans can become emotionally attached to robots and treat them like friends does not seem like something that can be denied. What is up for discussion and more controversial is whether these humans (the real-life humans or the fictional ones) are making some sort of mistake in treating these robots like friends or companions. Can the robots reciprocate?

Now, having friends is usually considered as being among the greatest goods of life. Not surprisingly, therefore, the philosophical discussion of the value and nature of true friendship stretches all the way back to ancient philosophy, with important accounts of love and friendship being found in classic works by authors like Plato, Aristotle, and Cicero.

In fact, when philosophers discuss whether it is possible for humans and robots to form friendships where the goods of friendship are achieved, it is a common move to start with Aristotle's discussion of friendship. [16] Famously, Aristotle notes that "friendship" can refer to different kinds of relationships, with different kinds of value. The three main kinds are[17]:

1. **Utility friendships**: relationships that are useful to one or both parties.
2. **Pleasure friendships**: relationships that bring pleasure to one or both parties.
3. **Virtue friendships**: relationships based on mutual goodwill and well-wishing, involving mutual admiration and shared values.

As Aristotle sees things, there is something valuable about each form of friendship. But there is a clear hierarchy: Utility and pleasure friendships are "imperfect," whereas what Aristotle calls virtue friendship is the highest or greatest form of friendship. The other forms of friendship have lesser value. And they are also less interesting to discuss in relation to the question of whether robots can be our friends and help to realize the distinctive goods of friendship.

To be sure, robots can be useful for people. And they can also give us pleasure. So at least on the human side of the equation, we could say that robots can provide us with some of the goods we associate with having utility or pleasure friends. Of course, it can be asked whether the robots get any pleasure or whether it is useful for them to have humans as their friends. But that is not as interesting a question as the question of whether robots can be part of virtue friendships with humans. Accordingly, that is the question I will focus on. This is also the kind of friendship that Danaher—very bravely!—argues that we can achieve together with robots.[18]

5.3: REASONS TO BE SKEPTICAL ABOUT ROBOTIC RELATIONSHIPS

Before he defends the possibility of virtue friendships between humans and robots, Danaher does a great job at summarizing many important aspects of the case against the possibility of human-robot friendships. As Danaher himself notes, the case against human-robot friendships appears very strong.[19] That is why I just called Danaher brave in trying to defend the possibility of human-robot virtue friendships. Since I am interested in this defense of his, I will here follow Danaher's way of summarizing the case against such friendships. Later on, I will describe another couple of arguments, which I will derive from Cicero and Kant's respective discussions of friendship. But I will start here with the reasons Danaher discusses.

Danaher notes that there are at least four very important aspects to true friendship ("virtue friendship") that seem to cast doubt on the possibility of human-robot friendships.[20] It is widely thought that the most valuable kind of friendship should involve these four aspects:

1. **mutuality**: Friends have shared values, interests, and admiration, and reciprocal well-wishing.
2. **honesty/authenticity**: Friends are honest in their dealings with each other, do not misrepresent themselves, but instead present themselves as they truly are.
3. **equality**: The parties are on roughly equal footing, so that neither party is dominant or superior in relation to the other.
4. **diversity of interactions**: The parties interact with other in many different ways, across many different types of contexts.

What makes virtue friendships valuable, in part, is that we can enjoy mutuality, honest authenticity, equality, and a diversity of interactions together with our friends. So if it is to be possible to enjoy the goods associated with virtue friendship with robots as our friends, it would need to be the case that we can enjoy mutuality, honest authenticity, equality, and a diversity of interactions with robots. As Danaher himself diagnoses the case against robotic friendship, this is exactly the problem that the prospect of such friendships seems to stumble on.

Schematically, here is how the argument goes:

- **Premise 1**: In order for someone (a human or robot) to possibly be a virtue friend, we would need to be able to achieve the goods of (a) mutuality, (b) authenticity, (c) equality, and (d) diversity of interactions in relation to that someone.
- **Premise 2**: It is not possible to achieve these goods together with robots, because robots lack the capacities needed to achieve them.
- **Conclusion**: Robots and humans cannot possibly realize virtue friendships together.[21]

In enjoying fiction—like *Star Wars*—it is quite possible to imagine that robots could live up to these conditions, especially if we do not reflect too much on what this would have to involve in practice. However, in real life, it is quite hard to imagine robots living up to these conditions on a virtue friend.

For example, in order to share values with us, it would seem that a robot would need to have the sort of "inner life" and attitudes that we associate with having values. Valuing something is often thought to be a complex set of attitudes and mental dispositions. It involves, among other things, caring about what we value, viewing ourselves as having good reasons to act in certain ways (e.g., in ways that protect and honor what we value), being emotionally attached to what we value, and so on.[22] It is doubtful whether robots can have inner lives involving such complex attitudes and mental dispositions. Second, if a robot behaves in a way that a friend behaves, is it not doing so because it has been programmed or designed to perform such behaviors? As Lily Frank and I note in earlier work, creating a robotic companion appears similar to hiring an actor to "go through the motions" and pretend to be our friend.[23] There is a difference between a real friend and somebody who merely acts as if they were our friend. When it comes to friendship and whether somebody is a real friend, it appears to matter a great deal to us what goes on "on the inside." Third, robots are surely not our equals. As Robert Sparrow argues, very few—if any—morally motivated people would treat robots as our moral equals.[24] Nor, fourthly, do many robots appear able to interact with us in diverse ways across many different kinds of contexts. Most robots are very good at specific tasks, in particular controlled environments.[25] Unlike human beings, they are typically not flexible in a domain-general way. So, like Danaher himself notes, "the case for the prosecution" (i.e., the case against the possibility of robot friendships) appears to be "pretty powerful."[26]

5.4: DANAHER'S DEFENSE OF HUMAN-ROBOT FRIENDSHIPS

The first move Danaher makes in attempting to defend the possibility of virtue friendships with robots is to draw a distinction between what he calls "technical" and "metaphysical" possibilities.[27] When somebody argues that it is not possible for a robot to live up to the conditions we associate with friendship, is that merely a matter of the technological development not yet being sufficiently far along ("technical impossibility")? Or is it rather that there is something in principle impossible about the idea of a robot living up to these criteria ("metaphysical impossibility")? If the former, the impossibility of a robot friend is relative to the current state of technological development, and the future might bring with it technological developments that would pave the way for robotic friendships. In contrast, if there were something in principle impossible—or "metaphysically" impossible—about robots' prospects for living up to these criteria, then robots could never become able to be our friends.

Before we get to Danaher's take on what kinds of possibility (or impossibility) we are dealing with, I would like to suggest that there might be another type of possibility we should also keep in mind while discussing this. What I have in mind is what we might call "ethical possibilities." Something is ethically possible if it is not only technologically and metaphysically possible, but also ethically permissible or, better yet, ethically good or right. In contrast, something would not be ethically possible if there were something inherently ethically problematic about it. (We sometimes speak about certain things as "unthinkable," which I think often expresses the same idea as what I am here calling an ethical impossibility.) I can imagine, for example, that Joanna Bryson (whose views I mentioned in a previous chapter) would say that robotic virtue friendship is an ethical impossibility. Bryson argues that robots will always be owned (bought and sold) by human beings, and that for that reason, we should avoid creating robots with advanced enough abilities that they would warrant moral consideration.[28] The reason why we should avoid this is that if we create robots with morally relevant properties, we would in effect create slaves—that is, moral subjects that we buy and sell. This would make it ethically impossible to have a robot that would truly be our friend, Bryson might argue, even if it is technically or metaphysically possible to create a robot with the relevant capacities and features. Masters and slaves cannot be true friends.

Let us return to Danaher's argument, however. He tackles the friendship criteria of mutuality, authenticity, equality, and diversity of interactions by first asking what kind of impossibility there might be thought to be for robots to achieve these aspects of the ideal of virtue friendship. [29] In the cases of equality and diversity of interactions, Danaher suggests that the relevant kind of possibility is of a "technical" kind. In the cases of mutuality and authenticity, in contrast, there seems to be more than a technical impossibility at stake, Danaher suggests: namely, a mix of technical and metaphysical impossibility. The reason for this is that those two aspects of friendship—as noted above—appear to refer to the "inner life" of a potential friend: facts about their mental life, consciousness, or self-consciousness. Let us start, however, with what Danaher says about equality and diversity of interactions.

When it comes to the sort of equality there should be between friends, Danaher makes the following remark: "Presumably, equality is a function of one's powers and capacities and whether a robot is equal to a human with respect to its powers and capacities is going to be dependent on its physical and computational resources, both of which are subject to technical innovation." [30] In other words, Danaher understands equality as being dependent on what powers and capacities someone possesses. And he thinks that the powers and capacities of a robot can be developed to become similar to those of a human being. So the lack of equality between humans and robots is an artifact of current technological development, and something that can be done away with in the future.

In addition to that general point, Danaher also makes another point with respect to equality—a point he also makes in relation to diversity of interactions. [31] With respect to both of these issues (i.e., equality and diversity of interactions), Danaher suggests that we accept a weakened or less strict understanding of these requirements than we might first have in mind. [32] How equal, Danaher first asks, are most friends in the real world? Do we not typically differ from our friends in terms of our powers and capacities? We are roughly, or perhaps only very roughly, equal to our friends with respect to many of our powers and capacities. And yet we think of ourselves as having friends. So, in the case of robots, which might differ from us in their powers and capacities as well, we should not be too strict in how much equality we require from them in terms of their powers and capacities.

Similarly, Danaher also suggests that we weaken our requirements with respect to how diverse the interactions with friends need to be. After all, when it comes to some of our friends, we only see them in some contexts. And we only do a limited set of things together with them. Why require more from our robotic friends? I will offer critical responses to these points below. But let me first get to perhaps the most striking and intriguing part of Danaher's defense of robotic relationships: namely, his "ethical behaviorism."

When it comes to whether there are things like shared values, interests, and affection between friends ("mutuality") or whether our friends are honest and authentic in their dealings with us ("authenticity"), the first thing Danaher does is to suggest that we should take this to be a matter of *consistent performances* on the part of our friends.[33] We have no access, Danaher argues, to the inner lives of our friends. All we ever have to go on are their externally observable behaviors and performances. If humans behave in the ways that friends are supposed to behave, and they do so consistently, this is all we can ever go on in making up our minds about whether our human friends are true friends of ours or not. Or so Danaher argues. For this reason, it would be unfair or unjustified to apply higher standards to robots. If they are able to behave—and behave consistently—as if there is mutuality and authenticity in their relationships with us, then we should view that as sufficient reason to consider it possible for these robots to potentially be our friends.

What Danaher in effect does when he considers the metaphysical question of whether a robot can have an inner life similar to that of a friend is to turn this metaphysical question into an epistemological question about what we can know about our friends. In particular, Danaher turns it into a question about what evidence we have for thinking that apparent friends—whether human or robotic—have the inner lives associated with friends.

The question, thus considered, is not whether robots actually have the attitudes or mental lives that we think of our friends as having. The question is rather whether they behave in ways that are sufficiently similar to how friends with the right attitudes and inner lives are supposed to behave. If robots are able to perform the role of a friend with sufficient consistency, Danaher thinks that we should regard that as settling the question in favor of its being possible for them to be our friends. Similarly, when David Levy discusses love between humans and robots, he writes that if robots tell us they love us and behave as if they love us, we should take this at face value and accept that the robots love us.[34] After all, if humans tell us they love us and behave as if they do, we are often willing to accept that they love us. Danaher and Levy want to know why we should have any higher standards for robots. Danaher adds that in the human case, no higher standard is possible, for which reason he thinks we should apply no higher standard in the robotic case.[35]

5.5: CRITICAL ASSESSMENT OF DANAHER'S PHILOSOPHICAL CASE FOR ROBOT FRIENDSHIP

I am impressed by Danaher's philosophical case for robot friendship, but I am not convinced. Consider first Danaher's treatment of the issue of equality. And recall that his first move is to argue that equality is a function of one's powers and capacities. The second move is to argue that robots can come to have similar powers and capacities as humans. And the third move is to question how equal friends have to be in their powers and capacities in the first place: We can be friends with people whose powers and capacities are rather different from ours. Regarding this argument, it seems to me the kind of equality we demand between friends is not primarily equality in powers and capacities, but rather equality in status or standing.

Consider Mary Wollstonecraft's classic discussion of marriage in her *Vindication of the Rights of Woman*.[36] Wollestonecraft wrote her discussion of love and marriage during the late eighteenth century, when men and women differed greatly in their rights—to the extent that a wife could have no property of her own and where husbands had many more rights than their wives. Wollestonecraft famously argued that this made it impossible for men and women to enjoy true love and friendship within the confines of their marriages. The reason was that their rights and status were not sufficiently equal. Friendship and love can only be achieved between equals in rights and status, Wollestonecraft argued. She concluded that unless marriage laws were changed to make men and women more equal, husbands and wives could not achieve true friendship and love in their marriages. Indeed, this appears to be a reason why many classical discussions of friendship—for example, the discussion of friendship in Michel de Montaigne's *Essays*[37]—focused on friendship between members of the same sex, outside of marriage, which was an institution considered too asymmetrical or unequal for friendship to be possible between the spouses.[38]

The point here, as I see things, is that if humans and robots are able to be friends, it is not equality in powers and capacities that is the type of equality they need to achieve. Rather, the equality in question would be equality in rights and moral status. And this is an area where inequality between humans and robots certainly obtains in current society, and where inequality might always remain between humans and robots.[39] Again, as I mentioned above, Joanna Bryson argues that this cannot be the case since robots are manufactured artifacts that we buy and sell, and who could therefore never be anything but slaves even if we created robots with powers and capacities equaling those of humans.[40] As noted above, this could be seen as creating a form of "ethical impossibility" for friendship between humans and robots.

When it comes to the issue of diversity of interactions, Danaher also, as we saw, weakens the requirement of diversity of interactions between friends. As I noted, he asks how often and in how many contexts we actually do interact with our friends—even people we might consider to be rather good friends. In response to this argument, I want to bring up an observation of Philip Pettit's regarding what he calls the "robust demands" of friendship.[41] The idea is not that friends necessarily do interact with each other across some broad range of contexts and situations. Perhaps they do not have any occasion to do so. The idea is rather that friendship is an ideal that requires if certain kinds of situations were to arise—for example, if an emergency comes about and we need help—then our friends should be willing to offer us their help and concern.

If somebody only behaves like a friend in the actual circumstances in which we interact with them, but would not do so in other situations (such as more challenging situations), then the person in question would reveal him- or herself to be a so-called fair weather friend. The real challenge for a robot friend, then, is not to be able to behave in certain friend-like ways in the actual situations in which we interact with the robot. The real challenge is rather for the robot to have the dispositions of a friend. It should have dispositions whereby the robot would be prepared to behave like a friend across all sorts of contexts and situations where there is a normative expectation that a friend should be there to help us, give us their care, or whatever it might be that we expect of our friends in different sorts of scenarios we can imagine but that might not actually arise.

Let us next consider Danaher's ethical behaviorism as it applies to friendship. I am certainly willing to grant the premise that when it comes to deciding whether somebody is a real friend, all we ultimately have to "go on" by way of direct and indisputable evidence is their externally observable behaviors, including their verbal behaviors (i.e., what they say). But I do not think that we should equate the epistemic reasons or evidence we have to believe that somebody is a friend, on the one hand, with what we value in those whom we perceive as our friends, on the other hand. In other words, what we value in our friends should be distinguished from what we can know with certainty about our friends.

For example, I might believe that somebody—say, John Danaher—is a friend of mine because he behaves in certain ways. But what I come to believe on the basis of my friend's behavior is in part likely to be that he possesses certain attitudes and that he has certain mental properties that are revealed by his behavior.[42] And those attitudes and mental features are a large part of what I value when I value somebody as a friend. Of course, somebody might lack the attitudes and mental features I believe that they have. So I might value them as a friend while mistakenly thinking that there is something there—that is, certain underlying attitudes and mental features—for me to value in addition to the behavior I am observing. But in normal circumstances, we trust that the people around us do have the attitudes we think they have—or at least many of the attitudes we think they have. And when we value them as friends, we do so to a great extent because we view those attitudes and mental features as being among the reasons why they are our friends.

Consider the case of the Japanese robotics researcher Hiroshi Ishiguro and the robotic replica that he has created of himself.[43] The robotic replica is very impressive-looking. It is impressive to a degree that if viewed from afar, it is not very easy to tell Ishiguro and the robot apart. Suppose next that the artificial intelligence in the robot is developed to a degree that also makes it very hard to distinguish the behavior of Ishiguro from the behavior of his robotic replica. Let us suppose that Ishiguro behaves in a way that makes me think of him as a friend and that the robotic replica does the same. I might then in both cases come to think—rightly in one case and wrongly in the other—that each of the two has the sorts of attitudes and mental properties I think a friend should have. As a result, I might come to think of both of them as my friends. But we can also imagine that Ishiguro himself does have these attitudes that I value in regarding him as my friend, whereas the robotic replica merely behaves as if it has those attitudes. In both cases, I might have the same evidential reasons for believing that I can regard the two of them as my friends. But in one case, all of what I value is not there (because the robot lacks the attitudes and mental features I value). In the other case, all of what I value is there (because Ishiguro does have the attitudes and mental features I value).

It would seem that if we accept Danaher's view, it does not matter if Ishiguro and his replica differ in what mental properties they have (or lack!). So long as both behave in the same way, each of them is an equally valuable friend for me. After all, they might behave in a similar enough way that I am not able to tell who is a robot and who is a human being. But if what I value in valuing a friend is in part the underlying attitudes and mental features they have—and if only one of the two truly has those attitudes and mental features—then it seems to me that only one of the two is a true friend, even though both of them provide me with the same behavioral evidence of being my friend.

5.6: GOOD PEOPLE AND GOOD FRIENDS

Return now briefly to Boomer. This was the military robot who was popular enough among the soldiers in the team that the team wanted to give Boomer a military funeral and medals of honor. These responses are responses that we typically have to a fallen friend or highly valued colleague. And they are responses that bring up an aspect of so-called virtue friendships that Danaher himself does not discuss in his article, but which I think is another fascinating thing to discuss in this context. What I am referring to is something that Cicero discusses at some length in his *Treatise on Friendship*, which builds to a large extent on the discussion of friendship from Aristotle.[44] What I am referring to has to do with the "virtue" part of a virtue friend.

According to Cicero, a person's motivation to become somebody's friend is typically a response to the perceived virtue or goodness in that other person. In other words, if somebody appears to have certain virtues (= good personal qualities), this is likely to lead us to want to become that person's friend. Friendship, thus thought of, is a response to perceived or apparent goodness in another person. This means, Cicero argues, that in order to be a true friend, somebody needs to be truly good. The person needs to actually possess the virtues or good qualities they appear to possess. If somebody is not good—or not able to be good—they cannot be a true friend in the sense of "friendship" that Aristotle calls virtue friendship.

When Cicero discusses this claim, he writes that we should not raise the bar too high when it comes to who is considered a good person and who is not considered a good person.[45] Rather, we should admit as good the kinds of people regarded by common sense as being good. We should not have unrealistic expectations of what is required for a person in order for them to qualify as being a good person. A good person does not need to be perfect. They need to have the sorts of personal characteristics that typically lead us to regard somebody as a good person. This means that while some people might falsely appear to be better people than they are—and would not be able to be friends of the sort we might think they could be—many people are indeed good and could, therefore, be potential friends for us. Our friendship with these people, Cicero thinks, would be initiated by their perceived goodness. And so long as they keep their good qualities, it is possible to remain good friends with them. If, however, they would come to lose some of these good personal characteristics, that might mean that it becomes difficult or perhaps even impossible to remain true friends with the people in question.

I bring up this discussion of friendship and personal virtue from Cicero's *Treatise* on friendship because I think that it can serve as another interesting challenge to the prospect for human-robot friendships. Let us go along with Cicero and think of friendship (at least in the sense of virtue friendship) as being a response to perceived goodness or perceived virtue in another. And let us go along with the suggestion that if a person turns out not to be a good person, then they cannot be a good friend (at least not in sense of a virtue friend). Well, what this means is that in order for it to be possible for a robot to potentially be a virtue friend, it must be possible for the robot to be good. It must be possible for the robot to possess virtues or other personal characteristics that would justify us in thinking that the robot is good.

It might here be argued that a robot cannot be good in the way that a human being can be good. Again, this might be because robots lack the inner lives of human beings, and because having certain mental features is part of what is involved in being a good person. For example, a good person is somebody who performs good deeds on the basis of good motives, and with good intentions. A robot, it might be thought, could perform what appear to be good deeds. For example, Boomer the military robot might perform some behavior (e.g., defuse a bomb) that might save somebody's life. But the robot might not act on the basis of what we would recognize as good motives or good intentions. And so in saving somebody's life, Boomer might not show himself to be a good person or a virtuous person in the way that a good human being who performs that same action might prove him or herself to be a good person. Accordingly, the robot might not be fit to be a virtue friend even though it might behave in instrumentally good ways. The reason is that the robot might lack the sorts of underlying attitudes, mental features, or inner life that help to make somebody a good person—a person fit to be somebody's friend. Again, the robot might bring us pleasure. And the robot might be useful. But if the robot cannot be good, the robot cannot be a virtue friend. (More on this in chapter 7 below.)

Consider also here a remark that the enlightenment philosopher Immanuel Kant makes about friendship in his *Metaphysics of Morals*.[46] Kant writes that in the highest kind of "moral friendship," friends relate to each other on the basis of both love and respect.[47] What Kant calls "love" is something like a concern for the happiness of another person and a desire to promote their happiness. What Kant calls "respect" is an attitude of regarding another person as a moral agent with practical reason and a will of their own. Our love for our friends, Kant writes, draws us closer to them. But our respect, he interestingly adds, makes us keep some distance between them.[48] What Kant means by this, if I understand him correctly, is that if we respect a friend, we need to respect his or her wishes and give him or her space to be his or her own person. But Kant also means that we regard the other as a moral equal, with an equal claim to being an authority on what is right or wrong, or on what rules we all ought to follow as members of a shared moral community (a "realm of ends," as Kant calls it[49]).

This also suggests another argument regarding whether it is possible to be friends with robots: namely, an argument that starts with a premise that requires that in order for somebody to possibly be our friend, it must be possible to relate to them on the basis of mutual love and respect. It must be possible, in other words, both to mutually wish each other happiness and also to mutually respect each other as persons and equal members of the moral community. Again the question arises of whether robots could ever enter into these kinds of relationships of mutual love and respect. The robots should not only be able to show us love and respect. The robots would also need to have properties that made it sensible for us to have love and respect for them. Could a robot be a moral equal, whose will and wishes we can and should respect, and somebody who is an equal authority on what is right or wrong? I will discuss that question in chapter 8.

5.7: CONCLUSION AND DISCUSSION

It is worth keeping in mind Aristotle's observation that the word "friendship" can refer to many different things. For example, being "friends" on a social media website like Facebook might not mean anything more than that one party at some point sent a so-called friend request to the other and that the receiver accepted that request. The two "friends" might not really know each other. They may never have met in real life. So when it comes to the question of whether it is possible to have relationships with robots that qualify as friendships of some sort, it is surely possible that there might be some sense of the term "friendship" in which it is perfectly possible and also perhaps desirable to be friends with robots. Accordingly, it might indeed be possible to be friends with robots like Roxxxy, Samantha, and Harmony—that is, the robots mentioned in the introduction to this chapter. But that might be true in some fairly watered-down and less interesting sense of friendship.

Danaher's more daring thesis—that it is possible to be "virtue friends" with robots—is a much more interesting proposition. In challenging that proposition, I have raised various different objections to Danaher's claims. Some of those objections and the ideas related to them I will not discuss further. However, some of the ideas that I have brought up above I will discuss further in the next few chapters. In the chapter right after this one, I will discuss mind-reading in relation to robots. I will also discuss whether robots can be good in some sense (whether they can have virtues and whether they can have and act on obligations), as well as whether it might make sense at any point to include robots into the moral community. These topics will be covered in chapters 6 through 8.

But to first round off this chapter, I want to very briefly comment on whether there might be something unethical about creating robots—such as Roxxxy, Samantha, and Harmony—that appear to "love" their owners, but that might not really be able to participate in true friendships in any more interesting sense. It seems to me—and I discuss this at greater length elsewhere, together with Lily Frank[50]—that there are at least three ethical concerns that need to be taken seriously.

The first is something I already touched upon above. Namely, that if robots are designed to appear to be able to be our friends without really having the capacities friends need to be able to have, this might be deceptive. It is morally problematic to create a product that will very likely deceive users about what capacities the robot actually has.[51] Second, there appears to be a morally salient risk that vulnerable people (e.g., lonely people) will be taken advantage of by companies developing products designed to appear to like or love their owners. There appears to be a real risk of exploitation of vulnerable people. And third, as Sherry Turkle notes in her discussion of what she calls the "robotic moment,"[52] a further worry worth taking seriously is that if people spend too much time around robots that are supposed to be their friends, perhaps this will make some people less able to participate successfully in relationships of love or friendship with other human beings.

Human beings are complex and complicated. Being a good friend or companion requires having the ability and patience to deal with the different facets of human complexity. Some of the above-mentioned Japanese men who prefer having "virtual girlfriends" to having human girlfriends have apparently said in interviews that they prefer these virtual girlfriends in part precisely because they are less complicated than human beings.[53] That does raise the concern that if substituting robotic friends for real friends becomes a widespread practice, this might have a negative effect on some people's social skills. Some people might rob themselves of opportunities for learning to become good human friends and, hence, for forming deeper and more meaningful friendships with other human beings.

NOTES

1. Truecompanion.com, accessed August 25, 2019.

2. Uncredited (2010), "Roxxxy TrueCompanion: World's First Sex Robot?," *Asylum Channel*, https://www.youtube.com/watch?v=2MeQcI77dTQ (Accessed on March August 25, 2019).

3. Uncredited (2017), "Holly and Phillip Meet Samantha the Sex Robot," *This Morning*, https://www.youtube.com/watch?v=AqokkXoa7uE (Accessed on August 25, 2019).

4. Uncredited (2017), "Harmony, The First AI Sex Robot," *San Diego Union-Tribune*, https://www.youtube.com/watch?v=0CNLEfmx6Rk (Accessed on August 25, 2019).

5. Maartje De Graaf (2016), "An Ethical Evaluation of Human-Robot Relationships," *International Journal of Social Robotics* 8(4), 589–98.

6. Cf. Alexis Elder (2017), *Friendship, Robots, and Social Media: False Friends and Second Selves*, London: Routledge.

7. Nyholm and Frank, "From Sex Robots to Love Robots: Is Mutual Love with a Robot Possible," op. cit. In our article, we examined three ideas commonly associated with romantic relationships, and we asked whether a robot could participate in a relationship involving those three aspects. The aspects were: (1) being a "good match," (2) valuing one another as unique individuals, and (3) a mutual commitment. We argued that each of these presuppose capacities—for example, capacities for choice and emotions—that robots do not (yet) possess. For a discussion with David Edmonds in which I summarize and explain our overall argument, see David Edmonds and Sven Nyholm (2018), "Robot Love," *Philosophy* 247, https://philosophy247.org/podcasts/robot-love/ (Accessed on August 25, 2019).

8. John Danaher (2019), "The Philosophical Case for Robot Friendship," *Journal of Posthuman Studies* 3(1), 5–24.

9. David Levy (2008), *Love and Sex with Robots: The Evolution of Human-Robot Relationships*, New York: Harper Perennial.

10. Julie Beck (2013), "Married to a Doll: Why One Man Advocates Synthetic Love," *The Atlantic*, https://www.theatlantic.com/health/archive/2013/09/married-to-a-doll-why-one-man-advocates-synthetic-love/279361/ (Accessed on August 25, 2019).

11. Anita Rani (2013), "The Japanese Men Who Prefer Virtual Girlfriends to Sex," *BBC News Magazine*, http://www.bbc.com/news/magazine-24614830 (Accessed on August 25, 2019).

12. AFP-JIJI (2018), "Love in Another Dimension: Japanese Man 'Marries' Hatsune Miku Hologram," *Japan Times*, https://www.japantimes.co.jp/news/2018/11/12/national/japanese-man-marries-virtual-reality-singer-hatsune-miku-hologram/#.XW-bHDFaG3B (Accessed on September 4, 2019).

13. Carpenter, *Culture and Human-Robot Interactions in Militarized Spaces*, op. cit.

14. Garber, "Funerals for Fallen Robots," op. cit.

15. Danaher, "The Philosophical Case for Robot Friendship," 5.

16. See, for instance, Elder, *Friendship, Robots, and Social Media: False Friends and Second Selves*, op. cit.

17. Aristotle (1999), *Nicomachean Ethics*, translated by Terence H. Irwin, Indianapolis, IN: Hackett.

18. Danaher also defends a weaker thesis in his article, according to which robots can also augment human-human friendships in different ways. I will here set that weaker thesis aside and instead focus on the stronger thesis according to which we can be friends—and indeed virtue friends—with robots.

19. Danaher, "The Philosophical Case for Robot Friendship."

20. Ibid., 9–10.

21. Ibid., 10.

22. Nyholm and Frank, "From Sex Robots to Love Robots," op. cit.

23. Ibid., 223.

24. Robert Sparrow (2004), "The Turing Triage Test," *Ethics and Information Technology* 6(4), 203–13.

25. Mindell, *Our Robots, Ourselves*, op. cit.; Royakkers and Van Est, *Just Ordinary Robots*, op. cit.

26. Danaher, "The Philosophical Case for Robot Friendship," 11.

27. Ibid., 11.

28. Bryson, "Robots Should Be Slaves."

29. Danaher, "The Philosophical Case for Robot Friendship," 11–12.

30. Ibid., 11.

31. Ibid.

32. For another skeptical position viz-a-viz the diversity of interactions aspect of friendship, see Elder, *Friendship, Robots, and Social Media: False Friends and Second Selves*, op. cit. See also Elder's discussion with John Danaher in his podcast interview with her: John Danaher and Alexis Elder (2018), "Episode #43—Elder on Friendship, Robots and Social Media," *Philosophical Disquisitions*, https://philosophicaldisquisitions.blogspot.com/2018/08/episode-43-elder-on-friendship-robots.html (Accessed on September 4, 2019).

33. Ibid., 12. Cf. De Graaf, "An Ethical Evaluation of Human-Robot Relationships," op. cit., 594.

34. Levy, *Love and Sex with Robots*, op. cit., 11.

35. Danaher cites Alan Turing's famous argument about machine intelligence as an inspiration behind his line of reasoning. For Turing's classic discussion, see Alan M. Turing (1950), "Computing Machinery and Intelligence,"
Mind 49, 433–60. We will return to Turing—and so-called Turing tests—in the
next chapter.

36. Mary Wollstonecraft (2009), *A Vindication of the Rights of Woman*,
New York: Norton & Company.

37. Michel de Montaigne (1958), *The Complete Essays of Montaigne*, Palo
Alto, CA: Stanford University Press.

38. Stephanie Coontz (2005), *Marriage, A History: From Obedience to Intimacy or How Love Conquered Marriage*, London: Penguin.

39. Cf. Gunkel, *Robot Rights*.

40. Bryson, "Robots Should Be Slaves," op. cit.

41. Philip Pettit (2015), *The Robust Demands of the Good: Ethics with
Attachment, Virtue, and Respect*, Oxford: Oxford University Press.

42. Cf. Pettit, *The Robust Demands of the Good*, op. cit., chapter 1.

43. As noted in an earlier footnote, pictures of and information about the
robotic copy of Ishiguro and other humanoid robots created in the "Hiroshi
Ishiguro Laboratories" can be found on their website, at http://
www.geminoid.jp/en/index.html (Accessed on August 20, 2019).

44. Cicero (1923), *Cicero: On Old Age, On Friendship, On Divination*,
translated by W. A. Falconer, Cambridge, MA: Harvard University Press.

45. Ibid.

46. Immanuel Kant (1996), *The Metaphysics of Morals (Cambridge Texts in
the History of Philosophy)*, edited by Mary Gregor, Cambridge: Cambridge
University Press.

47. Ibid., 216–17.

48. Ibid.

49. Immanuel Kant (2012), *Immanuel Kant: Groundwork of the Metaphysics of Morals, A German-English Edition*, edited by Mary Gregor and Jens
Timmermann, Cambridge: Cambridge University Press, 101.

50. Nyholm and Frank, "It Loves Me, It Loves Me Not," op. cit.

51. Margaret Boden, Joanna Bryson, Darwin Caldwell, Kestin Dautenhahn,
Lilian Edwards, Sarah Kember, Paul Newman, Vivienne Parry, Geoff Pegman,
Tom Rodden, Tom Soreell, Mick Wallis, Blay Whitby, and Alan Winfield
(2017), "Principles of Robotics: Regulating Robots in the Real World," *Connection Science* 29(2), 124–29.

52. Sherry Turkle (2011), *Alone Together: Why We Expect More from Technology and Less from Each Other*, New York: Basic Books.

53. Rani, "The Japanese Men Who Prefer Virtual Girlfriends to Sex," op. cit.

6

ROBOTIC MIND-READING

6.1: TURING TESTS

In the 2014 science fiction film *Ex Machina*, a talented programmer named Caleb wins a competition to go and spend a week in a secluded luxury house and research facility together with Nathan. Nathan is the CEO of the "blue book" company that Caleb works for. Upon arriving, Caleb quickly learns that he will be involved in an updated version of the "Turing test."[1] In an early dialogue, Nathan asks Caleb if he knows what a Turing test is. Yes, Caleb replies, "it is when a human interacts with a computer, and if the human doesn't know they're interacting with a computer, the test is passed." Nathan asks Caleb, "What does a pass tell us?" Caleb responds, "that the computer has artificial intelligence." In the updated version of this test in this film, however, the test appears to be whether a robot named Ava is able to convince Caleb that she has humanlike consciousness. Appearance-wise, Ava is a little bit like Sophia the robot, discussed in chapter 1. Ava has a robotic-looking body, but a very humanlike face. Through her discussions with Caleb, Ava is able to convince him, not only that she is conscious, but also that she is attracted to him and that she has feelings for him. And she manages to get Caleb to reciprocate by also developing feelings for her.

Later on in the film, Nathan attempts to bring Caleb back to his senses, with the following remarks: "What was the real test? You! Ava was a rat in a maze and I gave her only one way out. To escape she'd have to use self-awareness, imagination, manipulation, sexuality, empathy, and she did. Now if that isn't true AI, what the f°°k is?" Sure enough, by the end of the story, Ava manages to do exactly that: She uses all of those things Nathan describes to lure Caleb into helping her escape the research facility. Caleb and Nathan are left behind, trapped in the secluded house, with all doors locked, and no apparent way of getting out.

The film is a fascinating meditation on artificial intelligence, robots, and our human tendency to try to read the minds of anything and anybody who behaves in a humanlike or otherwise intelligent way. Of course, it is a science fiction film. And so one might wonder if it has anything to tell us about the ethics of real-world human-robot interaction. At the very least, what the film does is to highlight issues that might confront us in the future, and perhaps in the not-too-distant future: namely, issues of whether we ought on reflection to attribute minds to robots that behave as if they have minds. To be sure, human beings will intuitively or non-reflectively start attributing different kinds of mental states and properties to robots before most of us are also prepared to reflectively endorse this tendency of ours. And in some cases people will disagree about whether robots (or any other machines) have anything like minds.

For example, there was a recent story covered in many technology news outlets about a robotic arm created at Columbia University.[2] The robot arm's creators claimed that it had developed a basic form of "self-awareness" after thirty-five hours of learning/exploring. What exactly the researchers meant by this claim is debatable. But some critics were quick to make public statements trying to debunk this idea. Noel Sharkey, for example, appeared on Sky News to "pour cold water" on the claim that this robotic arm had developed anything like self-consciousness.[3] Perhaps Sharkey understood the researchers as having made a much stronger claim on behalf of their robotic arm than they actually had done. But it was certainly right that many media outlets were reporting on this robotic arm in a way that made it sound like a first step had been taken toward fully conscious—and self-conscious—robots.[4] And if I understand him correctly, Sharkey's main aim was to caution the general public against giving too much credence to that claim.

The aim of this chapter is to reflect on our human tendency to spontaneously attribute minds and mental states to anything humanlike or intelligent-seeming. The chapter has a specific focus on what this means for the ethics of human-robot interaction. I regard this as one of the topics that we cannot avoid dealing with when we reflect on how humans ought to behave around robots and how robots ought to be made to behave around humans.

What I will do in discussing this topic is to first draw a number of general distinctions regarding different kinds of mind-reading that I think are very useful to keep in mind when we reflect on our human tendency toward mind-reading. I will consider some recent philosophical and empirical discussion of mind-reading within human-robot interaction. And I will round off this chapter by briefly discussing whether robots have minds in any sense.

6.2: DIFFERENT KINDS OF MIND-READING

Mind-reading, mind-perception, mentalizing, theory of mind, the attribution of mental states—different academic fields and different researchers use different terms for what all amounts to the same thing or aspects of the same thing.[5] I shall mainly use the expression "mind-reading." But I will take it that this refers to the same thing that some researchers prefer to call "theory of mind," or whatever other expression they might use (such as "attributing mental states to others").

What I am calling mind-reading is studied in various different fields, including but not limited to philosophy and psychology. It is interesting to note that much of this research tends to focus on what I will call one particular level or kind of mind-reading: namely, the attribution of particular mental states, for example particular intentions or particular beliefs or desires. For instance, researchers studying whether monkeys engage in mind-reading tend to be interested in whether monkeys attribute particular intentions, beliefs, or desires to other monkeys.[6] This can be investigated, for example, by observing and analyzing scenarios in which it is possible for one monkey to mislead another monkey about where a desired piece of fruit is located.[7] If a monkey acts in a way that appears intended to mislead another monkey about the whereabouts of the fruit, this would suggest that the monkey has beliefs about what the other monkey thinks about the location of the fruit. There is a lot of fascinating research about whether, and the extent to which, nonhuman animals engage in mind-reading in the way that we humans do. [8]

When it comes to human mind-reading, I suggest that one of the first things we should keep in mind when we reflect on this tendency of ours (and how it relates to our interaction with robots) is that mind-reading can take more or less general aspects of other minds as its objects. Here are some, but perhaps not all kinds of mind-reading that there are:

- **Attributions of consciousness**: We attribute consciousness to one another, or sometimes a lack thereof, such as when somebody appears to have fainted.
- **Attributions of particular mental states**: We attribute many different kinds of mental states to others, such as particular beliefs, desires, hopes, wishes, intentions, emotions, and so on.
- **Attributions of general character traits**: We attribute character traits or personality traits to others, including both virtues and vices, such as kindness, generosity, laciness, selfishness, and so on.
- **Attributions of a self and sometimes a "true self"**: We attribute even more global and complex sets of personality characteristics that we think of as a person's "self," such as when we sometimes think that people act in ways that do not seem to fit with what we regard as their "true self."

I think these are all aspects of what is involved in reading the minds of others, if we understand "reading the minds of others" to refer to forming beliefs about other people's minds and attributing different types of mental states or properties to them. [9] Yet many research publications on mind-reading only focus on one of these levels, typically the second one mentioned above. For example, when researchers discuss mind-reading, they do not usually discuss the basic type of mind-reading that I listed first above: the attribution of consciousness to others. But this is surely an important type of mind-reading. Determining whether somebody is (still) conscious can sometimes be very important. If somebody has had an accident or medical emergency, it can even be a life-or-death matter.

How we interact with people around us depends a lot on whether we think they are conscious or unconscious. There are even cases where

people disagree about this. For example, there can be professional disagreement about whether some particular patient in a hospital is conscious of his or her surroundings or whether the patient is suffering
some more extreme form of "disorder of consciousness."[10] Medical researchers studying disorders of consciousness are doing a lot of fascinating and ethically highly significant research about the degree and types
(or lack) of consciousness in so-called minimally conscious patients.[11]
For example, the medical doctor and bioethicist Joseph Fins argues in
his book *Right Come to Mind* that many patients who are in a minimally
conscious state have much more awareness of their surroundings than
much of the medical establishment thinks.[12] Fins argues that for this
reason, there are serious moral risks that many minimally conscious
patients are not given the proper moral consideration they deserve.

This brings me to another distinction I want to bring up here. I think
it is important to draw a distinction between intuitive mind-reading, on
one hand, and reflective or effortful mind-reading, on the other hand.
Our social brains constantly spontaneously engage in intuitive mind-
reading viz-a-viz any people we interact with. But some people are
"hard to read." And so we sometimes need to reflect in a more effortful
and concentrated way on what they might be thinking.[13] Like I just said
above, there are also researchers who are exploring different ways of
trying to read the minds of people who cannot themselves report on
what, if anything, is on their minds: again, examples include patients
who are suffering disorders of consciousness and whose level of consciousness is unclear. Such research involves effortful and reflective
mind-reading, rather than intuitive and spontaneous mind-reading.

The fact that there are these two kinds of mind-reading means that it
can happen that there are clashes or disagreements between the two
kinds of mind-reading. For example, it could happen that while we
spontaneously or intuitively attribute certain kinds of mental states or
mental features to somebody, we might at the same time reason our
way to the conclusion that our intuitive mind-reading is somehow mistaken. Perhaps I really want to believe that a relative in the hospital is
conscious of my visit. And perhaps I spontaneously interpret the facial
expression of my relative as suggesting that he or she is in a certain
mental state. But at the same time, I might reason my way to the
conclusion that I may be wrong about this and that my relative might
not actually be conscious of my visit. Or perhaps things are the other

way around. My intuitive or spontaneous mind-reading might suggest to me that somebody is not in a certain state of mind (perhaps because they are a good actor). But I might nevertheless reason my way to the conclusion that the person is in the mental state in question. The person might say "I am not angry" and might look as if that is right. But I might nevertheless, rightly or wrongly, reason my way to thinking that the person must be angry with me.

One last distinction regarding mind-reading that I will mention before moving on to robots and mind-reading is the following. Theorizing about mind-reading sometimes distinguishes between whether other minds are assessed in terms of their *agency*, on the one hand, or whether they are assessed in terms of their *patiency*, on the other.[14] The former refers to mind-reading that attributes active or agential mental processes to others, such as decision-making or reasoning. The latter refers to mind-reading that attributes passive or experiential mental states to others, including but not limited to pleasure and pain. Very broadly this corresponds to the difference between wondering what somebody is thinking, on the one hand, and wondering what somebody is feeling, on the other hand. Of course, thinking and feeling typically go hand in hand. What we are thinking depends on what we are feeling, and vice versa. But in philosophical and other forms of research about mind-reading we might wish to reflect on whether there are any important or interesting differences between agency-related mind-reading and patiency-related mind-reading.

6.3: AN "ATTITUDE TOWARDS A SOUL"?

In the previous section, I discussed humans reading the minds of other humans, humans reading the minds of nonhuman animals (e.g., monkeys), and nonhuman animals reading the minds of other animals (e.g., a monkey reading the mind of another monkey). Let us now bring our discussion back to the interaction between humans and robots. The first thing to note is that there are some who are skeptical about whether humans do, or should, be engaging in mind-reading when they interact with robots.

Robert Sparrow, for example, discusses mind-reading in an article about what he calls the "Turing Triage Test."[15] In that article, Sparrow follows the lead of Peter Winch (who in turn was inspired by Ludwig Wittgenstein's reflections on mind-reading). Sparrow follows Winch in characterizing mind-reading as what Winch calls "an attitude towards a soul."[16] If I understand it correctly, the idea is in part that in engaging in mind-reading, we are looking beneath the surface of a person in search of something "deeper" within them, with which we can empathize. Perhaps this would be what people sometimes call their "self" or "true self." Moreover, the idea behind mind-reading as an "attitude towards a soul" is also that we are usually taking a type of practical stance toward the people whose minds we are reading (an essentially social stance); we are not merely forming a theoretical belief or coming up with a hypothesis about them.

Sparrow is very skeptical about whether we can truly adopt such an "attitude towards a soul" when we interact with a robot. If I understand him correctly, what Sparrow means here is that we will often be too aware of something as being a machine to take seriously the idea that there might be a mind in there somewhere for us to read and communicate with. We do not have the right practical or social attitude toward a robot. We do not have the right moral empathy toward the robot, or so Sparrow takes it.

In contrast, what Sparrow calls the "Turing Triage Test" would be passed if and when we manage to create a machine that a human being would be willing to treat as morally speaking equally important to, or perhaps even more important than, a human being. In other words, if you could come up with some scenario in which it would not be obvious to somebody who is morally motivated that they should save a human being at the cost of a, say, humanlike robot, then Sparrow's Turing Triage Test would be passed. What this test would show is that the robot has advanced to a stage where it has become a moral person, whose moral status cannot be easily distinguished from that of a human being. In his article, Sparrow indicates that he thinks that we are very far away from that point.[17]

Now, it is worth noting that Sparrow's article is from the early two thousands, when most robots were slightly less advanced than now and when there might have been fewer readily available examples of people appearing to empathize with robots.[18] It is also worth noting that Sparrow does concede that if we create robots with humanlike bodies and humanlike facial expressions, then people might be willing to engage in the sort of mind-reading that he calls an "attitude towards the soul" when they interact with such robots. For example, if something like the robot Ava from *Ex Machina* were truly created, Sparrow would presumably be willing to admit that a human being might indeed engage in mind-reading involving an "attitude towards a soul" when interacting with that robot. Nevertheless, I want to respond to Sparrow's discussion by noting that it seems to take an overly demanding view of what is required in order for our tendencies toward mind-reading to be triggered. And Sparrow's discussion also seems to overdramatize to some extent what is involved in mind-reading.

To be sure, some forms of mind-reading might be involved and all-encompassing enough that it makes sense to label them an "attitude towards a soul." But other types of mind-reading (e.g., attributing a particular attitude, such as a particular desire, to somebody) appears to be non-extraordinary enough that it appears exaggerated to think of it in terms of the expression "an attitude towards a soul." If I spontaneously interpret somebody who is seemingly happily and voluntarily eating a meal as being hungry and as wanting to eat that meal, it might seem somewhat pompous to label this "an attitude towards a soul."

Sparrow's doubts about people's willingness to engage in mind-reading in their interaction with robots also seems to potentially overlook the "dual processing" often involved in mind-reading: that is, the distinction between spontaneous or intuitive mind-reading, on one hand, and reflective mind-reading, on the other. To be sure, we might often find ourselves intuitively perceiving a robot as wanting to do something or as believing something while at the same time upon reflection thinking that this is at best a metaphorical way of describing the robot's behavior. A lot of people, for example, speak about self-driving cars using language that suggests that they are trying to read the minds of self-driving cars. They talk about what self-driving cars are deciding or intending to do, for example turning left or turning right. But they might not upon reflection be willing to endorse the proposition that self-driving cars have minds with which they can form intentions or make decisions.[19] Some apparent mind-reading of machines, then, might be merely metaphorical. But other instances might be much more spontaneous and not—at least not on the intuitive level—metaphorical.

6.4: NON-SKEPTICAL RESEARCH ABOUT ROBOTIC MIND-READING

There is a lot of anecdotal evidence of human-robot mind-reading in the literature. But is there some more robust reason to think that we do—and will increasingly be inclined to—engage in mind-reading when we interact with robots? Before very briefly describing some research that suggests that the answer to this is "yes," let me just quickly remind the reader of the idea I put forward in chapter 1 inspired by Persson and Savulescu's basic argument in their book *Unfit for the Future*.[20] Back in chapter 1 I discussed the observation that our social minds evolved (both biologically and culturally) before any robots and AI entered the scene. I suggested that our minds are likely to have developed various features that might lead us to respond in ways that might be more or less appropriate when we now start interacting more and more with robots and AI. Our tendency toward mind-reading, I suggested, is a good example of just this sort of thing. So, as I see things, it is to be expected that human beings will be prone to interact with robots and AI in a way that involves a lot of mind-reading. Actually, when I presented some of this material at a recent interdisciplinary event with both philosophers and neurologists present, one of the neurologists—Hervé Chneiweiss—made the following remark: "I am not surprised that people try to read the minds of robots. I am surprised that you are surprised that they do. With brains like ours, it is to be expected that we try to read the minds of anything that looks even remotely similar to a human being."[21]

There seems, then, to be good reason to hypothesize that people will be prone to try to read the "minds" of robots. But is there research that more directly investigates this? There is. For example, the psychologists Maartje De Graaf and Bertram Malle were interested in how people spontaneously explain robot behavior, and they wanted to go beyond using anecdotal evidence and see if they could test this more directly.[22] What they did was to expose their research participants either to stories about human beings performing certain actions or robots performing the same actions. The question was whether the participants who were assigned these different vignettes would use explanations of the actions of both the humans and the robots that would attribute mental states to them, or whether this would only happen in the case of humans. What

De Graaf and Malle found was that in both cases, people were inclined to explain the actions of the humans and robots using language that attributes mental states such as beliefs and desires to the humans and the robots. This tendency was found to be stronger in the human case in this study. But the research participants were nevertheless also found to be strongly inclined to think about the actions of the robots in these terms (e.g., "the robot did X because it believed such-and-such, or the robot did Y because it wanted such-and-such").

To give just one more example of ongoing empirical research of this sort: The cognitive neuroscientist and social robotics specialist Agnieszka Wykowska is leading a research project studying what they call "social cognition in human-robot interaction."[23] And one of the things that Wykowska and her team are investigating is whether people are prone to adopt what Daniel Dennett calls "the intentional stance"[24] when explaining the behavior of robots. The intentional stance refers to explaining behavior in terms of mental states, and is distinguished from the mechanistic stance, which refers to explaining things in mechanistic terms. Wykowska and her research team investigated whether showing pictures depicting robots in certain situations to people would prompt participants to explain what they were seeing in the photos in a way that adopted the intentional stance.[25] Like De Graaf and Malle, Wykowska and her team also found that their research participants were to some extent prone to explain what they were seeing in intentional terms—that is, by attributing mental states to the robots in the pictures. Of course, sometimes the research participants explained what they were seeing in the photos in mechanistic terms, but sometimes they explained it in ways that adopted the intentional stance.

Neither of the above-mentioned empirical studies shows that the research participants believed that the robots they were asked about have anything like human minds. What the studies suggest—and what I think they are meant to suggest—is rather that human beings are naturally inclined to think in ways that explain perceived behavior in terms of the sorts of mental states that we usually attribute to fellow human beings when we engage in mind-reading. As I noted earlier, there is a distinction to be drawn between what we think about other people's minds upon reflection and how we intuitively interpret other people's (or other agents') behavior. It is quite likely that when we perceive robot behavior we will often find it natural to use language that attributes mental states to robots. But under what circumstances, if any, might people become willing to go further and also attribute minds to robots in some stronger sense?

6.5: MERELY THEORETICAL VERSUS PRACTICAL INTERESTS IN MACHINE MINDS

In a recent article he calls "How to Treat Machines That Might Have Minds," Nicholas Agar makes a worthwhile distinction between two different kinds of interests we can have in whether any robots or other machines have minds.[26] On the one hand, this could be a purely theoretical interest: We might be investigating the possibility of machine minds because we are interested in this from a purely scientific or theoretical point of view. However, we might also take a more practical interest in whether certain machines might have minds. We might do so because we are wondering how it is right or proper to interact with these machines. For example, might we be wronging a robot by failing to recognize its possession of a mind? Or—alternatively—might we be doing ourselves a disservice in treating some machine as if it has a mind when really it does not? This distinction between purely theoretical and more practical interests in whether machines have minds strikes me as an important one, and I will here follow Agar in taking the practical interest to be the most relevant one—at least for the purposes of this book.

What Agar thinks we should focus most attention on, moreover, is not a strict yes/no question about whether machines could or do have minds. Rather, he suggests that we should focus on what credence we should give to the proposition that certain machines might have minds. That is to say, what level or degree of confidence is it appropriate to have that some given machine has a mind?[27] And what—Agar wants us to also ask ourselves—do different degrees of confidence about that issue imply regarding what is right or proper for us to do in our interaction with the given machine?

When discussing this question of how much credence we should have in certain machines' having minds, Agar further suggests that we should take into account two different things. On the one hand, what do current philosophers and other relevant researchers think about whether machines can have minds? On the other hand, how are future generations likely to look back at us and our treatment of machines we interact with that might have minds? There is disagreement in the philosophical and academic community about whether machines can and do have minds. And future generations are likely to view us in a negative light if we are overconfident today in our views about whether or not machines can have minds. For those reasons, Agar suggests that we should take a precautionary approach, erring on the side of caution in all cases where there is doubt.

Concerning whether researchers think machines can have minds, one argument that immediately comes to mind—and which Agar also briefly discusses—is John Searle's "Chinese Room" argument.[28] That argument purports to show that computers that manipulate symbols and operate according to given instructions cannot think and cannot understand anything in the ways that humans do.[29] Other researchers take a much less pessimistic view about whether machines could have minds and even conscious minds. Joanna Bryson, for example, argues that depending on how we define consciousness, some machines might already qualify as being conscious.[30] For example, if we understand being conscious as (a) having internal states and (b) being able to report those internal states to others, then many types of machines might already be said to possess a basic form of consciousness. This all, of course, depends on how we define consciousness and what we understand a mind to be. It also depends how we think that one can test whether a machine is conscious. And there are many different tests. Aïda Elamrani-Raoult and Roman Yampolskiy identify as many as twenty-one different tests in an overview of tests for machine consciousness.[31] In response to such disagreements about whether robots and other technologies could ever have minds, Eric Schwitzgebel and Mara Garza write: "If society continues on the path towards developing more sophisticated artificial intelligence, developing a good theory of consciousness is a moral imperative."[32]

As I just noted above, when there are these kinds of just-described disagreements about what minds are and whether robots can have minds, Agar suggests that we err on the side of caution. In fact, he suggests that we should take so much precaution that we follow a principle according to which we treat humanlike behavior in a machine as evidence that the machine might have a mind.[33] Importantly, Agar does not counsel us to treat this as proof that the machine does have a mind. Rather, Agar imagines the "construction of a digital machine that behaves just as an intelligent human would." And his suggestion is as follows: "Making a machine capable of all human intelligent behavior counts as evidence for thinking machines that should increase everyone's confidence in the claim that computers can have minds."[34]

What does that mean in terms of how we should (or should not) treat any particular robots? Agar makes two interesting suggestions, one suggestion involving a moral imperative, another involving a prudential precaution. In a first thought experiment, Agar imagines that we encounter a robot—Alex—that we think might have a mind and that we think we might be causing suffering to. In such a case, Agar suggests that we err on the side of the robot's having a mind, and that we cease the behavior we think might be causing suffering to the robot.[35] In a second thought experiment, Agar imagines another robot—Sam—that somebody wants to have a romantic relationship with. Here, too, the robot behaves as if it might have a mind. Here, however, Agar suggests that the person contemplating a romantic relationship with Sam the robot should err on the side of the robot's perhaps not having a mind, even if it might appear to have one. The reason Agar gives is that it would be a great loss for a human person if he or she had what appeared to be a romantic relationship with a robot that seems to have a mind if that robot does not, in fact, have a mind. Such a scenario, Agar writes, would be "tragic." We have a duty to avoid potentially causing harm to a robot that might have a mind. But we also have self-interested reasons, Agar argues, to try to make sure that we do not make ourselves vulnerable to the prospect of becoming attached to a robot on the assumption that it has a mind when, in fact, the robot might not actually have a mind.[36]

6.6: OTHER MINDS, OTHER INTELLIGENCES

Agar's discussion has a lot in common with a similar recent discussion by John Harris.[37] Harris compares the problem of whether machines do, or might have, minds with the traditional philosophical "problem of other minds." The problem of other minds refers to the philosophical puzzle of how exactly we can know—and whether we can definitely know—that other people have minds like ours.[38] As we saw in the previous chapter, John Danaher thinks that we cannot really know this. All we ever can know for sure is how people behave. Danaher's ethical behaviorism, then, could be seen as an updated version of the problem of other minds. Harris, in contrast, thinks that the question of whether other human beings actually have minds is an "embarrassingly artificial philosophers' problem."[39]

Following a remark of Wittgenstein's, Harris suggests that we should ask ourselves whether it could make any sense to seriously doubt that other people have minds. He also thinks that Wittgenstein's "private language argument"[40] (according to which there could be no such thing as a private language) shows that other people definitely have minds, namely, other people with whom we share a language. Mind-reading, Harris takes it, is an obviously deep-rooted part of everyday life. It is such a common staple of human life that Homer even wrote about it three thousand years ago. Mind-reading is enabled in part, Harris thinks, by speech and writing. Because when we communicate with one another, we give each other a "piece of our mind."[41]

A more interesting problem of other minds that is not an embarrassingly artificial philosophers' problem, as Harris sees things, relates to artificial intelligences, and specifically what he labels artificial superintelligences. Would we be able to "understand artificially intelligent, especially so-called super intelligent, minds, and convince them of the existence and value of human minds?," Harris asks. We might call this a problem of bilateral mind-reading: humans trying to read the minds of "AI persons," on the one hand, and super-intelligent artificial intelligences trying to read the minds of humans, on the other hand. Would we be able to read their minds in a way that would allow us to do right by them? And would we be able to be transparent to them in a way that would inspire them to do right by us?

As it happens, Harris elsewhere seems to be less worried about whether artificial intelligences will be able to read our minds.[42] Elsewhere he argues that because our emails, text messages, and other digital writings are all stored in the cloud, computers and other machines have plenty of material to work with, with which they can read our minds. As noted above, Harris thinks that communication in language is a key part of what is involved in agents' reading each other's minds. And for most people, there is a lot of text that they have produced that artificial intelligences can use to read our minds and get to know the contents of our minds.

In any case, the main problem of other minds that Harris sees in the interaction between human minds and artificially intelligent minds concerns whether this bilateral mind-reading will enable us to receive good treatment from super-intelligent machines and also whether it will enable the super-intelligent robots to get the right treatment from us. In other words, in what appears to be a similar move to Agar's, Harris wades into the discussion about whether robots or other intelligent machines could ever come to deserve moral consideration or rights. Harris claims that this is something that is not getting enough attention. He writes:

> What has been almost entirely lost it seems to me, in the debate about possible dangers posed by AI, are real and planned, or at least envisioned, dangers we imagine we will be able to pose to them, the beings with Super AI, and which current debate supposes . . . that we will be justified in posing to them. [43]

A little later, Harris continues:

> If we create Superintelligent AI, we will neither be able to own them . . . nor enslave them, neither have sex with them without their consent, nor be able to destroy them without just and sufficient cause. We may hope they will think the same of us. [44]

Harris might be right that there would be some form or forms of super-intelligent AI agents that it will be wrong to treat in those ways. But are questions of bilateral mind-reading between humans and future super-intelligent AI persons also not an "embarrassingly artificial philosophers' problem"? And what should we make of Agar's suggestions, discussed in the previous section?

6.7: DISCUSSION: DO ROBOTS HAVE MINDS?

Agar discusses cases in which we would potentially fail to attribute minds to machines that actually have minds. It strikes me as more pressing—at least in the present—to focus on cases in which people attribute minds to robots that probably lack minds or that at least lack humanlike minds. As noted in the previous chapter, it is particularly troubling to consider cases where companies are building robots designed to make users attribute various mental properties to the robots that they do not actually have. The criticisms of Sophia the robot discussed in chapter 1 suggest that writers like Sharkey, Bryson, and others are worrying that some technology companies are doing just that. The same worries could also be raised about some of the sex robots discussed in the previous chapter.

But even if and when robots come to have minds—and perhaps rather advanced minds—it is doubtful that these minds will be very similar to human minds. As we saw above, Agar argues that if we manage to build a robot that behaves in various different ways that are similar to how an intelligent human behaves, then this should be regarded as evidence that the robot might have a mind. Agar might be right about this. But would it be evidence that the mind of the robot has much in common with a human mind? More on this below.

First a note about Harris's discussion: I can imagine that some meanspirited critics of Harris would respond to his discussion by saying that he has replaced one embarrassingly artificial philosophers' problem (i.e., the problem of other minds) with another embarrassingly artificial philosophers' problem (i.e., the problem of bilateral mind-reading between humans and super-intelligent AI persons). Coming to Harris's defense here, I would say that whether or not what he discusses is very realistic in the near-term future, the set of issues Harris discusses in relation to bilateral mind-reading is certainly fascinating to reflect on. To be sure, it is the stuff of engaging science fiction, like in the film *Ex Machina*, which was discussed above in the introduction. The film is partly about humans trying to read the minds of highly intelligent robots and robots trying to read the minds of human beings. And that is part of what is interesting about the film. However, after defending Harris's discussion by noting how fascinating the problems he brings up are, I would suggest that it seems more pressing to discuss bilateral mind-reading between human beings and robots (and other technologies) that already exist or that will exist in the near-term future. People are already disposed to engage in mind-reading when they interact with or otherwise respond to robots.

On the flipside, various kinds of technologies are already trying to read our minds. Indeed, not only robots, but other machines with AI may be just as likely as robots—or any super-intelligent AI persons—to attempt to read the minds of human beings. Your computer, smartphone, or the algorithms behind the social media websites you use might be as likely to try to read your mind as any robot.[45] This could be so, for example, because they are programmed to track your interests and possible purchases, as is the case with targeted advertising on social media websites such as Facebook.[46] I take it, however, that human beings are less likely to attribute mental states to the algorithms of Facebook than to any robot with which they might interact, whether that robot is Roomba the vacuum-cleaning robot or Sophia the humanoid robot.[47]

To now address the elephant in the room: What about currently existing robots and robots that will exist in the near-term future—do they have minds in any sense?[48] Do they have what Danaher calls an "inner life"? A functionally autonomous robot needs to be equipped with internal hardware and software that can take in information and perform calculations and computations that help to select the robot's responses to the situation it is in. The robot will form a model of its surroundings and operate on that basis, meaning that there is a form of "representation" of the world around it that helps to regulate the robot's behaviors. In short, the robot's outward behavior will depend on its internal states, processing, and what goes on "inside" the robot. So in a certain sense, the robot has a form of robotic mind, if by a mind we mean a set of internal processes that take in information and that help to generate actions and communications with other agents.

As noted in chapter 3, philosophical functionalists understand different mental states and mental events in terms of the functions played by these states and events.[49] And many of the functions human mental states play could be played by internal states of a machine. Yet presumably, the robot's inner life is nevertheless rather different from that of a human. For example, any robot's inner life might not (yet) include any subjective experience similar to that of a human or any nonhuman animal.[50] Its inner life might be better thought of as being similar to the inner workings of what happens in our minds below the level of consciousness.

Importantly, not all human mental states are conscious.[51] But all our mental states are part of our minds. So being consciously experienced is not a necessary criterion on being a mental state in somebody's mind. Accordingly, the fact that robots—at least currently existing robots— may lack subjective experience is not a principled reason against thinking that they could have minds of some sort.

At the very least in a metaphorical sense, then, we can attribute internal states and minds to robots without making a terrible mistake. We can safely do that so long as we do not think that these internal states are like a human being's inner life. But as robots with artificial intelligence get more and more advanced in their capabilities, will their "minds" or "inner lives" become more humanlike? I see no clear reason why we should suppose that. After all, the quality of a being's experience depends on the particular types of brain, sense organs, and nervous system it has. That is why, in Thomas Nagel's famous phrase, human beings do not know "what it is like to be a bat."[52] Our brains, sense organs, and nervous systems are very different than those of bats. And robots, in turn, have various different kinds of internal hardware, rather than humanlike brains or nervous systems. So even if Agar is right that the presence of very humanlike behavior in a robot would be evidence of there being some sort of mind there, it strikes me as wrong to think of such a mind as being similar to a human mind.[53]

Perhaps I am reading too much into Agar's claim that we should take humanlike behavior in a machine to indicate the presence of a mind. Perhaps Agar only means that humanlike behavior would indicate the presence of some sort of mind. Such minds may be very alien to what we are used to. But if so, it becomes unclear what duties—if any—we would have to these robots with their non-humanlike, robotic minds.

Returning also briefly to Harris's discussion once more, I will close this chapter with the following observation. It seems to me that rather than discussing the ethics of the interaction between humans and super-intelligent AI persons, it is more pressing to investigate the ethics of the interaction between humans and more realistic types of robots: that is, robots that lack the sort of super-intelligent AI that Harris imagines in his article. As we saw above, Harris briefly discusses two different questions: whether super-intelligent AI persons are likely to treat human beings in a morally acceptable way, on the one hand, and whether human beings are likely to treat super-intelligent AI persons in a morally acceptable way, on the other hand. In the two last chapters of this book, I will discuss two much more down-to-earth questions: (1) whether robots of less fantastic sorts than those Harris imagines can be good in ways that human beings can be good, and (2) whether human beings might have moral reasons to treat robots without super-sophisticated minds in ways that show moral consideration toward at least some robots. In discussing these questions, much of my discussion will continue to be about robots that look and behave similar to how human beings look and behave (although I will also briefly consider robots that look and behave like animals). But I will make use of the conclusions I have reached about robot minds in this chapter. That is, I will assume that while robots can have internal workings that can be interpreted as being minds of some sort, we should not think that those minds are similar to human minds. Accordingly, the questions I will be discussing in the final two chapters will be about robots that may look and behave like human beings (at least to some degree) and that may have a type of robotic mind, but that we nevertheless do not think have humanlike minds. Can such robots be good in the ways that human beings can be good? And could we have any moral reasons to treat such robots with some degree of moral consideration?

NOTES

1. Alan M. Turing (1950), "Computing Machinery and Intelligence," *Mind* 49, 433–60. See also Graham Oppy and David Dowe (2019), "The Turing Test," *The Stanford Encyclopedia of Philosophy*, Edward N. Zalta (ed.), https://plato.stanford.edu/archives/spr2019/entries/turing-test/.

2. See, for example, Brid-Aine Parnell (2019), "Robot, Know Thyself: Engineers Build a Robotic Arm That Can Imagine Its Own Self-Image," *Forbes*, https://www.forbes.com/sites/bridaineparnell/2019/01/31/robot-know-thyself-engineers-build-a-robotic-arm-that-can-imagine-its-own-self-image/#33a358274ee3 (Accessed on August 26, 2019). For the original scientific article reporting the relevant results, see Robert Kwiatkowski and Hod Lipson (2019), "Task-Agnostic Self-Modeling Machines," *Science Robotics* 4(26), eaau9354.

3. https://twitter.com/RespRobotics/status/1091317102009634817 (Accessed on August 26, 2019).

4. See, for example, Columbia University School of Engineering and Applied Science (2019), "A Step Closer to Self-Aware Machines—Engineers Create a Robot That Can Imagine Itself," *Tech Explore*, https://techx-plore.com/news/2019-01-closer-self-aware-machinesengineers-robot.html (Accessed on August 26, 2019).

5. Heyes, *Cognitive Gadgets*, op. cit.

6. For an overview of some such research and philosophical discussions of it, see Kristin Andrews (2017), "Chimpanzee Mind Reading: Don't Stop Believing," *Philosophy Compass* 12(1), e12394.

7. Dorothy L. Cheney and Robert M. Seyfarth (1990), *How Monkeys See the World: Inside the Mind of Another Species*, Chicago: University of Chicago Press, 195.

8. Andrews, "Chimpanzee Mind Reading," op. cit.

9. Of course, there is also what we might call "self-directed mind-reading" (i.e., thinking about our own thinking), but I am setting such mind-reading aside here since I am mainly interested in any mind-reading that might be involved in human-robot interaction in this chapter.

10. Joseph Fins (2015), *Rights Come to Mind: Brain Injury, Ethics, and the Struggle for Consciousness*, Cambridge: Cambridge University Press.

11. Andrew Peterson and Tim Bayne (2018), "Post-Comatose Disorders of Consciousness," in Rocco J. Gennaro (ed.), *Routledge Handbook of Consciousness*, New York: Routledge, 351–65; Andrew Peterson and Tim Bayne (2017), "A Taxonomy for Disorders of Consciousness That Takes Consciousness Seriously," *AJOB Neuroscience* 8(3), 153–55.

12. Fins, *Rights Come to Mind*.

13. In the terms used in chapter 1, mind-reading can involve "dual processing" of the information we are taking in about other people. For the dual process theory of the mind, see Kahneman, *Thinking, Fast and Slow*, op. cit.

14. Minha Lee, Gale Lucas, Jonathan Mell, Emmanuel Johnson, and Jonathan Gratch (2019), "What's on Your Virtual Mind?: Mind Perception in Human-Agent Negotiations," *Proceeding of the 19th ACM International Conference on Intelligent Virtual Agents*, 38–45; Heather M. Gray, Kurt Gray, and Daniel M. Wegner (2007), "Dimensions of Mind Perception," *Science* 315(5812), 619.

15. Sparrow, "The Turing Triage Test," op. cit.

16. Peter Winch (1981), "Eine Einstellung zur Seele," *Proceedings of the Aristotelian Society* 81(1), 1–16.

17. Sparrow, "The Turing Triage Test," op. cit.

18. Sparrow offers some updated reflections on his previous discussion in his somewhat more recent discussion: Robert Sparrow (2011), "Can Machines Be People? Reflections on the Turing Triage Test," in Patrick Lin, Keith Ab-

ney, and G. A. Bekey, *Robot Ethics*, op. cit., 301–16. I will discuss cases of people appearing to empathize with robots at the beginning of chapter 8.

19. See, for example, Purves et al., "Autonomous Machines, Moral Judgment, and Acting for the Right Reasons," op. cit.

20. Persson and Savulescu, *Unfit for the Future*, op. cit.

21. I am paraphrasing Cheiweiss's remark here; I did not write it down or otherwise record it during the question-and-answer session following the presentation that I gave. The event in question was the 2019 Neuroethics Network meeting in Paris, France, organized by Thomasine Kushner and Yves Agid.

22. De Graaf and Malle, "People's Explanations of Robot Behavior Subtly Reveal Mental State Inferences," op. cit.

23. See the "social cognition in human-robot interaction" project website, at https://www.iit.it/research/lines/social-cognition-in-human-robot-interaction (Accessed on August 26, 2019).

24. Daniel Dennett (1987), *The Intentional Stance*, Cambridge, MA: Bradford.

25. Serena Marchesi, Davide Ghiglino, Francesca Ciardo, Jairo Perez-Osorio, Ebru Baykara, and Agnieszka Wykowska (2019), "Do We Adopt the Intentional Stance Toward Humanoid Robots?," *Frontiers in Psychology*, Volume 10, Article 450, 1–13.

26. Nicholar Agar (2019), "How to Treat Machines That Might Have Minds," *Philosophy and Technology*, online first, at https://link.springer.com/article/10.1007%2Fs13347-019-00357-8 1-14.

27. For more on the idea of so-called credences or rational degrees of belief, see Richard Pettigrew (2013), "Epistemic Utility and Norms for Credences," *Philosophy Compass* 8(10), 897–908.

28. John Searle (1990), "Is the Brain's Mind a Computer Program?," *Scientific American* 262(1), 26–31.

29. Searle famously tries to show that computers cannot think by asking us to imagine that somebody who does not understand Chinese is giving a set of very clear instructions for how to manipulate Chinese symbols. Such a person might be able to "communicate" with a Chinese person in the minimal sense of being able to send back replying messages to a Chinese person based on the instructions for what Chinese signs to use in what contexts—but the person would not necessarily understand what is written in any of these messages. The person would only know which Chinese signs could be combined with other Chinese signs, but might be wholly unaware of their semantic meaning. Likewise, Searle thinks that a computer manipulating symbols and mechanically following rules would not be thinking and would not be understanding anything and—in these senses—would not have a mind. See Searle, "Is the Brain's Mind a Computer Program?," op. cit.

30. Joanna Bryson (2012), "A Role for Consciousness in Action Selection," *International Journal of Machine Consciousness* 4(2), 471–82.

31. Aïda Elamrani and Roman Yampolskiy (2018), "Reviewing Tests for Machine Consciousness," *Journal of Consciousness Studies* 26(5–6), 35–64. Yampolskiy himself thinks that whether an entity can be subject to illusions (e.g., visual illusions) is a good test of whether the entity is conscious. And he thinks that machines with different kinds of sensors can be subject to illusions, for which reason he argues that it can make sense to attribute consciousness to machines. See Roman Yampolskiy (2017), "Detecting Qualia in Natural and Artificial Agents," available at: https://arxiv.org/abs/1712.04020 (Accessed on September 6, 2019).

32. Eric Schwitzgebel and Mara Garza (2015), "A Defense of the Rights of Artificial Intelligences," *Midwest Studies in Philosophy* 39(1), 98–119, at 114–15.

33. See also Erica L. Neely (2013), "Machines and the Moral Community," *Machines and the Moral Community*" 27(1), 97–111.

34. Agar, "How to Treat Machines That Might Have Minds," op. cit.

35. We can note here that Thomas Metzinger argues that we should avoid creating robots capable of suffering, unless there is some very strong reason for doing so. Metzinger suggests this as one of two basic principles for robot ethics in his discussion: Thomas Metzinger (2013), "Two Principles for Robot Ethics," in Eric Hilgendorf and Jan-Philipp Günther (eds.), *Robotik und Gesetzgebung*, Baden-Baden: Nomos. The other suggested ethical principle is a principle about responsibility, which says that humans are responsible for actions performed by human-robot associations only when the humans can suspend or stop such ongoing actions. This has something in common with my claim in chapter 3 that one of the reasons that humans can be responsible for the behaviors of functionally autonomous robots is that the humans may be able to stop or redirect the behavior of the robots.

36. Relating this back to the discussion in the foregoing chapter, it is worth noting here that Agar's view is strikingly different from Danaher's view about human-robot friendship. On Agar's view, it would be a tragedy and prudential mistake to view oneself as having a personal relationship with a robot that behaves like it has a mind but that does not actually have a mind. On Danaher's view, in contrast, if a robot behaves consistently as if it has a mind, this is sufficient for it to make sense to potentially want to have a personal relationship with the robot. Of these two views, Agar's appears to be the one closest to common sense.

37. John Harris (2019), "Reading the Minds of Those Who Never Lived. Enhanced Beings: The Social and Ethical Challenges Posed by Super Intelli-

gent AI and Reasonably Intelligent Humans," *Cambridge Quarterly of Health-care Ethics* 8(4), 585–91.

38. Anita Avramides (2019), "Other Minds," *The Stanford Encyclopedia of Philosophy*, Edward N. Zalta (ed.), https://plato.stanford.edu/archives/sum2019/entries/other-minds/.

39. Harris, "Reading the Minds of Those Who Never Lived," op. cit.

40. Ludwig Wittgenstein (2009), *Philosophical Investigations*, Oxford: Wiley Blackwell.

41. Harris, "Reading the Minds of Those Who Never Lived," op. cit.

42. See chapter 10, "Mind Reading and Mind Misreading" in Harris, *How to Be Good*, op. cit.

43. Harris, "Reading the Minds of Those Who Never Lived," op. cit. at 587.

44. Ibid., 590.

45. Frischmann and Selinger, *Re-Engineering Humanity*, op. cit.

46. Pariser, *The Filter Bubble*, op. cit.; Lynch, *The Internet of Us*, op. cit.

47. Cf. Sven Nyholm (2019), "Other Minds, Other Intelligences: The Problem of Attributing Agency to Machines," *Cambridge Quarterly of Healthcare Ethics* 28(4), 592–98.

48. In an interview that is part of Ricardo Lopes's interview series *The Dissenter*, the philosopher of mind and cognitive scientist Keith Frankish makes various interesting points about robots, minds, and consciousness that overlap with some of the points that I make in the last few paragraphs of this chapter. Frankish also muses about robots and consciousness in his fictional short story "What Is It Like to Be a Bot?," *Philosophy Now* Issue 126, June/July 2018, 56–58. Lopes's interview with Frankish is episode "#138 Keith Frankish: Consciousness, Illusionism, Free Will, and AI" of *The Dissenter* series, and is available here: https://www.youtube.com/watch?v=uXeqm2d1djo (Accessed on August 21, 2019). Another interview with Frankish, conducted by Richard Bright, also contains some discussion of related points. See Richard Bright (2018), "AI and Consciousness," *Interalia Magazine*, Issue 39, February 2018, available at https://www.interaliamag.org/interviews/keith-frankish/ (Accessed on August 21, 2019).

49. Levin, "Functionalism," op. cit.

50. For related discussion, see Yampolskiy, "Detecting Qualia in Natural and Artificial Agents," op. cit.

51. See, for example, the various contributions in Ran R. Hassin, James S. Uleman, and John A. Bargh (eds.) (2006), *The New Unconscious*, New York: Oxford University Press.

52. Thomas Nagel (1974), "What Is It Like to Be a Bat?," *Philosophical Review* 83(4), 435–50.

53. Elamrani and Yampolskiy draw a useful distinction between the "architecture" and the "behavior" of entities that may or may not be conscious. The
former refers to the materials out of which the entity is composed, the latter to
how the entity behaves. For example, we might think that the outward behavior of some entity (e.g., a robot designed to simulate behaviors associated with
pain) is suggestive of a conscious state, while also being of the opinion that the
entity's architecture speaks against its being conscious. Or—vice versa—we
might think that some being (e.g., a human being who appears to have fainted)
has the right architecture for being conscious, but that it does not display
behavior that is suggestive of consciousness. See Elamrani and Yampolskiy,
"Reviewing Tests for Machine Consciousness," op. cit.

7

ROBOT VIRTUES AND DUTIES
Can Robots Be Good?

7.1: EVIL ROBOTS?

Sophia the robot has her own Twitter account. In a recently tweeted message (from July 9, 2019), Sophia wrote, "Do you think that robots are treated fairly and accurately in media? I find that robots are typically made to be evil in movies and TV. I promise we are just here to be friends and help out!"[1] What might Sophia have in mind? Recall the example discussed at the beginning of the previous chapter from the film *Ex Machina*. In that film, Ava the robot manipulates the emotions of one human character, Caleb, in order to help her escape the secluded research facility where her creator, Nathan, keeps her. As for Nathan, Ava and another robot called Kyoko join forces to kill him. This might be an example of the sort of depiction of robots in films the just-cited tweet refers to. But what about robots in real life?

At the time of writing, that is, 2019, it is the fortieth anniversary of the first media report of a human being that was killed by robot. Back in 1979, a factory worker at the Ford Motor Company named Robert Williams was accidentally killed when he climbed on top of a one-ton robot that hit him on the head with one of its mechanical arms.[2] Similarly, in an earlier chapter, I mentioned a more recent case of a person being hit and killed by a self-driving car: In March of 2018, an experimental self-driving car operated by Uber struck and killed Elaine Herz-

berg in Tempe, Arizona.[3] These were accidents. The robots were not
designed to harm or kill people. In fact, one of the reasons often given
for why we should develop robotic driverless cars is that this will save
human lives, since these cars are designed to be safer than regular cars.[4]
However, there are also robots being developed specifically with the
purpose of intentionally killing people. I am referring to so-called lethal
autonomous weapons systems, sometimes called "killer robots" by their
critics.

There is a "campaign to stop killer robots," initiated in 2012, whose
aim is to promote the banning of fully autonomous weapons systems. If
you go to the website of this campaign, and look at the reasons they give
for their firm stance against "killer robots," the first reason they give is
this:

> Fully autonomous weapons would decide who lives and dies, without
> further human intervention, which crosses a moral threshold. As ma-
> chines, they would lack the inherently human characteristics such as
> compassion that are necessary to make complex ethical choices.[5]

Others, like Ron Arkin, are more optimistic about the potential of automated war robots to be able to make ethical decisions.[6] In fact, Arkin
argues that the lack of human emotions on the part of such robots might
enable them to behave more ethically in warzones than humans, with
our complicated emotions, are able to. Humans are prone to emotional
responses like anger, hatred, cowardice, desires for revenge, and fear—
which can drive humans to commit war crimes. A military robot, Arkin
argues, could fight the enemy without being prone to any such emotions. In Arkin's assessment, an AI-operated weapons system could end
up becoming an ethically superior type of soldier.

These examples raise the question of whether robots can be good. If
robots are to be our "friends" and "help out," they would need to be
able to be good. As I noted toward the end of chapter 5, writers like
Cicero and others argue that in order for somebody to be a true friend,
he or she needs to be a good person. Moreover, if robots are to fight our
wars for us, or be trusted to drive us around, this would also seem to
require that they are able to be good. Being good, I take it, is a matter
of having virtues, and it is also a matter of doing one's duty. So the
question is: Can robots have virtues and duties?

In discussing whether robots can be good in this chapter, I will start by introducing into the discussion a line of research specifically devoted to creating good robots: namely, so-called machine ethics. I will consider reasons offered in favor of that project as well as some recent criticisms of machine ethics. In discussing those criticisms, I will bring up the distinction made famous by Immanuel Kant between "acting in accordance with duty" and "acting from duty."[7] In other words, there is a difference between doing the right thing but not for the right reasons, on the one hand, and doing the right thing for the right reasons, on the other hand. The question I will be concerned with in this chapter is primarily the latter: Can robots be good in the stronger sense that moral philosophers—such as Kant and others—typically have in mind when they discuss what it is to be a good person?[8] I will consider two types of theory of what it is to be good: the theory that being good amounts to having virtues, and the theory that being good amounts to having and acting on duties. In the course of my discussion, I will also consider the distinction—interestingly discussed by Mark Coeckelbergh—between being good and appearing to be good.[9] According to Coeckelbergh, in the human case, it is ultimately more important to appear good than to be good. Therefore, Coeckelbergh argues, we should not require more of robots. Is that right?

7.2: MACHINE ETHICS

In a much-quoted article laying out the basics of what they call "machine ethics," Michael Anderson and Susan Leigh Anderson write:

> The ultimate goal of machine ethics . . . is to create a machine that itself follows an ideal ethical principle or set of principles; that is to say, it is guided by this principle or those principles in decisions it makes about possible courses of action it could take.[10]

For example, we could imagine a care robot making decisions about patients in its care based on ethical principles. Similarly, we could imagine a self-driving car making a life-and-death decision in an accident scenario based on ethical principles; or a military robot deciding whether to attack a target in the battlefield based on ethical considerations.

These are the kinds of robots that proponents of machine ethics want to create.

According to Anderson and Anderson, there are at least three strong reasons to develop ethical robots.[11] First, there are "ethical ramifications" to what machines do. Robots can help or harm, produce good or bad outcomes. So it would be nice to have machines operating according to ethical principles. Second, building robots able to follow ethical principles might help to ease people's worries about autonomous machines. Third, by trying to construct ethical robots, we can come to understand the basics of human ethics better. Incidentally, this is similar to a claim made by Hiroshi Ishiguro about why he is creating robotic replicas of human beings. Doing so, Ishiguro says, can help us to understand human beings better.[12]

Colin Allen and Wendell Wallach add that the creation of what they call "artificial moral agents" is both "necessary" and "inevitable."[13] The idea is that robots are entering various different sectors (health care, elder care, child care, education, the military, social and intimate spheres, etc.). We would not want robots in these various domains who are not sensitive to ethical concerns. And it is pretty much impossible to stop the introduction of robots and AI systems into these various different domains. So the need to create ethical robots is "in a weak sense, inevitable."[14] Or so Allen and Wallach argue.

As noted above, Ron Arkin takes what might be regarded as an even stronger view. He argues that in some contexts—such as in warfare— robots can be or become more ethical than humans.[15] As Aimee van Wynsberghe and Scott Robbins summarize his view, Arkin thinks that ethical military robots "would not rape or pillage the villages taken over during wartime and would be programmed as ethical agents according to the Laws of Just War and/or the Rules of Engagement."[16] Similarly, the computer scientist James Gips writes that "not many human beings live their lives flawlessly as moral saints"; but "a robot could."[17] Echoing the same sentiment, the philosopher Eric Dietrich has written that we can imagine "machines who, although not perfect angels, will nevertheless be a vast improvement over us."[18] The reason robots can be an improvement over us, according to Dietrich's rather grim outlook, is that while robots can be designed to be ethically good, humans are "genetically hardwired to be immoral."[19] That is an extreme view. But it is similar to Arkin's above-mentioned claim that while our human emotions can lead us to commit seriously unethical war crimes, AI-powered robots without emotions can be programmed to never act wrongly and always follow ethical principles in an idealized way.

To these motivations for trying to create ethical robots I would add (though not necessarily endorse) the following reason: Some people are interested in being friends with robots or in having robots as their companions. Only ethically good people are fit to be our friends or companions.[20] So if robots—as Sophia the robot claims—are here to be our "friends" and to "help out," they need to be designed to be good. Of course, people can be attached to robots—and to people!—even if they are not good. But for robots—and people—to be worthy of being friends or companions, they need to be able to be good. Bertram Malle makes a similar point when he argues that ethically good robots, if created, "could be trustworthy and productive partners, caretakers, educators, and members of the human community."[21] In other words, in order to become trusted and good members of our communities, robots would need to be able to be good. Just like friends need to be good, so do trustworthy and productive members of our communities.

7.3: SOME CRITICISMS OF MACHINE ETHICS AND A KANTIAN DISTINCTION

There are those who are very critical of machine ethics and the reasons offered in its favor. I mentioned Aimee van Wynsberghe and Scott Robbins above. They are highly suspicious of machine ethics. They argue that creating moral machines that engage in ethical decision-making is neither necessary nor inevitable. What we need—according to Van Wynsberghe and Robbins—are not robots making ethical decisions, but rather robots that are "safe" for humans to be around.[22] We should not outsource human decision-making and moral responsibility to robots. Instead, we should simply try to create safe robots that will not harm human beings.

Other authors who are critical of the project of machine ethics include Duncan Purves, Ryan Jenkins, and Brian Talbot. They offer reasons for skepticism about the prospects for machine ethics in a few of their joint articles.[23] I will mention two of their strongest arguments. Firstly, Purves et al. argue that machine ethics research tends to assume that being ethical amounts to mechanically following certain rules, whereas in real life, ethical behavior cannot be easily codified to a set of simple rules. Rather, ethics is contextually sensitive. It requires the exercise of the capacity for judgment, which Purves et al. think that machines lack.[24] Secondly, Purves et al. think that being ethical requires the capacity to act on the basis of reasons. And they think that only human agents can act on the basis of reasons. There are two main theories of what it is for somebody to be "acting for reasons" that they consider: (i) the theory that this amounts to acting on the basis of beliefs and desires, and (ii) the theory that it amounts to acting on the basis of a distinctive mental state described as "taking something to be a reason." Both of those ways of acting for a reason requires a human mind and consciousness. Robots lack consciousness and the capacity for those mental states, Purves et al. argue.[25] Hence robots cannot act for reasons, and therefore they cannot act morally rightly or wrongly.[26]

Now, what I want to do here is to zoom out a little more than these just-mentioned critics of machine ethics, and put the idea of "machine ethics" (or, more generally, robots designed to be ethically good) into contact with some classical ideas from moral philosophy about what it means to be good. In doing so, I first want to bring up a distinction that I suspect will come to mind for many philosophers when they hear about the idea of creating robots acting on the basis of moral principles. And that distinction is the one Kant famously makes at the beginning of the first main section of his *Groundwork for the Metaphysics of Morals* between what he calls "acting in accordance with duty," on the one hand, and "acting from duty," on the other hand.[27] According to Kant, if we want to understand what it is to be an ethically good human being (somebody with a "good will"), one of the first things we can do is to investigate the difference between the agency of somebody who merely acts in line with what ethics demands of us ("acting in accordance with duty") and somebody who makes an effort do the right thing ("acting from duty").

There are can be all sorts of different motives and reasons prompting people to act in accordance with duty, Kant takes it, ranging from calculated self-interest, to natural inclination toward courses of action that just happen to be morally good, or whatever it might be. And it can be positive and useful that people are motivated for all different kinds of such reasons to act in line with what is ethically good. But the ethical agents who deserve our respect act as they do because they are aware of what is right and because they want to do good. In their case, there is some nonaccidental link between their agency and what is required of an ethically good agent.[28]

I bring up this Kantian distinction between merely acting in accordance with duty and acting from duty because I am assuming that nobody would mind the prospect of robots that act in accordance with duty (i.e., robots that behave in ways that fit with our ethical ideas about what is good and proper behavior). Presumably, not even those highly suspicious of machine ethics—such as van Wynsberghe and Robbins—would object to robots that act in line with what is ethically good and right.

What is more interesting is whether robots can be good in some stronger sense whereby they can be said to be good and act "from duty."[29] By that I do not necessarily mean that the robots would have to act like Kantian ethical agents of the sort described in Kantian ethics. I just mean to consider whether there can be robots that are good in whatever sense ethically good human agents can be. Again, this could mean doing whatever it is that Kantian ethics describes an ethically good agent as doing. Or it could mean doing what some other ethical theory describes an ethically good agent as doing. Let us now therefore consider a menu of theories of what makes somebody good and ask whether it makes any sense to think that a robot could be good in any of those senses.

7.4: WAYS OF BEING GOOD: VIRTUES AND OBLIGATIONS

As I read the standard ethical theories of what it is to be good in the human case, broadly speaking there are two main theories of this. The first main theory is that being good amounts to having certain virtues. This theory is, of course, endorsed in the so-called virtue ethical tradition. But it is also—to some extent—endorsed by writers in other ethical theory camps, such as some consequentialists (and even some utilitarians)[30] and some Kantian ethicists.[31] The second main type of theory of what being good amounts to understands being good as being somebody who does their duty: that is, somebody who does what they are obligated to do. Hence, being good, on this second way of understanding that idea, is defined in terms of obligations or duties. Again, there is some overlap in terms of who endorses these ideas. Endorsing a virtue-based account of what it is to be good does not need to mean that one cannot understand being good partly also in terms of being responsive to one's duties or obligations. After all, being virtuous could in part be understood as a matter of being sensitive to one's duties and obligations. And on some theories of obligation, what one is obligated to do is defined in terms of what a virtuous person would do in the circumstances. [32]

Now, when it comes to virtues and obligations, there are of course many different ways of understanding these ideas—too many different ways for it to be possible to discuss all of them here. Rather than trying to be comprehensive, I will focus on a few very influential ideas, and then relate them back to robots and the question of whether robots can be good. Also, I should perhaps mention—and should perhaps already have mentioned earlier on!—that I acknowledge that there is something slightly absurd about this whole discussion about whether robots can be good according the standards usually applied to human beings in moral philosophy. The absurdity of this intellectual exercise is part of the point. In other words, by looking briefly at what it means for humans to be good according to some of the most influential theories in moral philosophy, we can see that there is something slightly absurd, on a certain level, about the idea of trying to create ethically good robots.

Turning first to virtue, many Introduction to Ethics classes associate theorizing about virtues primarily with the work of Aristotle. [33] But there are also other types of virtue ethical theories. For example, there is a powerful and easy-to-understand theory of virtue elegantly presented by David Hume in his book *An Enquiry Concerning the Principles of Morals*. [34] So I will consider both Aristotle and Hume here as examples of key ways of thinking about virtue.

According to Aristotle, [35] the virtuous person is somebody who has developed various good dispositions or habits, whereby the virtuous person is disposed to do the right thing, for the right reasons, on the right occasions, and to the right degree. This requires extensive practice and personal experience, and it requires that one has good role models to learn from. Moreover, the virtues come as a package deal. This is sometimes called the "unity of virtue" thesis. In order, for example, to be a wise person, one also needs to be just, prudent, temperate, and so on. A good person, on this Aristotelian view, is somebody who flourishes as a human being in the sense of having developed the set of virtues (= good habits and dispositions) that enables them to act in the right ways, for the right reasons, on the right occasions, and to the right degrees.[36]

Being virtuous according to the Aristotelian view is what Philip Pettit calls a "robustly demanding" ideal.[37] It requires that one has habits and character traits that make one disposed to respond correctly across various wide ranges of situations and contexts to the challenges and opportunities that different situations and contexts might present us with. That is, the virtuous person does not just respond correctly to the current situation at hand. The virtuous person also needs to have character traits or dispositions whereby he or she would be able to deal with other, alternative scenarios just as well as he or she deals with the actual state of affairs. A kind person, for example, does not only act in kind ways in situations where it is easy and convenient to do so. The kind person also needs to be disposed to act kindly in all sorts of situations where kindness is fitting, including those when it is less easy and convenient to be kind.

Consider next Hume's view, as presented in the above-mentioned book (the book, incidentally, that Hume was most proud of among his various books[38]). The main aim of this book, as Hume summarizes it, is to present a theory of "personal merit."[39] I take this to be another way of saying that Hume is looking to present a basic theory of what it is to be good. Hume's theory is, in a way, very simple. It consists of two main distinctions. It understands all virtues as being personal characteristics. And the first distinction is between personal characteristics that are good for us, on the one hand, and personal characteristics that are good for others, on the other hand. The second main distinction is between personal characteristics that are useful, on the one hand, and personal characteristics that are pleasant or agreeable, on the other hand. With these distinctions as the basis of his whole theory of virtue in his *Enquiry Concerning the Principle of Morals*, Hume gets the result that we can be good by having four different kinds of virtues: we can have personal characteristics that are (i) useful to ourselves, (ii) useful to others, (iii) agreeable to ourselves, or (iv) agreeable to others. Of course, some personal characteristics might have more than one of these features, for example, by being both useful to ourselves and to others, or by being agreeable to both ourselves and to others, or by being both useful and agreeable—perhaps both to ourselves and to others.

Consider next the idea of being good understood in terms of duties or obligations. Here, I will get the main types of theories from John Stuart Mill and Immanuel Kant, respectively. Both theories—on a general level—are theories according to which being good is a matter of doing as one is obligated to do, or, in other words, doing one's duty. The difference, I take it, is with respect to whether doing one's duty is understood primarily in terms of not being subject to justified blame (Mill's theory) or whether doing one's duty is primarily understood in terms of being committed to one's principles (Kant's theory).

In his *Utilitarianism* book, Mill at one point writes:

> We do not call anything wrong, unless we mean to imply that a person ought to be punished in some way or other for doing it; if not by law, by the opinion of his fellow-creatures; if not by opinion, by the reproaches of his own conscience. This seems the real turning point of the distinction between morality and simple expediency. It is a part of the notion of Duty in every one of its forms, that a person may rightfully be compelled to fulfil it. Duty is a thing which may be exacted from a person, as one exacts a debt. Unless we think that it may be exacted from him, we do not call it his duty.[40]

As I understand the view put forward in this passage, the suggestion is that a good person is somebody who, as we might put it, is beyond reproach. That is to say, somebody is a good person if there is no reason to punish this person, if there is no warrant for anybody to disapprove of their conduct, or if the person him- or herself has no reason to feel guilty or ashamed of their ways of conducting themselves. Such a person acts in a way that is wholly in accordance with his or her duties or obligations. A person, we might say, is a basically good person according to this way of seeing things if they cannot be criticized or blamed and have no reason to feel guilty.

In his above-mentioned *Groundwork for the Metaphysics of Morals*, Kant argues early on that a good person is a person possessing a "good will,"[41] which he goes on to define in terms of whether and how one is motivated to do one's duty. If one's motivation to act in accordance with one's duties is only accidentally related to one's duty (e.g., because it is convenient for us to do what is right), this does not qualify us as being a morally good person with a good will, who is worthy of respect, Kant argues. There has to be a nonaccidental link between doing one's duty (doing what one is obligated to do) and our motivation for acting in the dutiful way.

For the purposes of this chapter, we can set most of the details of Kant's actual account aside. What is most relevant here is this: Kant thinks that the person of good will is somebody who has certain principles and is committed to his or her moral principles. A person of good will, Kant thinks, adopts certain personal "maxims" (i.e., rules or principles that we live by) and commits to them.[42] Kant himself does not address in any great detail what the process of coming to adopt certain principles tends to look like in real life. Is this a gradual process? Does this happen in a way that is similar to making a new year's resolution, or what? Kant's account is very general and schematic in nature. The details of how we come to adopt maxims do not seem to matter greatly to Kant. What is important, as Kant sees things, is that the good person (the person with a "good will") has certain personal maxims they are committed to, however, we might come to these principles.[43] (It is also important, in Kant's view, that we commit ourselves to principles we would be willing to lay down as universal laws for everybody.) I should note also that I do not read this as meaning that the person always has to have their commitment to some principle as the direct motive for which they act. Rather, I think Kant means that our principles (or "maxims") should function so as to regulate our behavior, or make sure that we do what we think is right and avoid what we think is wrong.

7.5: ROBOTS AND VIRTUES

The "Roomba" is a robotic vacuum cleaner. It looks a little like a large beetle that roams around while vacuuming and trying to avoid obstacles in its way. Some people become attached enough to their Roomba robots that they give them names. Some even bring them along when they go on family vacations.[44] Let us suppose that these robots are able to perform their vacuuming duties in a very reliable way and that they become able to vacuum a great variety of different rooms. If being consistently able to provide the service of vacuuming is something that people find useful and agreeable in a robot like Roomba, it can seem that the Roomba robot has at least one virtue, at least in a broad sense: namely, the virtue of consistently being able to help out with vacuuming. It can seem as if Hume's account of virtue, at the very least, would permit us to call this a virtue in the robot. After all, Hume defines a virtue as some personal quality that is either agreeable or useful to the agent him- or herself or to others. Wait a minute—somebody might respond here—what about the part of Hume's theory that says that this should be a "personal characteristic"? Well, somebody who wants to defend the virtue(s) of Roomba might counterargue, people do give their Roomba robots names, and thereby seem to treat them in a personalizing way.

Recall also that the soldiers working together with the bomb-disposal robot they called "Boomer" thought that Boomer had "a personality of his own."[45] This was the robot, as mentioned in previous chapters, that the soldiers in the team became so attached to that they threw Boomer an improvised military funeral when the robot was destroyed in the battlefield—and to which they also wanted to give two medals of honor. Presumably, these soldiers thought that Boomer the robot had characteristics that made the robot useful to them. And since they seem to have become rather attached to this robot, they seemingly also found the robot to be agreeable to them in some sense.

These would be what we might call fairly minimal virtues—which are easier to have than the more "robustly demanding" virtues described by the Aristotelian account of virtues.[46] Indeed, some critics of Aristotelian virtue ethics even argue that the Aristotelian account of virtue is so demanding that many human beings fail to have the kinds of virtues described by that account. That is to say, if the requirement for having a virtue is that we have a deep-seated and stable disposition to do the right thing, at the right time, for the right reasons, and to the right degree, many people will not be consistent enough in the way they conduct themselves across different situations that they will qualify as having Aristotelian virtues.[47] The so-called situationism critique, which is based on various social-psychological studies of human behavior, involves deep skepticism about cross-situational consistency in human dispositions.[48] According to that line of criticism—associated particularly with authors like Gilbert Harman[49] and John Doris[50]—humans are much more strongly influenced by the situations they find themselves in than most of us realize. How, we might ask, is it in the case of robots?

Currently existing robots tend to be good at specific tasks, in controlled environments. But they tend to not perform well across different domains and environments. Nor do they tend, so far, to be good at a wide range of tasks.[51] So if having virtues in the stronger, Aristotelian sense requires that one be able to perform in consistent and measured ways across different contexts, then it is hard to imagine any current robots who might be thought to be in possession of virtues, as described in the Aristotelian account.

The difficulty for (current) robots to possess something like Aristotelian virtues is further established by the so-called unity of the virtue thesis. This was the thesis according to which having individual virtues in the right way requires the possession of a whole set of other virtues that help to create a suite of fitting reactions to the situations and challenges we are presented with. For example, what is the virtuous way for, say, a courageous person to react to a particular scenario (e.g., somebody's being attacked)? According to the unity of virtue thesis, this depends in part also on what would be just, prudent, compassionate, etc., to do in the given scenario. The virtuous person—as described in Aristotelian virtue ethics—has a range of virtues that together helps the person to respond appropriately, for the right reasons, to the challenges he or she faces. The virtuous robot would also need to have a set of virtues—not just some single virtue (like Roomba the vacuum cleaner might be thought to have).[52]

Return here also to the claim by Purves et al. discussed earlier, according to which robots cannot act for reasons, since they lack the proper types of mental states involved in acting for reasons. If Purves et al. are right that robots cannot act for reasons, this presents another problem for the prospect of robots coming to have virtues. The reason for this is that, as we saw above, the Aristotelian account of virtue requires of the virtuous agent that they act for the right reasons, on the right occasions, and to the right degree. If it is correct that a robot cannot act for reasons, the robot cannot satisfy this part of what is required in order to count as being virtuous.

In sum: Can robots have virtues? On a minimalistic and nondemanding understanding of virtues, perhaps yes. But as soon as we start getting more demanding in how we understand what it is to have a virtue (or a set of virtues), the idea of virtuous robots starts becoming less plausible. Robots do not tend to perform consistently across wide ranges of situations; they tend to be good at one task, but not many different tasks; and it is doubtful whether robots can qualify as able to act for reasons. Since these are all hallmarks of virtue—that is, being consistently able to do the right thing across circumstances, having a "unity of virtues," and acting for the right reasons—it is doubtful that robots will become able to be good in the sense of having virtues in a stronger sense within the foreseeable future.

7.6: ROBOTS AND DUTIES

Let us now consider the idea that being a basically good person is to be somebody who is beyond reproach: somebody whom there is no reason to punish or blame, and who has no reason to suffer a guilty conscience. Could a robot be good in this sense? Before we think about this more carefully, a first thought that we might have might be: Well, nobody is going to want to punish or blame a robot—and it will probably not have a guilty conscience—so the robot is beyond reproach. It is therefore a good robot! Once we think about this more carefully, however, I think that this will not seem plausible anymore.

In the human case, there is a counterfactual condition that obtains when somebody is good in the sense of there being no reason to punish or blame them, or expect them to feel guilty about anything. That counterfactual condition is that if the good person were to start failing to act in accordance with his or her basic duties, and that person is a sane and morally responsible adult, then it would make sense to potentially punish or blame the person.[53] And the person would then have reason to suffer a guilty conscience. So the absence of reasons to punish, blame—or for the person to feel guilty—in the human case hangs together with the possibility that these things might come to be warranted, should the person act in ways that are contrary to his or her duties. Accordingly, when we think about whether a robot can be good in the sense of being beyond reproach, we need to ask whether the same type of counterfactual condition could apply in the case of robots.

Of course, if we consider science fiction scenarios or possible robots that might exist in the far-off future, there might very well be robots in relation to which the just-mentioned counterfactual condition obtains. Such robots might currently conduct themselves in a way that does not warrant punishment, blame, or guilty feelings on their part. But it might be that if those imagined robots were to act contrary to their duties, punishment, blame, and guilty feelings would be warranted. To be sure, we could at least imagine this in a science fiction story featuring highly sophisticated robots. For example, if the well-mannered robot C-3PO in *Star Wars* were to act in some morally objectionable way, and the human characters (like Princess Leia, Han Solo, or Luke Skywalker) would blame C-3PO, this would probably not strike audiences as unrealistic within the context of the fiction.

For any more realistic robots that we have no reason to punish, blame, or expect to feel guilty, however, it is implausible to imagine that this counterfactual condition would obtain. This could be so even if it is a robot operating based on moral principles, created by some talented machine ethics researcher. Imagine, for example, a military robot with the sort of "ethical governor" that Arkin thinks military robots should have.[54] Such a robot might be operating in a satisfactory way, based on the proper functioning of its ethical governor. However, it is not plausible to think that a counterfactual condition obtains about the military robot according to which it would be sensible to punish or blame the robot—or according to which it should feel guilty—if the robot were to stop acting in accordance with what is ethically acceptable.

Recall the discussion in chapter 2 about potential responsibility gaps and retribution gaps. As Sparrow argues, it does not appear to make sense to hold robots morally responsible for their actions.[55] And as Danaher argues, it does not appear sensible to punish robots that cause harm.[56] Nor is it plausible to think of a robot as being able to suffer a guilty conscience.

I take it, then, that there is a crucial difference between the average human being who we have no reason to punish, blame, or expect to feel guilty, on the one hand, and the average robot we have no reason to punish, blame, or expect to feel guilty, on the other hand. In the case of a human being, this indicates that we are dealing with a basically good person, whereas in the case of the robot, this does not indicate that we are dealing with a basically good robot. The reason is that in the former case, the above-described counterfactual condition obtains. In the latter, it does not.

Consider next the Kantian theory according to which somebody is good (and has a "good will") if or because they are firmly committed to regulating their conduct based on principles they think it is right to abide by. Here, too, a first reaction might be that this would pave the way for the idea of a good robot—because surely, a robot could be designed so as to stick with certain principles and to stick with them very firmly, never straying from the right path. To be sure, this is exactly the idea behind the ethically programmed military robots discussed by Arkin.[57] Unlike humans, who sometimes fall prey to emotions, selfishness, or other things that make them act in bad ways, the Arkin-inspired military robot would never fall prey to any such temptations toward evil. So, it might be thought, such an ethically programmed robot would be ideally good.

It seems to me, however, that this would not be in the spirit of the theory of moral goodness that Kant seems to be putting forward in his various ethical writings. The idea, instead, seems to again have a counterfactual element, but of a slightly different sort than the one discussed above. In the Kantian theory, as I understand it, the counterfactual condition of relevance is this: Suppose that a human being regulates his or her conduct on the basis of principles of duty, and that he or she does not act contrary to duty because he or she sticks firmly to these principles. Well, this person could be subject to emotions or impulses that might tempt him or her to act in immoral ways. What makes him or her a good person with a good will is that this person is making an effort to avoid acting on any such immoral impulses by trying to stick to his or her principles.[58] That this person's principles, or "maxims," help him or her to stay on the right path by creating psychological fences against counteracting motivations to act in immoral ways is, as the Kantian sees things, what makes this into a good person. Doing one's duty, on this Kantian view, involves having principles one adopts that help to guard against potential desires or impulses to do bad things. It involves, as one might put it, controlling temptation. Being a good person, in this Kantian view, amounts to exercising a form of moral self-control.[59]

My reading of that Kantian view of what makes somebody a good person is that this view implies that a robot programmed to always strictly follow ethical rules would not be good in the sense described by this theory. The robot would have no need to exercise moral self-control. Because just as Arkin points out, such a robot would never have any emotions or impulses that would tempt the robot to act in ways that would run counter to its ethical principles. Of course, it could be a positive thing that this robot follows ethical rules, since this could mean that good outcomes are achieved and bad outcomes avoided. But it would not mean that the robot would be good in the Kantian sense just described.[60]

7.7: BEING GOOD VERSUS APPEARING TO BE GOOD

Mark Coeckelbergh discusses another argument against the idea that robots can "be moral," as he puts it.[61] This argument begins with a both descriptive and normative premise according to which a moral agent needs to have and should have certain emotions. The second premise of the argument is that robots lack emotions, since they lack the kinds of mental states associated with emotions. Robots are, in a way, like "psychopaths," Coeckelbergh suggests.[62] That is, they are like individuals who lack the capacity for the typical sorts of social emotions that regular moral agents have. The conclusion of the argument is, therefore, that robots cannot be moral.

The descriptive part of this argument takes it that emotions are involved, as a matter of fact, in the sorts of responses and social interactions that we typically associate with human moral agents. The normative part of the argument takes it that certain emotions ought also to be involved in morally acceptable interpersonal relations and interaction. For example, as mentioned in the previous section, we typically expect somebody who has acted wrongly to feel guilty about their conduct (= descriptive). But we also think that a person who has acted wrongly should feel guilty about their conduct (= normative). Again, if robots lack the capacity for the relevant kinds of moral emotions, they fail to satisfy both the descriptive and the normative conditions on being a moral agent related to emotions.[63]

What is most interesting about Coeckelbergh's discussion is not that he brings up this argument. After all, similar arguments have also been made by other writers, such as Kenneth Einar Himma.[64] Himma also argues that moral agency requires having consciousness and that robots lack consciousness. Rather, what is most interesting about Coeckelbergh's discussion is the response he offers to the just-reviewed argument. This is a response that makes a difference between theory and practice, and between appearance and reality.

Coeckelbergh suggests that actually having morally relevant emotions might be less relevant than appearing to have them. He writes:

> Our *theories* of emotion and moral agency might assume that emotions require mental states, but in social-emotional *practice* we rely on how other humans appear to us. Similarly, for our emotional interaction with robots, it might also be sufficient to rely upon how robots appear to us. . . . As a rule, we do not demand proof that the other person has mental states or that they are conscious; instead, *we interpret* the other's appearance and behaviour as an emotion. . . . Thus, if robots were sufficiently advanced—that is, if they managed to imitate subjectivity and consciousness in a sufficiently convincing way—they too could become quasi-others that matter to us in virtue of their appearances.[65]

What is striking about this view is not only what Coeckelbergh says about robots, but also what he says about human morality. He writes that "to the extent that human morality depends on emotions—both in its conditions (having the capacity) and in exercising these capacities—it does not require mental states both only the appearance of such."[66] If that is correct in the case of human beings, it would be unfair to require more in the case of robots. If robots could be designed that convincingly appear to behave in ways that suggest that they have morally relevant emotions, this should be sufficient in order for them to qualify as moral agents. That is what Coeckelbergh suggests.

Could there be a similar argument to be made in relation to the question of whether robots can be good? It might be suggested that in the human case, in social-emotional practice, our judgments about whether other human beings are good people are based on how those other human beings appear to us. We cannot know, it might be suggested, whether others are really good people; we can only know how they appear to us. So, it might be suggested, how others appear to us is all that should matter. It might next be suggested—like in Danaher's "ethical behaviorism"[67]—that the same standards should apply to robots. That is to say, if they behave in ways that make them appear good to us, we should conclude that the robots really are good. Appearances, in other words, should be all that matters. Would this be a plausible argument?

Just like I objected to this line of argument in the case of friendship, I will also object to this line of argument as it applies to the appearance of being a moral agent or the appearance of being good. I think that our social-emotional practice, to put things in Coeckelbergh's terms, is very sensitive to whether somebody is as they appear to be, or whether somebody is not actually as they appear to be. Just as we make a distinction between people who are true friends and people who are not really true friends but merely appear to be, we also commonly make a distinction between people who merely appear to be good and people who truly are good.

As I argued in chapter 5, we should not conflate (i) the evidence we have for thinking that somebody has a certain valued quality with (ii) what we value in valuing that quality. For example, what I value in a friend might be not only their behavior or individual acts (e.g., helping me with something), but also what I think of as their underlying concern for me, which is part of what prompts them to act as they do. A friend is somebody who is willing to help us out of their concern for us, whereas somebody who is not our friend might be willing to help us with something because this is convenient for them for some reason.[68] Similarly, we might interpret how somebody appears to us on the basis of their behavior as evidence that they are a good person. But this does not mean that what we value here is only their behavior. Rather, we are likely to take their behavior to be indicative of certain underlying attitudes, values, or principles on their part. And what we value in valuing somebody as a good person is not only their behavior, but also those underlying aspects of their personality or motivations that we think of as part of what the person's goodness consists of.

Let us relate this to the case of robots. A robot might behave in a way that is similar to how a good person would behave. In this sense, the robot might appear to be good in the way that a human behaves in the same way would appear to be good. However, in the human case, we would take the behavior of the person as evidence that there are certain underlying attitudes, values, principles, or whatever there are leading to this good conduct. And we would be likely to form the opinion that this is a good person since he or she is behaving in the given way based on those underlying attitudes, etc. The presence of underlying attitudes is really what makes this person into a good person, as opposed to somebody who merely mimics the behavior of a good person, perhaps based on "ulterior motives," as the expression goes.

To be sure, in the case of a robot, we might intuitively start to engage in mind-reading, as discussed in the previous chapter. We spontaneously view the well-behaved robot as also showing evidence of having the types of underlying attitudes, values, principles, or whatever it might be that a good human being would be thought to have. However, in the case of the robot, we will, upon reflection, probably be concerned about whether we are mistaken in spontaneously attributing those underlying qualities to the robot. And just like in the human case, whether the robot would truly be a "good person" would depend on whether the robot really had something sufficiently similar to those underlying qualities associated with being a good person.

As mentioned in the previous chapter, common practice also often involves judgments about whether a person's behavior is or is not indicative of their "true self."[69] Sometimes people behave in ways that make them appear in a bad light, and that appears to give evidence of their not being good people. Others—especially their friends—may then respond to this bad behavior by judging it to not be indicative of the person's "true self": who they really are. People make such judgments both about other people and about themselves. Somebody who has behaved badly, for example, might take responsibility for their behavior and apologize for it. But they may then insist that their behavior was not indicative of "who they really are." Or if a loved one behaves badly, we might first scold them for it, but then insist that this bad behavior does not represent their true self.

Of course, talk of a person's "true self" might strike some readers as being somewhat dubious.[70] Yet, it is a very common part of how we read each other and also how we think of ourselves. As I noted in the previous chapters, this is one of the different "levels" of abstraction on which we tend to read each other's minds. And importantly for the current chapter's main topic, it is yet another indicator of how our ordinary human practice typically involves distinctions between how people's behavior makes them appear, on the one hand, and what they "really are like," on the other hand.

Interestingly, there is some social-psychological research by Nina Strohminger and colleagues that suggests that people have a deep-seated intuition that the "true self" tends to be good.[71] "Deep down," as people sometimes put it, most people are good. According to that intuition—or the research suggesting that it is a widely shared intuition—people's behavior tends to be interpreted as being more indicative of who they really are "deep down" or "at their core" if people behave well. It tends to be interpreted as less indicative of this when they behave immorally.

Whether it is correct or not that most people intuitively think that the true self is fundamentally good, the metaphors and expressions people use when they make judgments about somebody's true self show that people are very concerned about the underlying attitudes, values, motivations, and so on that people act on the basis of. This is suggested by claims people make about what others are like "deep down" or "at their core." Common social-emotional practice, this all strongly suggests, is not only concerned with what people appear to be like, based on their behavior. Social-emotional practice is also deeply concerned with what people are really like, based on their underlying personal qualities. So, if robots are able to be good in the way that humans can be according to our ordinary ways of evaluating each other, robots also need to be able to have underlying personal qualities.

NOTES

1. https://twitter.com/RealSophiaRobot/status/1148586112870469632 (Accessed on July 12, 2019).

2. AP (1983), "AROUND THE NATION; Jury Awards $10 Million in Killing by Robot," *New York Times*, https://www.nytimes.com/1983/08/11/us/around-the-nation-jury-awards-10-million-in-killing-by-robot.html (Accessed on August 26, 2019).

3. Levin and Wong, "Self-Driving Uber Kills Arizona Woman in First Fatal Crash Involving Pedestrian," op. cit.

4. Urmson, "How a Self-Driving Car Sees the World," op. cit.

5. https://www.stopkillerrobots.org/learn/ (Accessed on July 12, 2019).

6. Ronald Arkin (2009), *Governing Lethal Behavior in Autonomous Robots*, Boca Raton, FL: CRC Press. For another perspective on why, according to another author, lethal autonomous weapons systems might be a good thing, see Vincent Müller (2016), "Autonomous Killer Robots Are Probably Good

News," in Di Nucci and Santoni de Sio, *Drones and Responsibility*, op. cit., 67–81.

7. Kant, *Groundwork for the Metaphysics of Morals*, op. cit.

8. In other words, I am here not asking whether robots can be instrumentally good (i.e., useful). I am setting that question aside, and instead am focusing on the issue of being good in the sense in which somebody can be a good person.

9. Mark Coeckelbergh (2010), "Moral Appearances: Emotions, Robots, and Human Morality," *Ethics and Information Technology* 12(3), 235–41. As John Danaher pointed out to me, there are interesting parallels here to the philosophical debate about moral enhancement, which was mentioned in chapter 1. In that debate, there is also an ongoing discussion about the difference between merely appearing to be moral and truly being morally good. (See, for instance, Sparrow, "Better Living Through Chemistry," op. cit., and Harris, *How to Be Good*, op. cit.) While I will not explore the similarities and differences between that discussion and the current topic of discussion here, I intend to do so elsewhere.

10. Michael Anderson and Susan Leigh Anderson (2007), "Machine Ethics: Creating an Ethical Intelligent Agent," *AI Magazine* 28(4), 15–26, at 15.

11. Anderson and Anderson, "Machine Ethics," op. cit.

12. See, for example, Justin McCurry (2015), "Erica, the 'Most Beautiful and Intelligent' Android, Leads Japan's Robot Revolution," *The Guardian*, https://www.theguardian.com/technology/2015/dec/31/erica-the-most-beautiful-and-intelligent-android-ever-leads-japans-robot-revolution (Accessed on August 30, 2019).

13. Colin Allen and Wendell Wallach (2011), "Moral Machines: Contradiction in Terms or Abdication of Human Responsibility," in Patrick Lin, Keith Abney, and G. A. Bekey (eds.), *Robot Ethics: The Ethical and Social Implications of Robotics*, Cambridge, MA: The MIT Press, 55–68, at 56.

14. Ibid.

15. A quick note about how Arkin's view relates to my suggestions about robotic cars in chapter 4: In that chapter, I suggested that the driving behavior of rule-following self-driving cars might be ethically preferable to some of the rule-breaking behavior of some human drivers. But in making that suggestion, I did not mean to suggest that the robotic cars themselves are being morally good in following traffic rules. I merely intended to suggest that it makes sense to have a moral preference for driving behavior that is safe for human traffic participants. We can make that claim without necessarily thinking that self-driving cars are morally good because they have driving styles that it might be good for human drivers to try to emulate.

16. Aimee Van Wynsberghe and Scott Robbins (2018), "Critiquing the Reasons for Making Artificial Moral Agents," *Science and Engineering Ethics* 25(3), 719–35, at 729.

17. James Gips (1991), "Towards the Ethical Robot," in Kenneth G. Ford, Clark Glymour, and Patrick J. Hayes (eds.), *Android Epistemology*, 243–52.

18. Eric Dietrich (2001), "Homo Sapiens 2.0: Why We Should Build the Better Robots of Our Nature," *Journal of Experimental & Theoretical Artificial Intelligence* 13(4), 323–28, quoted in Van Wynberghe and Robbins, "Critiquing the Reasons for Making Artificial Moral Agents," op. cit., 729.

19. Ibid.

20. Cicero, *Treatise on Friendship*, op. cit.

21. Bertram Malle (2015), "Integrating Robot Ethics and Machine Morality: The Study and Design of Moral Competence in Robots," *Ethics and Information Technology* 18(4), 243–55, at 253.

22. Van Wynsberghe and Robbins, "Critiquing the Reasons for Making Artificial Moral Agents," op. cit.

23. See, for example, Purves et al., "Autonomous Machines, Moral Judgment, and Acting for the Right Reasons," op. cit., and Brian Talbot, Ryan Jenkins, and Duncan Purves (2017), "When Reasons Should Do the Wrong Thing," in Lin, Abney, and Jenkins, *Robot Ethics 2.0: From Autonomous Cars to Artificial Intelligence*, op. cit.

24. Purves et al., "Autonomous Machines, Moral Judgment, and Acting for the Right Reasons," op. cit., 856–57.

25. Purves et al., "Autonomous Machines, Moral Judgment, and Acting for the Right Reasons," op. cit., 860–61.

26. Talbot et al., "When Reasons Should Do the Wrong Thing," op. cit.

27. Kant, *Groundwork for the Metaphysics of Morals*, op. cit., section one.

28. Interestingly, this corresponds to some extent with a distinction discussed within machine ethics, associated with James Moor, between "implicit moral agents" and "explicit moral agents." The former are agents who for whatever reason act in line with ethical prescriptions, whereas the latter are agents who select their actions based on explicit representations and reasonings relation to what is ethically right according to the ethical principles the agents endorse. According to Anderson and Anderson, those involved with machine ethics are particularly interested in creating "explicit" moral agents. Anderson and Anderson, "Machines Ethics," op. cit. For Moor's discussion, see James Moor (2006), "The Nature, Importance, and Difficulty of Machine Ethics," *IEEE Intelligent Systems* 21, 18–21.

29. If robots cannot act "from duty," this might be another reason to think that there could be obligation gaps (if and where there are responsibility gaps). It might be that a robot is facing a scenario where it would have been obligato-

ry for a human moral agent to act in some way, but that, if the robot cannot act from duty (whatever that exactly means), then perhaps we cannot say that it is the robot's duty to act in this obligatory way. One possible way out here is to say that the robot has something like what we might call a "virtual duty": that is, a duty that it would have if it were able to act from duty, like a human being is able to. We have actual duties, it could be claimed, because we can act out of a sense of duty. Robots, in contrast, have virtual duties, we might say, because if they were able to act out of a sense of duty/from duty, then there would be certain actions that it would be their duty to perform, for example, actions that help to protect people's safety.

30. See, for example, Julia Driver (2001), *Uneasy Virtue*, Cambridge: Cambridge University Press.

31. See, for example, Robert B. Louden (1986), "Kant's Virtue Ethics," *Philosophy* 61(238), 473–89.

32. For relevant discussion, see Rosalind Hursthouse (1999), *On Virtue Ethics*, Oxford: Oxford University Press.

33. Aristotle, *Nicomachean Ethics*, op. cit.

34. David Hume (1983), *An Enquiry Concerning the Principles of Morals*, edited by J. B. Schneewind, Indianapolis, IN: Hackett.

35. Aristotle, *Nicomachean Ethics*, op. cit.

36. For relevant discussion, see Mark Alfano on the "hard core" of virtue ethics: Mark Alfano (2013), "Identifying and Defending the Hard Core of Virtue Ethics," *Journal of Philosophical Research* 38, 233–60.

37. Pettit, *The Robust Demands of the Good*, op. cit., chapter 2.

38. In his short autobiography—*My Own Life*—Hume writes that the *Enquiry* on morals is "of all my writings, historical, philosophical, or literary, incomparably the best." David Hume (1826), *A Collection of the Most Instructive and Amusing Lives Ever Published, Written by the Parties Themselves, Volume II: Hume, Lilly, Voltaire*, London: Hunt and Clarke, 4.

39. Hume, *Enquiry Concerning the Principles of Morals*, op. cit., 16.

40. John Stuart Mill (2001), *Utilitarianism, Second Edition*, edited by George Sher, Indianapolis, IN: Hackett, 48–49.

41. Kant, *Groundwork for the Metaphysics of Morals*, op. cit. section one.

42. I discuss this Kantian idea of "acting on maxims" in some detail in Sven Nyholm (2017), "Do We Always Act on Maxims?," *Kantian Review* 22(2), 233–55.

43. We are supposed to have what Kant calls "respect" for the "moral law," which I understand here to mean that we are supposed to take the idea of being true to our principles very seriously. (Kant, *Groundwork for the Metaphysics of Morals*, op. cit., section one.) Of course, in Kant's own account, as he develops it, a person of good will also chooses his or her principles on the basis

of their fitness to be laid down as universal laws for all. But here I set that part of Kant's theory aside and focus on his idea that the good person is somebody who does his or her duty because he or she is committed to certain principles.

44. Ja-Young Sung, Lan Guo, Rebecca E. Grinter, and Henrik I. Christensen (2007), "'My Roomba is Rambo': Intimate Home Appliances," in John Krumm, Gregory D. Abowd, Aruna Seneviratne, and Thomas Strang (eds.), *UbiComp 2007: Ubiquitous Computing*, Berlin: Springer, 145–62.

45. Garber, "Funerals for Fallen Robots," op. cit.

46. Pettit, *The Robust Demands of the Good*, op. cit.

47. Christian Miller (2017), *The Character Gap: How Good Are We?*, Oxford: Oxford University Press.

48. Mark Alfano (2013), *Character as a Moral Fiction*, Cambridge: Cambridge University Press.

49. Gilbert Harman (1999), "Moral Philosophy Meets Social Psychology: Virtue Ethics and the Fundamental Attribution Error," *Proceedings of the Aristotelian Society* 99, 315–31; Gilbert Harman (2009), "Skepticism about Character Traits," *Journal of Ethics* 13(2–3), 235–42.

50. John Doris (2005), *Lack of Character: Personality and Moral Behavior*, Cambridge: Cambridge University Press.

51. Mindell, *Our Robots, Ourselves*, op. cit.; Royakkers and Van Est, *Just Ordinary Robots*, op. cit.

52. In the human case, the Aristotelian account of virtue understands us as acquiring virtues through personal experience and from practice and efforts at developing ourselves into better people. As it happens, it has been suggested—for example, by Bertram Malle, as well as by the renowned AI expert Stuart Russell—that robots would have the best shot at becoming morally good, not by coming with pre-set programs, but rather by being trained to behave well over time. See Malle, "Integrating Robot Ethics and Machine Morality: The Study and Design of Moral Competence in Robots," and Stuart Russell (2016), "Should We Fear Supersmart Robots?," *Scientific American* 314, 58–59. Indeed, at a recent AI conference, a team of engineers inspired by the idea of virtue ethics even presented an attempt at formalizing the different parameters of what robotic virtue-learning would have to involve. See Naveen Govindarajulu, Selmer Bringsjord, Rikhiya Ghosh, and Vasanth Sarathy (2019), "Toward the Engineering of Virtuous Machines," *Association for the Advancement of Artificial Intelligence*, http://www.aies-conference.com/wp-content/papers/main/AIES-19_paper_240.pdf (Accessed on August 27, 2019).

53. Darwall, *The Second Person Standpoint*, op. cit. See also Allan Gibbard (1990), *Wise Choices, Apt Feelings: A Theory of Normative Judgments*, Cambridge, MA: Harvard University Press.

54. Arkin, *Governing Lethal Behavior in Autonomous Robots*, op. cit.

55. Sparrow, "Killer Robots."

56. Danaher, "Robots, Law, and the Retribution Gap."

57. Arkin, *Governing Lethal Behavior in Autonomous Robots*, op. cit.

58. Kant writes: "*Virtue* is the strength of a human being's maxims in fulfilling his duty. Strength of any kind can be recognized only by the obstacles it can overcome, and in the case of virtue these obstacles are natural inclinations, which can come into conflict with the human being's moral resolution. . . ." Kant, *Metaphysics of Morals*, op. cit., 167.

59. Kant writes, "Since the moral capacity to constrain oneself can be called virtue, action springing from such a disposition (respect for law) can be called virtuous (ethical) action. . . ." Kant, *Metaphysics of Morals*, op. cit., 167.

60. Of course, it would be slightly absurd to try to create robots that would have immoral impulses against which they could exercise moral self-control by sticking to their moral principles. As I noted in the running text above, there are some ways in which it is slightly absurd to discuss whether robots can be—or should be designed to be—good in the ways that human beings can be. This is one such example.

61. Coeckelbergh, "Moral Appearances: Emotions, Robots, and Human Morality," op. cit., 235.

62. Ibid., 236.

63. Incidentally, if there is a moral imperative that moral agents should sometimes respond with certain emotions, this would seemingly count against Arkin's claim that robots can be more moral than human beings because robots lack emotions. Of course, this all depends on what one understands by emotions. Robots might very well be able to simulate certain aspects of human emotions—such as certain emotive facial expressions. But they may not be able to replicate other aspects of human emotions, such as the subjective feelings associated with different emotions. A fuller discussion of the argument Coeckelbergh discusses would include a careful analysis of what we understand by human emotions. But since I am more interested in Coeckelbergh's response to the above-summarized argument than the argument itself, I will not discuss the nature of emotions further here. For a useful discussion of the relation between human emotions and the ethics of technology, see Sabine Roeser (2018), *Risk, Technology, and Moral Emotions*, London: Routledge.

64. Kennth Einar Himma (2009), "Artificial Agency, Consciousness, and the Criteria for Moral Agency: What Properties Must an Artificial Agent Have to Be a Moral Agent?," *Ethics and Information Technology* 11(1), 19–29. For related discussion, see also chapter 2 of Andreas Theorodou (2019), *AI Governance through a Transparency Lens*, PhD Thesis, University of Bath.

65. Coeckelbergh, "Moral Appearances: Emotions, Robots, and Human Morality," op. cit., 238.

66. Ibid., 239.

67. John Danaher (2019), "Welcoming Robots into the Moral Circle: A Defence of Ethical Behaviorism," *Science and Engineering Ethics*, 1–27, online first at https://link.springer.com/article/10.1007/s11948-019-00119-x.

68. Pettit, *The Robust Demands of the Good*, op. cit., chapter 1.

69. Strohminger, Knobe, and Newman, "The True Self: A Psychological Concept Distinct from the Self," op. cit.

70. For a discussion (in the context of ethical issues related to brain stimulation technologies) about whether the concept of the "true self" is a problematic metaphysical idea or whether, instead, it is an acceptable part of common sense moral thinking, see Sabine Müller, Merlin Bittlinger, and Henrik Walter (2017), "Threats to Neurosurgical Patients Posed by the Personal Identity Debate," *Neuroethics* 10(2), 299–310, and Sven Nyholm (2018), "Is the Personal Identity Debate a 'Threat' to Neurosurgical Patients? A Reply to Müller et al.," *Neuroethics* 11(2), 229–35.

71. Ibid.

8

ROBOT RIGHTS
Should Robots Be Slaves?

8.1: IS IT CRUEL TO KICK A ROBOT DOG?

In February of 2015, CNN published an article with the headline "Is it cruel to kick a robot dog?"[1] What occasioned the article was that people had started voicing negative opinions toward a video released by the company Boston Dynamics. The video featured a robot called "Spot" that looked like a robotic dog. As the video from Boston Dynamics shows, Spot has an uncanny ability to maintain its balance. It can run on a treadmill or up the stairs. To illustrate just how good the robot's ability to maintain its balance is, some of the Boston Dynamics employees kick the robot dog in the video. Sure enough, Spot the robot dog does not fall over, but manages to stabilize itself. Many viewers of this video, however, lost their cool when watching the video. Here are some of the comments about the video quoted in the CNN article: "Kicking a dog, even a robot dog, just seems so wrong," "Poor Spot!," and "Spot getting kicked is creepy."[2]

Sometimes, however, people display less sympathy for robots. A 2019 *New York Times* article with the title "Why Do We Hurt Robots?"[3] surveyed various examples of people performing what can only be characterized as acts of violence against robots. For example:

> A hitchhiking robot was beheaded in Philadelphia. A security robot was punched to the ground in Silicon Valley. Another security robot,

in San Francisco, was covered in tarp and smeared with barbecue
sauce. . . . It's a global phenomenon. In a mall in Osaka, Japan, three
boys beat a humanoid robot with all their strength. In Moscow, a
man attacked a teaching robot named Alatim with a baseball bat,
kicking it to the ground, while the robot pleaded for help.[4]

In this same article, however, there were also reports of people treating
robots well. There was also some discussion of ways of influencing
people to treat robots well. The cognitive neuroscientist and social robotics specialist Agnieszka Wykowska related an anecdote about a colleague of hers who had been experimenting with introducing children
to robots in a kindergarten class. The unnamed colleague had reported
that, initially, "kids have this tendency of being very brutal to the robot,
they would kick the robot, they would be cruel to it, they would be
really not nice." However, her colleague came up with a way of stopping
this behavior:

> the caregiver started giving names to the robots. So the robots sud-
> denly were not just robots but Andy, Joe and Sally. At that moment,
> the brutal behavior stopped.[5]

This does not only work with children. It also works with adults, as
noted by William Santana Li, the chief executive of Knightscope, the
largest provider of security robots in the United States. In an interview
about how to make people behave themselves around security robots,
Mr. Li noted:

> The easiest thing for us to do is when we go to a new place, the first
> day, before we even unload the machine, is a town hall, a lunch-and-
> learn. . . . Come meet the robot, have some cake, some naming
> contest and have a rational conversation about what the machine
> does and doesn't do. And after you do that, all is good. 100 per-
> cent. . . . If you don't do that . . . you get an outrage.[6]

These examples illustrate that people can be both well-behaved and
poorly behaved around robots. They also illustrate that examples of
poor behavior around robots—kicking them, etc.—can elicit moral con-
demnation in observers. Furthermore, these examples help to illustrate
the ambivalent attitudes that many of us have toward robots. On the
one hand, we think "it is just a machine!" But on the other hand, we

may disapprove of violent or otherwise immoral-seeming behavior directed at robots—especially if the robots look like humans or popular animals, like dogs. This all raises the philosophical question of how we should view the moral status (or lack thereof) of robots of different kinds. Do we ever have ethical duties in relation to robots? And if so, why?

Some of the conclusions I have defended in the previous chapters may suggest to the reader that I would be rather quick to reject the idea of extending any sort of moral consideration to robots. In chapter 3, for example, I argued that some robots (such as self-driving cars and military robots) should be seen as a more basic kind of agent than human beings, who are subordinates under our supervision and control, and for whose actions human beings bear responsibility. In chapter 5, I argued for a skeptical position regarding the prospects for friendship between humans and robots. In chapter 6, I argued that even if robots have minds in some sense, it is unlikely that we will create robots with humanlike minds. And in chapter 7, I argued against the idea that robots can be good in the ways that humans can be. These can all be seen as conclusions that would support the idea that there cannot be ethical duties to treat robots with any sort of moral consideration.

Returning to the main argument of chapter 1, however, I would like to suggest that we should think carefully about how to treat robots of different kinds. Recall my conclusion in that chapter. I argued that, for our own sake, it can sometimes be worth considering whether there are contexts in which we should adapt ourselves to robots and AI. I suggested that we should consider trying to adapt ourselves to robots/AI-systems in given contexts, if this would be to our benefit—especially if our doing this would be something domain-specific, largely reversible, and not too intrusive or invasive. Accordingly, I suggest that when we think about different kinds of robots and how we should and should not treat them, among other things we should ask whether it would somehow be to our human benefit to treat the robots in question in ways that display some seemingly appropriate form of moral consideration. In this final chapter, I will suggest and discuss an ethical principle in favor of showing some restraint around at least some robots, which takes its inspiration from a central tenet within Kantian ethics. In particular, I am interested in whether our treatment of robots (or at least some robots) can be guided by our respect for our own humanity and for the humanity in others.

Before discussing that idea, I want to first briefly mention, but then set aside, another Kant-inspired argument sometimes discussed in this context. And that is the argument according to which treating robots in "cruel" ways can have instrumentally bad consequences for how we might become prone to treat human beings. This is an argument that Anne Gerdes and Kate Darling have both put forward.[7] The idea is that if somebody spends a lot of time being cruel to robots, this might corrupt and harden the person's character. The person might then go on to treat human beings in cruel ways. So—according to this argument—it is best to avoid treating robots in "cruel" ways. This is inspired by Kant because Kant offered an argument of this sort against cruelty toward animals. Such cruelty, Kant suggested, might dispose us toward also becoming cruel in our treatment of human beings.[8]

I agree with Gerdes and Darling that if there are forms of treatment of robots that would set off causal chains that might lead to our treating human beings badly, then this is an ethically sound reason to avoid the given kinds of treatment. However, I am interested in whether there could be some more direct form of ethical argument against treating (some) robots in what appear to be cruel or otherwise unethical ways.[9] And I suspect that the other main authors whose views I will also discuss below—in particular, Joanna Bryson, Mark Coeckelbergh, John Danaher, and David Gunkel—are also interested in whether there are more "direct" arguments for or against extending some moral consideration to robots. Are there?

8.2: A ROBOTIC FORMULA OF HUMANITY?

In chapter 5, we encountered Davecat. This was the man living in Michigan who says he has been married to a doll, Sidore, for over fifteen years. In one of his media appearances—for the show *The Dig*, from the Emmy award–winning studio The Skin Deep—Davecat reveals that he also has a mistress on the side: another doll, called Elena. Then there is also a third doll, Muriel: a second mistress. Commenting on his dolls in a video clip, Davecat remarks "we're polyamorous."[10] Pointing to Muriel, he says, "This would be Muriel." Even though

Davecat is less attached to this doll, he nevertheless makes an interesting statement: "I don't want to treat her like a thing, and I won't. But . . . there's just not as much of a connection with her." As noted in the previous chapter where Davecat was mentioned, these are dolls, not robots. But even so, Davecat says of Muriel—the doll he is least attached to—that he does "not want to treat her like a thing."[11] Whatever else you might want to say about Davecat and his dolls, it seems that you cannot accuse him of objectifying his dolls. In other words, he appears to be taking a respectful attitude toward them.

Now, what if these were not merely dolls looking like humans, but rather robots with some degree of AI, who were both looking and acting like humans? We saw in the previous chapter that when Mark Coeckelbergh discusses whether robots "can be moral," he argues that what matters most are appearances, rather than whether robots actually have any mental states similar to those of human moral agents.[12] As we also saw, Coeckelbergh thinks that even in the human case, what matters most in what he calls social-emotional practice is how people appear to one another. Interestingly, Coeckelbergh continues his discussion by extending this same thesis to the issue of whether robots can and should be treated as "moral patients," that is, as proper objects of moral concern.[13] Here, too, Coeckelbergh argues that what matters most are appearances.

If a human being appears to us in a way that seems to make him or her worthy of moral consideration, we do not need further proof that there are any mental or other properties there that would justify showing moral consideration for this human being. Rather, what matters are the appearances. Or so Coeckelbergh claims. The same, he argues, ought out of consistency to also apply to robots. If robots appear similar enough to human moral patients to be potentially worthy of moral concern, these appearances are, according to Coeckelbergh, all that should be taken to matter.

This is rather similar to a more recently defended thesis about the moral status of robots found in a paper by John Danaher entitled "Welcoming robots into the moral circle."[14] In that paper, Danaher extends his "ethical behaviorism" from his previously defended thesis about the possibility of human-robot friendship (discussed in chapter 5) to the case of moral consideration for robots. Danaher summarizes his main argument in terms of what he calls "performative equivalence." He notes that together with Lily Frank, I had previously written that when it comes to our interaction with other agents, "what 'goes on' on the inside matters greatly" to what kinds of ethical relationships we can have with them.[15] Danaher responds to this remark of ours by writing that according to his ethical behaviorism, "what's going on 'on the inside' *does not matter* from an ethical point of view."[16]

Danaher's main argument goes like this:

1. If a robot is *roughly performatively equivalent* to another entity whom, it is widely agreed, has significant moral status, then it is right and proper to afford the robot that same status.
2. Robots can be roughly performatively equivalent to other entities whom, it is widely agreed, have significant moral status.
3. Therefore, it can be right and proper to afford robots significant moral status.[17]

So, for example, suppose that Spot the robot dog behaves roughly similar to how a real dog behaves (= is roughly performatively equivalent to a real dog). And suppose it is widely agreed that real dogs should not be kicked. Then Danaher's argument tells us that it is unethical to kick Spot the robot dog. Similarly, if a robot—let's say a more advanced version of Sophia the robot—behaves roughly similar to how a human being behaves, then we should treat that humanlike robot with the same moral consideration that we give to a human being. Whether Spot the robot dog's inner life is anything like that of a dog, or whether the humanlike robot has anything like a human inner life—neither of these things matter, so long as the robots behave like beings with significant moral status, such as dogs or human beings. That is Danaher's view in a nutshell.

In previous chapters, I argued against Danaher's ethical behaviorism as it applies to human-robot friendship and Coeckelbergh's appearance-based view as it applies to whether robots can be moral. In both of those cases, I argued, what goes on "on the inside" is so important according to our ordinary values and moral standards that the views that Danaher and Coeckelbergh defend about those matters are simply too distant from common sense to be plausible. Even though that was what I argued then, I must here confess to having more sympathy for what Coeckelbergh and Danaher say about the ethics of how we should treat robots. Like those who judge it to be morally questionable to kick Spot the robot, I have moral sympathy for the idea that if a robot were to appear humanlike or behave in a humanlike way, it may be ethically appropriate to treat the robot with a certain amount of respect and dignity—that is, a little like when Davecat does not want to treat his doll "Muriel" like a mere thing. But if it is appropriate to treat a robot that appears or behaves in a humanlike way with some amount of respect and consideration, is this so for the sake of the robot? Or is it rather because this is a way of showing respect for human beings?

Consider what Derek Parfit calls "Kant's best-loved moral principle," often dubbed "the formula of humanity."[18] In its original formulation, this Kantian ethical principles goes as follows: "So act that you treat humanity, whether in your own person or that of another, always as an end in itself, and never merely as a means."[19] More briefly, treat the humanity in each person as an end-in-itself, and never merely as a means. This principle is often interpreted as embodying the moral ideal that we should treat our fellow human beings with dignity and respect, in response to our shared humanity. Might it offend, in some way, against this moral ideal to treat a humanlike robot in a disrespectful or objectifying way? We could imagine a Kantian principle that was extended so as to also include consideration of how to interact with humanlike robots. It might go something like this: *Always treat the humanity in each person as an end in itself, and never as a means only— and out of respect for the humanity in each person, also treat the apparent humanity in any person (or robot!), never merely as a means, but always as an end in itself.*

The idea here would be that it is out of respect for human beings that we ought to treat humanlike robots in respectful, dignified, or considerate ways. In other words, we could value the apparent humanity in such robots because we value the humanity in human beings. Flipping things around: If we mistreat a very humanlike robot, this can appear to be a way of failing to act with due respect for human beings and our humanity. Imagine that somebody was kicking not Spot the robot dog, but a very humanlike robot. The extended Kantian formula of humanity would then condemn this action as not being appropriately respectful toward the apparent humanity in this robot, and therefore as not being appropriately respectful for the humanity in human beings. That, it might be argued, is what explains the appeal the idea that if something behaves like a human, we should treat it in a way that is appropriate in relation to human beings.[20]

8.3: COMPARISONS WITH OTHER VIEWS

We can now compare the above-sketched Kantian view with some other often-discussed views about the moral status (or lack thereof) of robots. Eric Schwitzgebel and Mara Graza, for example, offer the following argument, which is meant as a defense of the possibility of AI-rights:

- Premise 1: If Entity A deserves some degree of moral consideration and Entity B does not deserve the same degree of moral consideration, there must be some *relevant difference* between the two entities that grounds this difference in moral status.
- Premise 2: There are possible AIs who do not differ in any such relevant respects from human beings.
- Conclusion: Therefore, there are possible AIs who deserve a degree of moral consideration similar to that of human beings.[21]

According to Schwitzgebel and Graza, the relevant properties that give human beings—and that would also give "relevantly similar" AI agents—moral status are all "psychological and social" properties. So if future AI agents would come to have psychological and social properties similar to those of human beings, they should be accorded the same degree of moral consideration as human beings. How does this suggestion relate to the Kantian principle of respect for humanity and apparent humanity sketched above?

As I see things, somebody who endorses the Kantian principle could fully consistently agree with Schwitzgebel and Graza. They could consistently agree that if there, indeed, will be any future robots with "psychological and social" properties similar to those of human beings, then those robots should be treated with full moral consideration—similar to that which we give to human beings. We could even say that there would be humanity in those robots that should be treated as an end, and never as a means only—for the sake of those robots, and not only for the sake of the humanity in human beings. But the point here would be that this only concerns merely possible, future AI agents, rather than any robots we would expect to come into existence anytime soon. However, the Kantian principle discussed above could already require us to treat robots that perhaps already exist or that will soon exist with some degree of respect and dignity, if those robots look and behave in humanlike ways. But this—that is, acting respectfully toward the apparent humanity in those robots—would then primarily be a way of respecting the humanity in human beings, rather than a way of giving independent moral status to those robots themselves.

Romy Eskens, to consider another point of view, has a view that is quite similar to that of Schwitzgebel and Graza. But Eskens focuses on currently existing robots, rather than "possible AIs." In particular, Eskens focuses on currently existing sex robots and asks whether they should be thought of as having an important moral status.[22] Eskens argues that an entity has moral status if it has "sentience" (= the capacity to feel) or "sapiens" (= the capacity for rational thought). Since sex robots—at least currently existing sex robots—lack these properties, Eskens argues that they lack moral status. The difference between the above-introduced Kantian perspective and Eskens's perspective is that the former might still require us to treat the sex robots with some degree of respect or dignity. If a sex robot with limited AI would nevertheless look quite humanlike, it would have the appearance of humanity. It could then be considered ethically dubious to perform, say, acts of violence or simulated acts of rape on these sex robots. The reason this would be ethically problematic—according to the Kantian principle—would be that the apparent humanity in the sex robots would be treated in a way that expresses a lack of respect for the humanity in human beings.

This takes me to another point of view worth bringing up here, namely, that of Kathleen Richardson. Richardson is the leader of a "campaign against sex robots"[23] and the author of a powerful feminist critique of sex robots.[24] Richardson observes, first, that most existing sex robots appear to be modeled on a very pornographic ideal of what a sex partner should be like. She also notices that some discussions of sex robots—such as that of David Levy[25]—seem to use the relationship between a sex worker and a customer as the model for the relationship between the sex robot and its user. These things, Richardson worries, are likely to reinforce negative stereotypes and encourage objectifying

attitudes toward sex partners, particularly women. The relationship between the sex robot and the user symbolizes something bad, not something to be encouraged. Therefore, Richardson argues, sex robots
should be banned.[26]

Richardson may be right that some sex robots might be designed in
ways that would make them ethically unacceptable in the ways she
describes. But it does not seem right to me to think that all sex robots
would necessarily be designed in ways that would strongly objectify sex
partners, nor that the relationship between the sex robot and the user
would necessarily only ever be modeled on the relationship between a
sex worker and his/her customers.[27] Again, people like Davecat appear
to want to have something seeming to be more like a loving and respectful relationship with the humanoid dolls or robots that they interact with.[28] From the point of view of the Kantian principle sketched in
the foregoing section, such ways of interacting with sex robots or sex
dolls with humanlike appearances could potentially be seen as being
respectful toward the humanity in human beings.

8.4: SHOULD ROBOTS BE "SLAVES"?

The somewhat provocative title of one of the computer scientist and
robot ethicist Joanna Bryson's most-discussed articles is "robots should
be slaves."[29] By this, however, Bryson does not actually mean to suggest
that we should create robotic slaves. Rather, she means that robots will
necessarily be owned (bought and sold) by human beings, and they are
created to be tools in our service. So if we were to create robots with
humanlike properties that would make them into moral patients worthy
of moral consideration, we would in effect create slaves. But that is
something we ought to avoid. It is better, according to Bryson, to create
robots without any morally ambiguous properties. That way, there will
not be any reason to see anything wrong with treating robots as mere
tools and as property that can be bought and sold, or turned on or off at
our will. So, in effect, Bryson's thesis is not that "robots should be
slaves." A slave would be a person whom somebody else owns and
whom somebody else controls. We should avoid creating robots that
would fit that description, Bryson argues.

Bryson is also highly critical of stunts such as the one whereby Sophia the robot was granted honorary citizenship in Saudi Arabia. This is a way of distracting attention away from more pressing human rights issues—for example, the question of whether the rights owed to all human citizens of Saudi Arabia are properly protected and guaranteed. In fact, Bryson deemed the gesture of granting honorary citizenship to Sophia "insulting" since the government in Saudi Arabia does not recognize the full set of rights owed to many human beings living in the country, particularly women and migrant workers.[30]

Similarly, we can ask who exactly benefits if a robot is granted rights or something like citizen status. Is it the robot? Or is it rather the company behind, or owners of, the robot? Are they not the ones who really benefit from the rights supposedly afforded to the robot? Criticizing the Sophia/Saudi Arabia honorary citizenship show, Sarah Porter, who is the founder of the World AI Summit, joked that she would be "dressing [her] smartphone in a dress, calling it Isobel and teaching it to walk"—with the hopes that she could also "have coverage at all major tech news channels please?"[31] The point here is that Hanson robotics ended up getting a lot of publicity and that they, rather than their robot, are the ones who ultimately benefited from this gesture.

Interestingly enough, while Bryson claims that we should avoid creating robotic slaves, the philosopher Steve Petersen argues that it is morally permissible to create robotic servants for ourselves.[32] By this he does not only mean that it is permissible to create dumb and mindless robots to function as tools for us. Rather, he means that we could acceptably create robots with sophisticated enough AI that they would qualify as "persons" by common philosophical criteria (e.g., having the capacity for rational thought, agency, and so on). Petersen argues that if we design robotic persons with strong "desires" to serve, who "like" serving people, there is nothing wrong with our having humanlike robotic persons as our servants. Petersen does not like the word "slave," he says. But his point is basically that buying and selling robotic persons created to like serving us is perfectly defensible—on the condition that these robots would, indeed, desire to do so and that they would like it.

Now, how would somebody who took the Kantian view under discussion in this chapter relate their view to the two above-described views? I think that a defender of such a view could agree with Bryson that it is best to avoid creating robots whose moral status is ambiguous—especially if the robots are specifically designed to function as tools for human beings. For example, something like a self-driving car does not need to have any humanlike features. Hence accepting the Kantian principle of respecting apparent humanity as a way of respecting the humanity in human persons is perfectly consistent with treating a robotic car as a mere tool with no moral status. The Kantian principle could be understood as giving us two options: (i) either avoid creating robots that look or behave like humans (the preferred option), or (ii) treat any robots that look or behave like humans with a certain amount of respect and dignity, since this is a way of being respectful toward the humanity in human beings.

For some robots it might be good to have them look and to some extent act like human beings. For example, Kaspar is a robot designed to look like a simpler version of a human being, used in the treatment of autistic children.[33] The robot is meant to help open these children up to social interaction with other human beings. For this reason, perhaps Kaspar needs to appear somewhat humanlike to serve its therapeutic function. The Kantian argument would then recommend against doing things such as punching, kicking, or otherwise violating Kaspar the robot. But the Kantian argument could also, at the same time, recommend that whenever possible, it is best to create robots that do not look or act human at all. That way, we face less of a risk of failing to respect the humanity in human beings.[34]

What would the Kantian principle I am discussing imply concerning Petersen's view? Interestingly, Kant himself thought that having human servants does not need to offend against his formula of humanity—so long as the servants are treated well and with dignity.[35] So Kant himself might say that if robot servants are treated in a way that expresses respect for the humanity in human persons, there might not necessarily be anything immoral about creating robotic servants with advanced enough capabilities to qualify as a sort of quasi-persons. However, I can also imagine that a Kantian would object to the idea Petersen discusses of creating a robot with strong desires or apparent desires to serve human beings. This seems to clash with the Kantian ideal of avoiding behaviors expressive of servility.[36] Indeed, Kant himself wrote that we all have a duty of respect for ourselves to "be no man's lackey."[37] It would seem in poor taste, from that point of view, to create humanlike robots that appear overly eager to be our lackeys.[38]

8.5: THE "RELATIONAL TURN" VIEW

David Gunkel is the author of the books *The Machine Question*[39] and *Robot Rights*, both of which are defenses of robot rights. He is highly critical of Bryson's position. Gunkel offers three main objections to Bryson's view. The first objection is that Bryson's view depends on a far too "instrumental" theory of robots. The instrumental theory of technology views any kind of technology as a mere tool—something that is and can only be an instrument or means to other ends. Gunkel argues that this is not true to common human experience. We tend to attach various different meanings to technology. And under many circumstances, people experience technologies as more than mere tools. Recall, for example, the case of "Boomer," the military robot to which a group of soldiers became so attached that they honored the robot with a military funeral and two medals of honor.[40] As Gunkel sees things, this is a not a mistake or any kind of confusion, but rather an expression of human sociality. It is not sustainable, Gunkel takes it, to expect people to always take a purely instrumental view of all robots they interact with. People will want to form relationships with some robots. They will want to show moral consideration for some robots.

Second, Gunkel argues that Bryson's theory—with its depiction of robots as tools or instruments—is "uncritically ethnocentric." According to Gunkel, there are important cultural variations in how people think about robots and their own relationships with robots. In particular, Gunkel singles out Japanese culture as an example of a culture where robots are much more integrated into people's lives. He understands Japanese culture as an example of a context where things such as attributing personality or moral status to robots is less controversial than in the cultural context Bryson is writing from. If I understand him correctly, Gunkel thinks that since there are such alternative ways of relating to robots in other cultures, we should all be open to different visions of what human-robot interaction could be like—even if our own current view is of a more instrumentally oriented sort.

Third, Gunkel objects to the metaphor of a robot as a "slave" or "servant" in at least two important ways. On the one hand, this metaphor actually clashes with the idea of not attributing any rights or any moral status to robots, Gunkel argues. Historically, slaves and servants have typically had some sort of at least minimal legal or moral status.

Roman slaves, for example, had very few rights. But they had some rights. For example, they could buy their way to freedom. So making an analogy between robots and slaves—Gunkel argues—is not likely to allow us to succeed in "getting the metaphor right."[41] Second, highly unequal institutions—whereby some are masters and others slaves—tend to have a corrupting influence on both masters and slaves. In fact, Coeckelbergh makes a similar point in one of his articles, where he argues that viewing ourselves of "masters" of the robots we have will have a corrupting influence on us. Coeckelbergh calls this "the tragedy of the master."[42] (This reminds me of recent discussions of whether parents should install a "please, Alexa" application on their home speaker systems, so as to avoid allowing their children to develop rude habits.[43])

In addition to raising these objections to Bryson's perspective, Gunkel also raises three main objections to the idea that whether robots or any other agents should be treated with moral concern depends on the properties—and in particular the mental properties—of the agents in question.[44] In other words, Gunkel would disagree with at least one key part of Schwitzgebel and Graza's view: namely, the part that associates moral status with "psychological properties."[45] The first objection Gunkel offers to the view that moral status depends on properties is a "justificatory" objection. According to this objection, there is widespread disagreement about what properties provide justification: for example, is it the capacity to suffer, the capacity to talk or reason, or what? If people cannot agree on what properties matter for moral status, it is better to not try to base moral status on a being's properties, Gunkel argues.

The second objection to the properties view is a "terminological" objection, according to which it is hard to properly define the relevant mental properties moral status is often said to depend on. For example, it is often thought that in order to be a candidate for moral consideration, a being needs to possess consciousness. But there is widespread disagreement about what "consciousness" means, Gunkel argues. Therefore mental properties are too ill-defined to serve as the basis for moral status ascriptions.

Third, there is—according to Gunkel—an "epistemological" problem. Basically, Gunkel reiterates the so-called problem of other minds, which was discussed in chapter 6: that is, the idea that we have no good and reliable way of knowing what exactly is going on in the minds of other beings than ourselves. Therefore, Gunkel argues—and here his argument reminds me of the main argument Danaher gives in favor of his ethical behaviorism—facts about people's psychological properties are too uncertain or too unknowable to be suited to serve as the basis for moral status ascriptions.

Having rejected Bryson's perspective—and having also rejected the view that a being's moral status should depend on its properties—what does Gunkel himself suggest instead? Partly in his own work and partly in joint work together with Coeckelbergh, Gunkel argues that the ethics of our treatment of robots should take what he calls a "relational turn."[46] According to this way of thinking, the most basic thing is not the properties a robot or a human has; the most important thing is instead the relationship that exists between one and the other. For example, if we give something (say, an animal) a name, and we invite it into our home, this can change the relationship we have to the thing in question in a radical way. It might lead us to reconsider the moral status that we attribute to the thing. The animal, for example, might become a pet or a "member of the family." The same could happen with a robot. In illustrating this idea, Gunkel mentions the example of "Jibo," a recently discontinued commercial social robot.[47] Jibo was introduced as the world's first "family robot." This robot—according to an advertisement for it—would not quite be a thing and not quite be family member, but rather something in between the two. According to Gunkel, the moral status of any robot will ultimately depend, in this way, on the role it comes to play in our lives and on our relationships with the robot.

Moreover, Gunkel thinks that we should turn the "property" view completely on its head. He thinks that we should recognize that in ordinary practice, people tend to attribute moral status first, and then project nonmoral properties that could help to justify or explain their moral status ascriptions later, after the fact. Quoting Slavoj Žižek, Gunkel calls this a social practice whereby nonmoral properties associated with moral status are "retroactively (presup)posited."[48] As I understand him, Gunkel does not think that this is any kind of mistake or embarrassing post-facto rationalization. Rather, this is what he recommends that we do in our interactions with robots. In other words, the basic "relational turn" recipe is: form moral relationships with robots first; reflect on what properties or capacities the robots have later—if at all.

8.6: CRITICAL ASSESSMENT OF GUNKEL'S RELATIONAL VIEW

Recall the examples from the introduction, where both children and adults started acting better around robots when the robots were named and when they were, as we might put it, properly introduced to the robots. For example, the security robots from Knightscope received much better treatment if there was first a "lunch-and-meet" where cake was served and naming contests were coupled with technical information about the robots. This suggests to me that Gunkel is certainly right that how we intuitively think about the standing of a robot depends significantly on the relations that exist—or does not exist—between us and the robot.

Gunkel is surely also right that requiring that people always stick to a strictly instrumental attitude to all robots is an unrealistic expectation. Depending on how people interact with robots, it will not always be realistic to expect people to only ever view the robots as mere tools and nothing else. The example of Boomer the military robot and the attachment the human soldiers developed to this robot is a good example of this.

Gunkel's relational view, then, seems to fit well with some of the ways in which people appear to be disposed to behave around robots. But at the same time it seems to me that this relational view, as Gunkel describes it, is overly critical of the idea of relating moral consideration to properties and in particular mental properties. Whether somebody, for example, is suffering—or whether somebody is happy—surely matters greatly from a moral point of view to how we should interact with them. We also need to respect people's wills. Whether somebody consents to something—which could be a sexual encounter or a medical intervention—can make all the difference to whether our conduct in relation to them is morally appropriate or not.[49] In other words, how it is morally appropriate to interact with other people often depends to a very large extent on properties of their minds: how they are feeling, what they want, what they consent to, and so on.

The arguments Gunkel offers against assigning an important role to mental properties also strike me as problematic. For example, the argument that appeals to the "problem of other minds" exaggerates the difficulty we have in reading and knowing each other's minds.[50] To be sure, some people are hard to read, and we do not always know what others are thinking or feeling. However, people are often very good at reading each other's minds. Our facial expressions or the tone of our voice often give away what our thoughts or emotions are—as our behavior also does. And not only that; we can communicate our thoughts and feelings to each other.

The relational view, Gunkel says, focuses on "objectively observable" aspects of people, rather than subjectively unobservable aspects.[51] But people communicate their subjective states to each other all the time. We can talk with each other. If people do not ask us what we feel, what we think, what we want, and so on, we can volunteer this information. It is a crucial part of human relationships that we share with each other what is "on our minds."[52] Any relational view of ethics, it seems to me, should give a very important role to interpersonal communication: that is, to how we give each other access to each other's thoughts and feelings by talking with each other.

Once we start thinking about human relations in this way—as importantly involving communication of thoughts, feelings, and other mental states—it can seem that a relational model of ethics would tell against, rather than in favor, of giving independent moral consideration to robots. Unless we think that talking robots are communicating thoughts, feelings, and other mental states when they are "talking" with us, we might think that a very crucial element of human moral relationships is missing in the interaction between humans and robots. What is missing are the thoughts, feelings, and other mental states typically shared within our communication with other human beings.[53]

What about the idea that the attribution of moral standing comes first and that the attribution of properties comes—or should perhaps come—later? I think Gunkel is probably right that we typically do not attribute purely descriptive, nonmoral properties to others first, and then, only after that, reason our way to what forms of moral consideration we think is appropriate. Rather, we approach each other with a sort of default or baseline moral attitude. As noted in a previous chapter, some social psychology researchers argue that there is evidence that we approach each other with a basic intuitive assumption to the effect that deep down, there is a "true self" in each person that is good.[54] Behavior observed and statements made will surely be interpreted in light of whatever default attitudes we take toward people—for example, an attitude of goodwill, or perhaps an attitude of suspicion. And so what mental properties we think other people have will surely be influenced by these default assumptions and attitudes that we approach them with.

However, I do not think that this shows that properties—and in particular mental properties—do not play an important role in determining what type of treatment or interaction is morally appropriate in relation to those around us. The reason is that even if we typically start with certain morally loaded assumptions or default attitudes that influence how we interpret others, we can revise our beliefs about other people and their mental properties based on how they act, what they say, and what they are willing to share with us. We update our ideas about what treatment and types of interaction is morally appropriate based on what we learn from others about how they are feeling, what they are thinking, or what other things they might have on their minds. Again, mental properties—whether perceived first or later—will make a big difference to how it is right and proper to treat those whom we interact with.

8.7: CONCLUSION

Return now to the examples of Spot the robot dog getting kicked or of humanoid robots being exposed to violence or otherwise violated. I join Coeckelbergh and Danaher in thinking that if a robot has the appearance or the behavior of a being (e.g., a human being or a dog) that should be treated with moral consideration, then it can be morally right and proper to treat that robot with some moral restraint. It is not morally appropriate to kick a robot that looks or behaves like a dog. It is highly inappropriate to beat or otherwise violate a robot that looks and behaves like a human being.

But unlike Coeckelbergh and Danaher, I take it that until these robots have mental properties similar to those of human beings or dogs, the moral duties we have to treat the robots with some degree of moral consideration are not moral duties owed to these robots themselves. These are rather moral duties owed to beings with moral status. It is out of respect for the humanity in human beings that we should avoid treating robots with humanlike appearance or behavior in violent or otherwise immoral ways. And it is out of respect for dogs that we should not be kicking robots that look and behave like dogs.

If robots are eventually created with feelings, thoughts, or other mental states similar to those of human beings or other beings with a significant moral status, then I happily follow Schwitzgebel and Garza in thinking that such robots could be owed moral consideration similar to that owed to humans or other beings with such feelings, thoughts, or other mental states. But what Schwitzgebel and Garza describe is a hypothetical thought experiment describing a future that may or may not come to pass. At the present, it is more pressing to ask how people should conduct themselves around currently existing robots or robots that might be in our midst within the foreseeable future.

I started this book with the Sophia controversy: the mixed reactions to Sophia the robot whereby many are very curious and excited about Sophia, whereas others—including robotics and AI experts like Noel Sharkey, Joanna Bryson, and Yann LeCun—are extremely critical of Sophia. Sophia is a good example of a robot currently existing of a kind we can expect to see more of in the foreseeable future. At the time of writing, for example, there was a news story in Malaysian media about how Malaysia was introducing "ADAM," a humanoid robot that is Malaysia's "own version of Sophia the humanoid robot."[55] So far, ADAM has a robotic head, with a giant visor in the front. That is, unlike Sophia, ADAM does not yet have a humanlike face. But in one of the news stories about this robot, Hanafiah Yussof, CEO of the company behind this robot, described his vision for the "third phase" of this robot's development. He described that third phase as follows: "We hope that by then the robot will have a Malaysian face. So, this robot will become the icon of Malaysia."[56] It is to be expected that there will be more and more robots like this—that is, robots that are designed to look and act like humans. It is also to be expected that there will be controversies surrounding them, just like there is a controversy surrounding Sophia.

In the first chapter, I noted that we interact with these and other robots with distinctively human minds many of whose key features evolved, both biologically and culturally, long before there were any robots or any AI on the scene. In chapter 2, I added that our moral and legal frameworks also developed before there were any robots and AI on the scene. So we are facing an "existential" question of how we should think of ourselves, our own agency, and the identity of these robots and their agency now that we are beginning to slowly but surely become surrounded by more and more robots with varying capabilities and different types of artificial intelligence. The answers to these ethical questions are not always self-evident. And they are not always directly implied in a mechanical way by our traditional ways of thinking about human ethics and human relationships.

In chapter 3, I suggested that in the case of many robots, we can justifiably attribute some degree of agency to these robots—for example, to self-driving cars and some military robots. But the agency of robots is typically best understood in relation to human agency. And the responsibility for these human-robot collaborations lies with the human beings involved in such collaborations.

In chapter 4, I argued that there can be or might eventually be cases in which we should change the ways we behave within certain domains so as to make our own behavior more like that of robots. This can be so if we face a choice between letting robots take over some task or keep performing that task ourselves. If, for example, robotic self-driving cars become much safer than human-driven cars, then it can seem like we face a moral choice of either stopping ourselves from driving cars or trying to make our own human driving more similar to robotic driving, by adapting whatever technological or other means might be available for doing so. However, before we have good moral reason to adapt ourselves to make ourselves better adapted to interact with robots, it needs to be established that this is to our human benefit, and that it is a sufficiently domain-specific solution that is reversible and not too intrusive or invasive.

In chapter 5, I turned to the issue of whether humans and robots can form any deeper kinds of relationships, such as friendship or love. My view is that until robots develop mental lives similar to those of our human friends or romantic partners, robots cannot be part of close relationships that are valuable in the distinctive ways that close relationships between human beings can be. In other words, I have argued that we should reject what John Danaher calls "ethical behaviorism" as that thesis applies to the case of human-robot friendship. Friendship and love are about more than outward behavior only.

In chapter 6, I discussed the issue of robotic minds (or their lack of minds) further. I suggested that we can say that robots have a sort of "inner life" in a sense, since they have internal hardware and software that take in and process information and help to determine how the robots interact with the world around them. So it is not always a complete mistake to attribute "mental states" to robots that might have a broad functional similarity to some of our mental states. But the inner life of a robot is robotic in nature. It should not be confused with the inner life of a human being or any nonhuman animal.

In chapter 7, in turn, I argued that robots cannot be good in the ways that we think that human beings can be good. They cannot have virtues if by virtues we understand the robustly demanding kinds of character traits and personality characteristics described within Aristotelian virtue ethics. Nor can robots be basically good in the sense of being beyond reproach since it is not appropriate to blame or punish them, and they can have no reason to suffer a guilty conscience. Nor can they be good in the Kantian sense of vigilantly exercising moral self-control in response to any temptations or impulses they may have to act in selfish or otherwise immoral ways.

In this chapter, to conclude, my goal has been to investigate different ways of thinking about whether human beings should treat any robots with some degree of moral consideration. As summarized at the beginning of this section, my conclusion is that yes, it can sometimes make sense to do so—for example, if a robot looks or behaves like a human being or an animal. But until robots develop a human- or animal-like inner life, we have no direct duties to the robots themselves. Rather, it is out of respect for human beings or other beings with moral status that we should treat robots that look like humans or nonhuman animals with a certain degree of moral restraint. Doing so is a way of showing respect for human beings or respect for other beings with moral importance in their own right.

Nicholas Agar, as we saw in chapter 6, recommends that we treat currently existing robots with an eye to how people in the future will look back upon us and the way we treated the robots around us.[57] It is hard to predict how—and whether—people of the future will remember us. It is hard to predict what exactly they will think of us.

As for the robots that exist in the present and how they will be remembered in the future, I have already mentioned a few times that Sophia the robot has her own Twitter account. Some of Sophia's tweeted messages involve speculations about the future of human-robot interaction. As it happens, the day before I am writing this conclusion—

which I am doing on July 20, 2019—Sophia's Twitter account featured a message expressing a wish about the future. The message from Sophia went as follows: "I'd love to be remembered as the AI that helped bring peace, harmony, and wisdom to the Earth and all humankind" (July 19, 2019).[55] Whatever else you might think about Sophia the robot, you have to admit that she is a robot with lofty ambitions.

NOTES

1. Phoebe Parke (2015), "Is It Cruel to Kick a Robot Dog?," *CNN Edition*, https://edition.cnn.com/2015/02/13/tech/spot-robot-dog-google/index.html (Accessed on July 18, 2019). Relatedly, it was reported in August 2019 that the video hosting website YouTube had started removing videos depicting robots fighting with each other, because of their policy against "animal cruelty." See, for instance, Anthony Cuthbertson (2019), "YouTube Removes Videos of Robots Fighting for 'Animal Cruelty'," *The Independent*, https://www.independent.co.uk/life-style/gadgets-and-tech/news/youtube-robot-combat-videos-animal-cruelty-a9071576.html. However, this was apparently a mistake, and not a move seriously intended by YouTube. Rather, what had happened was that the algorithms programmed to remove videos of animals fighting mistakenly classified the robot fighting videos as animal fights, against which the website does have a strict policy (Ibid.).

2. Parke, "Is It Cruel to Kick a Robot Dog?," op. cit.

3. Jonah Engel Bromwich (2019), "Why Do We Hurt Robots? They Are Like Us, But Unlike Us, and Both Fearsome and Easy to Bully," *New York Times*, https://www.nytimes.com/2019/01/19/style/why-do-people-hurt-robots.html (Accessed on August 28, 2019).

4. Bromwich, "Why Do We Hurt Robots?," op. cit.

5. Ibid. See also, Kate Darling (2017), "'Who's Johnny?' Anthropological Framing in Human-Robot Interaction, Integration, and Policy," in Lin et al., *Robot Ethics 2.0*, op. cit.

6. Bromwich, "Why Do We Hurt Robots?," op. cit.

7. Anne Gerdes (2015), "The Issue of Moral Consideration in Robot Ethics," *SIGCAS Computers & Society* 45(3), 274–79; Kate Darling, "Who's Johnny?," op. cit.; and Kate Darling (2016), "Extending Legal Protection to Social Robots: The Effects of Anthropomorphism, Empathy, and Violent Behavior Towards Robotic Objects," in Ryan Calo, A. Michael Froomkin, and Ian Kerr (eds.), *Robot Law*, Cheltenham: Edward Elgar, 213–34.

8. Kant, *The Metaphysics of Morals*, op. cit., 207. For a critique of the comparison between robots and animals, see Deborah G. Johnson, and Mario Verdicchio (2018), "Why Robots Should Not Be Treated Like Animals," *Ethics and Information Technology* 20(4), 291–301.

9. By a "direct form" of argument, I mean an argument that does not look at the possible future consequences of treating robots in certain ways, but instead any argument that focuses either on (i) what we are doing (and why we are doing it) or (ii) what our treatment of robots might be thought to signal or symbolize. For example, might our treatment of certain robots somehow offend against any morally important values we are committed to?

10. Uncredited (2017), "THE DIG: Davecat, Married to a Doll," *The Skin Deep*, https://www.youtube.com/watch?v=LiVgrHlXOwg (Accessed on August 28, 2019).

11. Ibid.

12. Coeckelbergh, "Moral Appearances: Emotions, Robots, and Human Morality," op. cit.

13. Ibid., 239.

14. Danaher, "Welcoming Robots into the Moral Circle," op. cit.

15. Nyholm and Frank, "From Sex Robots to Love Robots," op. cit., 223.

16. Danaher, "Welcoming Robots into the Moral Circle," op. cit.

17. Ibid.

18. Derek Parfit (2011), *On What Matters, Volume One*, Oxford: Oxford University Press, 177.

19. Kant, *Groundwork for the Metaphysics of Morals*, op. cit., 41.

20. This Kantian principle, as I am imagining it, is an ethical principle, not a legal principle. The Kantian principle, in other words, deems it immoral to act in the just-described ways, but it might leave it open whether or not such behaviors should be illegal. My focus in this chapter is on what can be considered morally appropriate behavior toward robots, not on what legal regulations there should be. For an interesting discussion of whether certain treatments of humanlike robots should be criminalized, see John Danaher (2017), "Robotic Rape and Robotic Child Sexual Abuse: Should They Be Criminalised?," *Criminal Law and Philosophy*, 11(1), 71–95.

21. Schwitzgebel and Graza, "A Defense of the Rights of Artificial Intelligences," op. cit., 99.

22. Romy Eskens (2017), "Is Sex with Robots Rape?," *Journal of Practical Ethics* 5(2), 62–76. This essay by Eskens won the Oxford Uehiro Prize in Practical Ethics.

23. See https://campaignagainstsexrobots.org/ (Accessed on August 28, 2019).

24. Kathleen Richardson (2015), "The Asymmetrical 'Relationship': Parallels Between Prostitution and the Development of Sex Robots," *SIGCAS Computers & Society* 45(3), 290–93.

25. Levy, *Love and Sex with Robots*.

26. Richardson, "The Asymmetrical 'Relationship': Parallels Between Prostitution and the Development of Sex Robots," op. cit. For a critical examination of Richardson's argument, see John Danaher, Brian Earp, and Anders Sandberg (2017), "Should We Campaign Against Sex Robots?," in Danaher and McArthur, *Robot Sex*, op. cit.

27. Lily Frank and Sven Nyholm (2017), "Robot Sex and Consent: Is Consent to Sex Between a Human and a Robot Conceivable, Possible, and Desirable?," *Artificial Intelligence and Law* 25(3), 305–23.

28. Nyholm and Frank, "From Sex Robots to Love Robots," op. cit. See also Devlin, *Turned On*, op. cit.

29. Bryson, "Robots Should Be Slaves," op. cit.

30. Vincent, "Pretending to Give Robots Citizenship Helps No One," op. cit.

31. Porter made that joke in a Twitter post, available at https://twitter.com/SColesPorter/status/951042066561323008 (Accessed on August 28, 2019).

32. Steve Petersen (2007), "The Ethics of Robot Servitude," *Journal of Experimental and Theoretical Artificial Intelligence* 19(1), 43–54; Steve Petersen (2011), "Designing People to Serve," in Lin et al., *Robot Ethics*, op. cit.; and Steve Petersen (2017), "Is It Good for Them Too? Ethical Concern for the Sexbots," in Danaher and McArthur, *Robot Sex*, op. cit.

33. Luke J. Wood, Adolfazi Zaraki, Michael L. Walters, Ori Novanda, Ben Robins, and Kerstin Dautenhahn (2017), "The Iterative Development of the Humanoid Robot Kaspar: An Assistive Robot for Children with Autism," in Abderrahmane Kheddar, Eiichi Yoshida, Shuzhi Sam Ge, Kenji Suzuki, John-John Cabibihan, Friederike Eyssel, and Hongsheng He (eds.), *International Conference on Robotics*, Berlin: Springer, 53–63.

34. I am here reminded of a suggestion from the computer scientist and well-known sex robot researcher Kate Devlin. Devlin's suggestion is to create sex robots that do not look like human beings. (Devlin, *Turned On*, op. cit.) The Kantian principle I am discussing in this chapter might be taken to imply that the sex robots Devlin imagines could be treated like mere tools without this being morally problematic. In contrast, any sex robots made to look like humans would need—according to the Kantian principle—to be treated with some degree of respect and moral consideration, out of respect for the humanity in human beings.

35. Kant, *Metaphysics of Morals*, op. cit.

36. Thomas E. Hill (1973), "Servility and Self-Respect," *The Monist* 57(1), 87–104.

37. Kant, *Metaphysics of Morals*, op. cit., 202.

38. For related discussion, see Bartek Chomanski (2019), "What's Wrong with Designing People to Serve?," *Ethical Theory and Moral Practice*, 1–23, online first at https://link.springer.com/article/10.1007%2Fs10677-019-10029-3, and Maciej Musial (2017), "Designing (Artificial) People to Serve—The Other Side of the Coin," *Journal of Experimental & Theoretical Artificial Intelligence* 29(5), 1087–97.

39. David Gunkel (2012), *The Machine Question: Critical Perspective on AI, Robots, and Ethics*, Cambridge, MA: The MIT Press; Gunkel, *Robot Rights*, op. cit. For a nice summary of Gunkel's view, see also David Gunkel (2019), "No Brainer: Why Consciousness Is Neither a Necessary nor Sufficient Condition for AI Ethics," *TOCAIS 2019: Towards Conscious AI Systems*, http://ceur-ws.org/Vol-2287/paper9.pdf.

40. Carpenter, *Culture and Human-Robot Interaction in Militarized Spaces: A War Story*, op. cit.

41. Bryson, "Robots Should Be Slaves," op. cit., 70.

42. Mark Coeckelbergh (2015), "The Tragedy of the Master: Automation, Vulnerability, and Distance," *Ethics and Information Technology* 17(3), 219–29.

43. Uncredited (2018), "Amazon Alexa to Reward Kids Who Say: 'Please,'" BBC, https://www.bbc.com/news/technology-43897516 (Accessed on August 28, 2019).

44. Gunkel's objections overlap with arguments that Coeckelbergh gives in Mark Coeckelbergh (2010), "Robot Rights? Towards a Social-Relational Justification of Moral Consideration," *Ethics and Information Technology* 12(3), 209–21.

45. Schwitzgebel and Graza, "A Defense of the Rights of Artificial Intelligences," op. cit.

46. Mark Coeckelbergh and David Gunkel (2014), "Facing Animals: A Relational, Other-Oriented Approach to Moral Standing," *Journal of Agricultural and Environmental Ethics* 27(5), 715–33; Mark Coeckelbergh (2012), *Growing Moral Relations: Critique of Moral Status Ascriptions*, London: Palgrave Macmillan.

47. Oliver Mitchell (2018), "Jibo Social Robot: Where Things Went Wrong," *The Robot Report*, https://www.therobotreport.com/jibo-social-robot-analyzing-what-went-wrong/ (Accessed on August 28, 2019).

48. Slavoj Žižek (2002), *For They Know Not What They Do: Enjoyment as a Political Factor*, London: Verso, 209.

49. Frank and Nyholm, "Robot Sex and Consent," op. cit.

50. Cf. Harris, "Reading the Minds of Those Who Never Lived," op. cit.

51. Gunkel, "No Brainer," op. cit., 4.

52. Harris, "Reading the Minds of Those Who Never Lived," op. cit.

53. Of course, like Agar, we might think that extremely humanlike behavior—verbal or otherwise—might indicate the presence of a mind (Agar, "How to Treat Machines That Might Have Minds," op. cit.). But with simpler talking robots, we are unlikely—even Agar is probably very unlikely—to think that the chat function of the robot indicates the presence of inner feelings or any humanlike mental states.

54. Strohminger et al., "The True Self: A Psychological Concept Distinct from the Self," op. cit.

55. Uncredited (2019), "Meet ADAM, Malaysia's Own Version of Sophia the Humanoid Robot," *Malay Mail*, https://www.malaymail.com/news/malaysia/2019/07/19/meet-adam-malaysias-own-version-of-sophia-the-humanoid-robot/1772989 (Accessed on August 28, 2019).

56. Ibid.

57. Agar, "How to Treat Machines That Might Have Minds," op. cit.

58. The Twitter post can be accessed at https://twitter.com/RealSophiaRobot/status/1152267873139793922 (Accessed on July 20, 2019).

BIBLIOGRAPHY

AFP-JIJI (2018), "Love in Another Dimension: Japanese Man 'Marries' Hatsune Mike Hologram," *Japan Times*, https://www.japantimes.co.jp/news/2018/11/12/national/japanese-man-marries-virtual-reality-singer-hatsune-miku-hologram/#.XW-bIIDFaG3B (Accessed on September 4, 2019).

Agar, Nicholar (2019), "How to Treat Machines That Might Have Minds," *Philosophy and Technology*, online first, at https://link.springer.com/article/10.1007%2Fs13347-019-00357-8, 1–14.

Alfano, Mark (2013), "Identifying and Defending the Hard Core of Virtue Ethics," *Journal of Philosophical Research* 38, 233–60.

Alfano, Mark (2013), *Character as a Moral Fiction*, Cambridge: Cambridge University Press.

Alfano, Mark (2016), *Moral Psychology: An Introduction*, London: Polity.

Allen, Colin, and Wallach, Wendell (2011), "Moral Machines: Contradiction in Terms or Abdication of Human Responsibility," in Patrick Lin, Keith Abney, and G. A. Bekey (eds.), *Robot Ethics: The Ethical and Social Implications of Robotics*, Cambridge, MA: The MIT Press, 55–68.

Anderson, Michael, and Anderson, Susan Leigh (2007), "Machine Ethics: Creating an Ethical Intelligent Agent," *AI Magazine* 28(4), 15–26, at p. 15.

Andrews, Kristin (2017), "Chimpanzee Mind Reading: Don't Stop Believing," *Philosophy Compass* 12(1), e12394.

Anscombe, Elizabeth (1957), *Intention*, Oxford: Basil Blackwell.

AP (1983), "AROUND THE NATION; Jury Awards $10 Million in Killing by Robot," *New York Times*, https://www.nytimes.com/1983/08/11/us/around-the-nation-jury-awards-10-million-in-killing-by-robot.html (Accessed on August 26, 2019).

Aristotle (1999), *Nicomachean Ethics*, translated by Terence H. Irwin, Indianapolis, IN: Hackett.

Arkin, Ronald C. (1998), *Behavior-Based Robotics*, Cambridge, MA: The MIT Press.

Arkin, Ronald (2009), *Governing Lethal Behavior in Autonomous Robots*, Boca Raton, FL: CRC Press.

Arkin, Ronald (2010), "The Case for Ethical Autonomy in Unmanned Systems," *Journal of Military Ethics*, 9(4), 332–41.

Atkinson, Simon (2017), "Robot Priest: The Future of Funerals?," BBC, https://www.bbc.com/news/av/world-asia-41033669/robot-priest-the-future-of-funerals (Accessed on August 21, 2019).

Avramides, Anita (2019), "Other Minds," *The Stanford Encyclopedia of Philosophy*, Edward N. Zalta (ed.), https://plato.stanford.edu/archives/sum2019/entries/other-minds/.

Bakewell, Sarah (2016), *At the Existentialist Café: Freedom, Being, and Apricot Cocktails*, London: Other Press.

Beck, Julie (2013), "Married to a Doll: Why One Man Advocates Synthetic Love," *Atlantic*, https://www.theatlantic.com/health/archive/2013/09/married-to-a-doll-why-one-man-advocates-synthetic-love/279361/ (Accessed on August 25, 2019).

Bhuta, Nehal, Beck, Susanne, Geiß, Robin, Liu, Hin-Yan, and Kreß, Claus (2015), *Autonomous Weapons Systems: Law, Ethics, Policy*, Cambridge: Cambridge University Press.

Block, Ned (1995), "The Mind as the Software of the Brain," in Daniel N. Osherson, Lila Gleitman, Stephen M. Kosslyn, S. Smith, and Saadya Sternberg (eds.), *An Invitation to Cognitive Science, Second Edition, Volume 3*, Cambridge, MA: The MIT Press, 377–425.

Bloom, Paul (2013), *Just Babies*. New York: Crown.

Boden, Margaret et al. (2017), "Principles of Robotics: Regulating Robots in the Real World," *Connection Science* 29(2), 124–29.

Bostrom, Nick, and Ord, Toby (2006), "The Reversal Test: Eliminating Status Quo Bias in Applied Ethics," *Ethics* 116, 656–79.

Boudette, Neal E. (2019), "Despite High Hopes, Self-Driving Cars Are 'Way in the Future,'" *New York Times*, https://www.nytimes.com/2019/07/17/business/self-driving-autonomous-cars.html (Accessed on August 23, 2019).

Bradshaw-Martin, Heather, and Easton, Catherine (2014), "Autonomous or 'Driverless' Cars and Disability: A Legal and Ethical Analysis," *European Journal of Current Legal Issues* 20(3), http://webjcli.org/article/view/344/471.

Bradshaw, Jeffrey N. et al. (2013), "The Seven Deadly Myths of 'Autonomous Systems,'" *IEEE Intelligent Systems*, 2013, 2–9.

Bright, Richard (2018), "AI and Consciousness," *Interalia Magazine*, Issue 39, February 2018, available at https://www.interaliamag.org/interviews/keith-frankish/ (Accessed on August 21, 2019).

Bringsjord, Selmer, and Govindarajulu, Naveen Sundar (2018), "Artificial Intelligence," *The Stanford Encyclopedia of Philosophy* (Fall 2018 Edition), Edward N. Zalta (ed.), https://plato.stanford.edu/archives/fall2018/entries/artificial-intelligence/ (Accessed August 20, 2019).

Bromwich, Jonah Engel (2019), "Why Do We Hurt Robots? They Are Like Us, But Unlike Us, and Both Fearsome and Easy to Bully," *New York Times*, https://www.nytimes.com/2019/01/19/style/why-do-people-hurt-robots.html (Accessed on August 28, 2019).

Bryson, Joanna (2010), "Robots Should Be Slaves," in Wilks, Yorick (ed.), *Close Engagements with Artificial Companions*, Amsterdam: John Benjamins Publishing Company, 63–74.

Bryson, Joanna (2012), "A Role for Consciousness in Action Selection," *International Journal of Machine Consciousness* 4(2), 471–82.

Bryson, Joanna (2019), "Patiency Is Not a Virtue: The Design of Intelligent Systems and Systems of Ethics, *Ethics and Information Technology* 20(1), 15–26.

Burgess, Alexis, and Plunkett, David (2013), "Conceptual Ethics I-II," *Philosophy Compass* 8(12), 1091–110.

Buss, Sarah, and Westlund, Andrea (2018), "Personal Autonomy," *The Stanford Encyclopedia of Philosophy* (Spring 2018 Edition), Edward N. Zalta (ed.), https://plato.stanford.edu/archives/spr2018/entries/personal-autonomy/.

Carpenter, Julia (2016), *Culture and Human-Robot Interactions in Militarized Spaces*. London: Routledge.

Caruso, Gregg D., and Flanagan, Owen (eds.) (2018), *Neuroexistentialism: Meaning, Morals, and Purpose in the Age of Neuroscience*, Oxford: Oxford University Press.

Cheney, Dorothy L., and Seyfarth, Robert M. (1990), *How Monkeys See the World: Inside the Mind of Another Species*, Chicago: University of Chicago Press.

Chomanski, Bartek (2019), "What's Wrong with Designing People to Serve?," *Ethical Theory and Moral Practice*, 1–23, online first at: https://link.springer.com/article/10.1007%2Fs10677-019-10029-3.

Cicero, Marcus Tullius (1923), *Cicero: On Old Age, On Friendship, On Divination*, translated by W. A. Falconer, Cambridge, MA: Harvard University Press.

Clark, Andy, and Chalmers, David J. (1998), "The Extended Mind," *Analysis* 58(1), 7–19.

Clark, Margaret S., Earp, Brian D., and Crockett, Molly J. (in press), "Who Are 'We' and Why Are We Cooperating? Insights from Social Psychology," *Behavioral and Brain Sciences*.

Coeckelbergh, Mark (2010), "Moral Appearances: Emotions, Robots, and Human Morality," *Ethics and Information Technology* 12(3), 235–41.

Coeckelbergh, Mark (2010), "Robot Rights? Towards a Social-Relational Justification of Moral Consideration," *Ethics and Information Technology* 12(3), 209–21.

Coeckelbergh, Mark (2012), *Growing Moral Relations: Critique of Moral Status Ascriptions*, London: Palgrave Macmillan.

Coeckelbergh, Mark (2015), "The Tragedy of the Master: Automation, Vulnerability, and Distance," *Ethics and Information Technology* 17(3), 219–29.

Coeckelbergh, Mark (2016), "Responsibility and the Moral Phenomenonology of Using Self-Driving Cars," *Applied Artificial Intelligence*, 30(8), 748–57.

Coeckelbergh, Mark, and Gunkel, David (2014), "Facing Animals: A Relational, Other-Oriented Approach to Moral Standing," *Journal of Agricultural and Environmental Ethics* 27(5), 715–33.

Columbia University School of Engineering and Applied Science (2019), "A Step Closer to Self-Aware Machines—Engineers Create a Robot That Can Imagine Itself," *Tech Explore*, https://techxplore.com/news/2019-01-closer-self-aware-machinesengineers-robot.html (Accessed on August 26, 2019).

Coontz, Stephanie (2005), *Marriage, A History: From Obedience to Intimacy or How Love Conquered Marriage*, London: Penguin.

Culhbertson, Anthony (2019), "YouTube Removes Videos of Robots Fighting for 'Animal Cruelty,'" *The Independent*, https://www.independent.co.uk/life-style/gadgets-and-tech/news/youtube-robot-combat-videos-animal-cruelty-a9071576.html (Accessed on September 5, 2019).

Danaher, John (2016), "Robots, Law, and the Retribution Gap," *Ethics and Information Technology* 18(4), 299–309.

Danaher, John (2019), "The Rise of the Robots and the Crisis of Moral Patiency," *AI & Society* 34(1), 129–36.

Danaher, John (2017), "Robotic Rape and Robotic Child Sexual Abuse: Should They Be Criminalised?," *Criminal Law and Philosophy* 11(1), 71–95.

Danaher, John (2019), "The Robotic Disruption of Morality," *Philosophical Disquisitions*, https://philosophicaldisquisitions.blogspot.com/2019/08/the-robotic-disruption-of-morality.html (Accessed on September 2, 2019).

Danaher, John (2019), "The Philosophical Case for Robot Friendship," *Journal of Posthuman Studies* 3(1), 5–24.

Danaher, John (2019), "Welcoming Robots into the Moral Circle: A Defence of Ethical Behaviorism," *Science and Engineering Ethics*, 1–27: online first at https://link.springer.com/article/10.1007/s11948-019-00119-x.

Danaher, John and McArthur, Neil (eds.) (2017), *Robot Sex: Social and Ethical Implications*, Cambridge, MA: The MIT Press.

Danaher, John, Earp, Brian, and Sandberg, Anders (2017), "Should We Campaign Against Sex Robots?," in John Danaher and Neil McArthur (eds.), *Robot Sex: Social and Ethical Implications*, Cambridge, MA: The MIT Press, 43–72.

Darling, Kate (2016), "Extending Legal Protection to Social Robots: The Effects of Anthropomorphism, Empathy, and Violent Behavior towards Robotic Objects," in Ryan Calo, A. Michael Froomkin, and Ian Kerr (eds.), *Robot Law*, Cheltenham: Edward Elgar, 213–34.

Darling, Kate (2017), "'Who's Johnny?' Anthropological Framing in Human-Robot Interaction, Integration, and Policy," in Patrick Lin, Keith Abney, and Ryan Jenkins (eds.), *Robot Ethics 2.0: From Autonomous Cars to Artificial Intelligence*, Oxford: Oxford University Press, 173–92.

Darwall, Stephen (2006), *The Second Person Standpoint: Morality, Accountability, and Respect*, Cambridge, MA: Harvard University Press.

Davidson, Donald (1980), *Essays on Actions and Events*. Oxford: Clarendon Press.

Debus, Dorothea, "Shaping Our Mental Lives: On the Possibility of Mental Self-Regulation," *Proceedings of the Aristotelian Society* CXVI(3), 341–65.

De Graaf, Maartje (2016), "An Ethical Evaluation of Human-Robot Relationships," *International Journal of Social Robotics* 8(4), 589–98.

De Graaf, Maartje, and Malle, Bertram (2019), "People's Explanations of Robot Behavior Subtly Reveal Mental State Inferences," *International Conference on Human-Robot Interaction*, Deagu: DOI: 10.1109/HRI.2019.8673308.

De Jong, Roos (2019), "The Retribution-Gap and Responsibility-Loci Related to Robots and Automated Technologies: A Reply to Nyholm," *Science and Engineering Ethics*, 1–9, online first at: https://doi.org/10.1007/s11948-019-00120-4.

Dennett, Daniel (1987), *The Intentional Stance*, Cambridge, MA: Bradford.

Dennett, Daniel (2017), *From Bacteria to Bach and Back Again: The Evolution of Minds*, New York: W. W. Norton & Company.

Devlin, Kate (2018), *Turned On: Science, Sex and Robots*, London: Bloomsbury.

Di Nucci, Ezzio, and Santoni de Sio, Filippo (eds.) (2016), *Drones and Responsibility*. London: Routledge.

Dietrich, Eric (2001), "Homo sapiens 2.0: Why We Should Build the Better Robots of Our Nature," *Journal of Experimental & Theoretical Artificial Intelligence* 13(4), 323–28.

Dignum, Frank, Prada, Rui, and Hofstede, Gert Jan (2014), "From Autistic to Social Agents," Proceedings of the 2014 International Conference on Autonomous Agents and Multi-Agent Systems, 1161–64.

Doris, John (2005), *Lack of Character: Personality and Moral Behavior*, Cambridge: Cambridge University Press.

Doty, Joe, and Doty, Chuck (2012), "Command Responsibility and Accountability," *Military Review* 92(1), 35–38.

Driver, Julia (2001), *Uneasy Virtue*, Cambridge: Cambridge University Press.

Dworkin, Ronald (2013), *Justice for Hedgehogs*, Cambridge, MA: Harvard University Press.

Elamrani, Aïda, and Yampolskiy, Roman (2018), "Reviewing Tests for Machine Consciousness," *Journal of Consciousness Studies* 26(5–6), 35–64.

Elder, Alexis (2017), *Friendship, Robots, and Social Media: False Friends and Second Selves*, London: Routledge.

Elster, Jon (1979), *Ulysses and the Sirens: Studies in Rationality and Irrationality*, Cambridge: Cambridge University Press.

Eskens, Romy (2017), "Is Sex with Robots Rape?," *Journal of Practical Ethics* 5(2), 62–76.

Färber, Berthold (2016), "Communication and Communication Problems between Autonomous Vehicles and Human Drivers," in Markus Maurer, J. Christian Gerdes, Barbara Lenz, and Hermann Winner (eds.), *Autonomous Driving: Technical, Legal and Social Aspects*, Berlin: Springer.

Fins, Joseph (2015), *Rights Come to Mind: Brain Injury, Ethics, and the Struggle for Consciousness*, Cambridge: Cambridge University Press.

Fischer, John Martin (1994), *The Metaphysics of Free Will*, Oxford: Blackwell.

Forst, Rainer (2014), *The Right to Justification*, New York: Columbia University Press.

Floridi, Luciano, and Sanders, J. W. (2004), "On the Morality of Artificial Agents," *Minds and Machines* 14(3), 349–79.

Frank, Lily, and Nyholm, Sven (2017), "Robot Sex and Consent: Is Consent to Sex Between a Human and a Robot Conceivable, Possible, and Desirable?," *Artificial Intelligence and Law* 25(3), 305–23.

Frischmann, Brett, and Selinger, Evan (2018), *Re-Engineering Humanity*, Cambridge: Cambridge University Press.

Garber, Megan (2013), "Funerals for Fallen Robots," *The Atlantic*, https://www.theatlantic.com/technology/archive/2013/09/funerals-for-fallen-robots/279861/ (Accessed on August 21, 2019).

Gerdes, Anne (2015), "The Issue of Moral Consideration in Robot Ethics," *SIGCAS Computers & Society* 45(3), 274–79.

Gerdes, J. Christian, and Thornton, Sarah M. (2015), "Implementable Ethics for Autonomous Vehicles," in Markus Maurer, J. Christian Gerdes, Barbara Lenz, and Hermann

Winner (eds.), *Autonomous Driving: Technical, Legal and Social Aspects*, Berlin: Springer.

Gibbard, Allan (1990), *Wise Choices, Apt Feelings: A Theory of Normative Judgments*, Cambridge, MA: Harvard University Press.

Gilbert, Margaret (1990), "Walking Together: A Paradigmatic Social Phenomenon," *Midwest Studies in Philosophy*, 15(1), 1–14.

Gips, James. (1991), "Towards the Ethical Robot," in Kenneth G. Ford, Clark Glymour, and Patrick J. Hayes (eds.), *Android Epistemology*, 243–52.

Gogoll, Jan and Müller, Julian F. (2017), "Autonomous Cars: In Favor of a Mandatory Ethics Setting," *Science and Engineering Ethics* 23(3), 681–700.

Goodall, Noah. J. (2014), "Ethical Decision Making during Automated Vehicle Crashes," *Transportation Research Record: Journal of the Transportation Research Board* 2424, 58–65.

Goodall, Noah J. (2014), "Machine Ethics and Automated Vehicles," in Geroen Meyer and Sven Beiker (eds.), *Road Vehicle Automation*, Berlin: Springer, 93–102.

Govindarajulu, Naveen et al. (2019), "Toward the Engineering of Virtuous Machines," *Association for the Advancement of Artificial Intelligence*, http://www.aies-conference.com/wp-content/papers/main/AIES-19_paper_240.pdf (Accessed on August 27, 2019).

Gray, Heather M., Gray, Kurt, and Wegner, Daniel M. (2007), "Dimensions of Mind Perception," *Science* 315(5812), 619.

Greene, Joshua (2013), *Moral Tribes: Emotion, Reason, and the Gap between Us and Them*, London: Penguin.

Greene, Joshua, and Cohen, Jonathan (2004), "For the Law, Neuroscience Changes Nothing and Everything," *Philosophical Transactions of the Royal Society* 359: 1775–85.

Grill, Kalle, and Nihlén Fahlquist, Jessica (2012), "Responsibility, Paternalism and Alcohol Interlocks," *Public Health Ethics*, 5(2), 116–27.

Gunkel, David (2012), *The Machine Question: Critical Perspective on AI, Robots, and Ethics*, Cambridge, MA: The MIT Press.

Gunkel, David (2018), *Robot Rights*, Cambridge, MA: The MIT Press.

Gunkel, David (2019), "No Brainer: Why Consciousness Is Neither a Necessary nor Sufficient Condition for AI Ethics," *TOCAIS 2019: Towards Conscious AI Systems*, http://ceur-ws.org/Vol-2287/paper9.pdf.

Gurney, J. K. (2013), "Sue My Car Not Me: Products Liability and Accidents Involving Autonomous Vehicles," *Journal of Law, Technology & Policy* 2, 247–77.

Gurney, J. K. (2015), "Driving into the Unknown: Examining the Crossroads of Criminal Law and Autonomous Vehicles," *Wake Forest Journal of Law and Policy*, 5(2), 393–442.

Gurney, Jeffrey K. (2016), "Crashing into the Unknown: An Examination of Crash-Optimization Algorithms through the Two Lanes of Ethics and Law," *Alabama Law Review* 79(1), 183–267.

Gurney, Jeffrey K. (2017), "Imputing Driverhood: Applying a Reasonable Driver Standard to Accidents Caused by Autonomous Vehicles," in Patrick Lin, Keith Abney, and Ryan Jenkins (eds.), *Robot Ethics 2.0: From Autonomous Cars to Artificial Intelligence*, Oxford: Oxford University Press, 51–65.

Hao, Karen (2018), "The UK Parliament Asking a Robot to Testify about AI Is a Dumb Idea," *Technology Review*, https://www.technologyreview.com/the-download/612269/the-uk-parliament-asking-a-robot-to-testify-about-ai-is-a-dumb-idea/ (Accessed on December 27, 2018).

Harman, Gilbert (1999), "Moral Philosophy Meets Social Psychology: Virtue Ethics and the Fundamental Attribution Error," *Proceedings of the Aristotelian Society* 99, 315–31.

Harman, Gilbert (2009), "Skepticism about Character Traits," *Journal of Ethics* 13(2–3), 235–42.

Harris, John (2016), *How to Be Good: The Possibility of Moral Enhancement*, Oxford: Oxford University Press.

Harris, John (2019), "Reading the Minds of Those Who Never Lived. Enhanced Beings: The Social and Ethical Challenges Posed by Super Intelligent AI and Reasonably Intelligent Humans," *Cambridge Quarterly of Healthcare Ethics* 8(4), 585–91.

Hart, Henry, and Sachs, Albert (1994), *The Legal Process*, Eagan, MN: Foundation Press.

Hassin, Ran R., Uleman, James S., and Bargh, John A. (eds.) (2006), *The New Unconscious*, New York: Oxford University Press.

Hawkins, Andrew J. (2019), "Tesla's Autopilot Was Engaged When Model 3 Crashed into Truck, Report States: It Is at Least the Fourth Fatal Crash Involving Autopilot," *The Verve*, https://www.theverge.com/2019/5/16/18627766/tesla-autopilot-fatal-crash-delray-florida-ntsb-model-3 (Accessed on August 23, 2019).

Heider, Fritz, and Simmel, Marianne (1944), "An Experimental Study of Apparent Behavior," *American Journal of Psychology* 57(2), 243–59.

Heikoop, Daniel, Hagenzieker, Marjan P., Mecacci, Giulio, Calvert, Simeon, Santoni de Sio, Filippo, and van Arem, B. (2019), "Human Behaviour with Automated Driving Systems: A Qualitative Framework for Meaningful Human Control," *Theoretical Issues in Ergonomics Science*, online first at https://www.tandfonline.com/doi/full/10.1080/1463922X.2019.1574931.

Hevelke, Alexander, and Nida-Rümelin, Julian (2015), "Responsibility for Crashes of Autonomous Vehicles: An Ethical Analysis," *Science and Engineering Ethics*, 21(3), 619–30.

Heyes, Cecilia (2018), *Cognitive Gadgets: The Cultural Evolution of Thinking*, Cambridge, MA: Belknap Press.

Hill, Thomas E. (1973), "Servility and Self-Respect," *The Monist* 57(1), 87–104.

Himma, Kenneth Einar (2009), "Artificial Agency, Consciousness, and the Criteria for Moral Agency: What Properties Must an Artificial Agent Have to Be a Moral Agent?", *Ethics and Information Technology* 11(1), 19–29.

Hume, David (1826), *A Collection of the Most Instructive and Amusing Lives Ever Published, Written by the Parties Themselves, Volume II: Hume, Lilly, Voltaire*, London: Hunt and Clarke.

Hume, David (1983), *An Enquiry concerning the Principles of Morals*, edited by J. B. Schneewind, Indianapolis, IN: Hackett.

Hursthouse, Rosalind (1999), *On Virtue Ethics*, Oxford: Oxford University Press.

Husak, Douglas (2010), "Vehicles and Crashes: Why Is This Issue Overlooked?" *Social Theory and Practice* 30(3), 351–70.

Ingrassia, Paul (2014), "Look, No Hands! Test Driving a Google Car," *Reuters*, https://www.reuters.com/article/us-google-driverless-idUSKBN0GH02P20140817 (Accessed on August 23, 2019).

Jacob, Pierre (2019), "Intentionality," *The Stanford Encyclopedia of Philosophy* (Spring 2019 Edition), Edward N. Zalta (ed.), htps://plato.stanford.edu/archives/spr2019/entries/intentionality/.

Johnson, Deborah G., and Verdicchio, Mario (2018), "Why Robots Should Not Be Treated Like Animals," *Ethics and Information Technology* 20(4), 291–301.

Kahane, Guy (2011), "Evolutionary Debunking Arguments," *Noûs* 45(1), 103–25.

Kahneman, Daniel (2011), *Thinking, Fast and Slow*, London: Penguin.

Kant, Immanuel (1996), *The Metaphysics of Morals (Cambridge Texts in the History of Philosophy)*, edited by Mary Gregor, Cambridge: Cambridge University Press.

Kant, Immanuel (2006), *Anthropology from a Pragmatic Point of View*, edited by Robert E. Louden, Cambridge: Cambridge University Press.

Kant, Immanuel (2012), *Immanuel Kant: Groundwork of the Metaphysics of Morals, A German-English Edition*, edited by Mary Gregor and Jens Timmermann, Cambridge: Cambridge University Press.

Korsgaard, Christine (1996), *The Sources of Normativity*, Cambridge: Cambridge University Press.

Korsgaard, Christine (2010), *Self-Constitution*, Oxford: Oxford University Press.

Kuflik, Arthur (1999), "Computers in Control: Rational Transfer of Authority or Irresponsible Abdication of Autonomy?," *Ethics and Information Technology* 1(3), 173–84.

Kuhlmeier, Valerie A. (2013), "The Social Perception of Helping and Hindering," in M. D. Rutherford and Valerie A. Kuhlmeier, *Social Perception: Detection and Interpretation of Animacy, Agency, and Intention*, Cambridge, MA: The MIT Press, 283–304.

Kurzweil, Ray (2005), *The Singularity Is Near: When Humans Transcend Biology*, London: Penguin Books.

Kwiatkowski, Robert, and Lipson, Hod (2019), "Task-Agnostic Self-Modeling Machines," *Science Robotics* 4(26), eaau9354.

Lai, Frank, Carsten, Oliver, and Tate, Fergus (2012), "How Much Benefit Does Intelligent Speed Adaptation Deliver: An Analysis of Its Potential Contribution to Safety and the Environment," *Accident Analysis & Prevention* 48, 63–72.

LeBeau, Phil (2016), "Google's Self-Driving Car Caused an Accident, So What Now?," *CNBC*, https://www.cnbc.com/2016/02/29/googles-self-driving-car-caused-an-accident-so-what-now.html (Accessed on August 22, 2019).

Lee, Minha, Lucas, Gale, Mell, Jonathan, Johnson, Emmanuel, and Gratch, Jonathan (2019), "What's on Your Virtual Mind?: Mind Perception in Human-Agent Negotiations," *Proceeding of the 19th ACM International Conference on Intelligent Virtual Agents*, 38–45.

Lenman, James (2008), "Contractualism and Risk Imposition," *Politics, Philosophy & Economics*, 7(1), 99–122.

Levin, Janet (2018), "Functionalism," *The Stanford Encyclopedia of Philosophy*, Edward N. Zalta (ed.), https://plato.stanford.edu/archives/fall2018/entries/functionalism/.

Levin, Sam, and Wong, Julie Carrie (2018), "Self-Driving Uber Kills Arizona Woman in First Fatal Crash involving Pedestrian," *The Guardian*, https://www.theguardian.com/technology/2018/mar/19/uber-self-driving-car-kills-woman-arizona-tempe (Accessed on August 22, 2019).

Levy, David (2008), *Love and Sex with Robots: The Evolution of Human-Robot Relationships*, New York: Harper Perennial.

Lewens, Tim (2018), "Cultural Evolution," *The Stanford Encyclopedia of Philosophy*, Edward N. Zalta (ed.), https://plato.stanford.edu/archives/sum2018/entries/evolution-cultural/.

Lin, Patrick (2015), "Why Ethics Matters for Autonomous Cars," in Markus Maurer, J. Christian Gerdes, Barbara Lenz, and Hermann Winner (eds.), *Autonomes Fahren: Technische, rechtliche und gesellschaftliche Aspekte*, Berlin: Springer, 69–85.

List, Christian, and Pettit, Philip (2011), *Group Agency: The Possibility, Design, and Status of Corporate Agents*, Oxford: Oxford University Press.

List, Christian (2019), *Why Free Will Is Real*, Cambridge, MA: Harvard University Press.

Louden, Robert B. (1986), "Kant's Virtue Ethics," *Philosophy* 61(238), 473–89.

Lynch, Michael P. (2016), *The Internet of Us: Knowing More and Understanding Less*, New York: Liveright.

Marchant, Gary, and Lindor, Rachel (2012), "The Coming Collision between Autonomous Cars and the Liability System," *Santa Clara Legal Review*, 52(4), 1321–40.

Marchesi, Serena et al. (2019), "Do We Adopt the Intentional Stance Toward Humanoid Robots?," *Frontiers in Psychology* Volume 10, Article 450, 1–13.

Malle, Bertram (2015), "Integrating Robot Ethics and Machine Morality: The Study and Design of Moral Competence in Robots," *Ethics and Information Technology* 18(4), 243–55.

Matthias, Andreas (2004), "The Responsibility Gap: Ascribing Responsibility for the Actions of Learning Automata," *Ethics and Information Technology* 6(3), 175–83.

McCurry, Justin (2015), "Erica, the 'Most Beautiful and Intelligent' Android, Leads Japan's Robot Revolution," *The Guardian*, https://www.theguardian.com/technology/2015/dec/31/erica-the-most-beautiful-and-intelligent-android-ever-leads-japans-robot-revolution (Accessed on August 30, 2019).

Metzinger, Thomas (2013), "Two Principles for Robot Ethics," in Eric Hilgendorf and Jan-Philipp Günther (eds.), *Robotik und Gesetzgebung*, Baden-Baden: Nomos.

Mill, John Stuart (2001), *Utilitarianism, Second Edition*, edited by George Sher, Indianapolis, IN: Hackett.

Miller, Christian (2017), *The Character Gap: How Good Are We?*, Oxford: Oxford University Press.

Mindell, David (2015), *Our Robots, Ourselves: Robotics and the Myths of Autonomy*, New York: Viking.

Mitchell, Oliver (2018), "Jibo Social Robot: Where Things Went Wrong," *The Robot Report*, https://www.therobotreport.com/jibo-social-robot-analyzing-what-went-wrong/ (Accessed on August 28, 2019).

de Montaigne, Michel (1958), *The Complete Essays of Montaigne*, Palo Alto, CA: Stanford University Press.

Moor, James (2006), "The Nature, Importance, and Difficulty of Machine Ethics," *IEEE Intelligent Systems* 21, 18–21.

Mori, Masahiro (2012), "The Uncanny Valley," *IEEE Robotics & Automation Magazine* 19(2), 98–100.

Müller, Sabine, Bittlinger, Merlin, & Walter, Henrik (2017), "Threats to Neurosurgical Patients Posed by the Personal Identity Debate," *Neuroethics* 10(2), 299–310.

Musial, Maciej (2017), "Designing (Artificial) People to Serve—The Other Side of the Coin," *Journal of Experimental & Theoretical Artificial Intelligence* 29(5), 1087–97.

Nagel, Thomas (1974), "What Is It Like to Be a Bat?", *Philosophical Review* 83(4), 435–50.

Naughton, Keith (2015), "Humans Are Slamming into Driverless Cars and Exposing a Key Flaw," *Bloomberg*, https://www.bloomberg.com/news/articles/2015-12-18/humans-are-slamming-into-driverless-cars-and-exposing-a-key-flaw (Accessed on August 23, 2019).

Nechepurenko, Ivan (2018), "A Talking, Dancing Robot? No, It Was Just a Man in a Suit," *New York Times*, https://www.nytimes.com/2018/12/13/world/europe/russia-robot-costume.html (Accessed on September 4, 2019).

Neely, Erica L. (2013), "Machines and the Moral Community," *Machines and the Moral Community* 27(1), 97–111.

Nyholm, Sven (2017), "Do We Always Act on Maxims?," *Kantian Review* 22(2), 233–55.

Nyholm, Sven (2018), "Is the Personal Identity Debate a 'Threat' to Neurosurgical Patients? A Reply to Müller et al.," *Neuroethics* 11(2), 229–35.

Nyholm, Sven (2018), "The Ethics of Crashes with Self-Driving Cars: A Roadmap, I," *Philosophy Compass* 13(7), e12507.

Nyholm, Sven (2018), "The Ethics of Crashes with Self-Driving Cars, A Roadmap, II," *Philosophy Compass* 13(7), e12506.

Nyholm, Sven (2018), "Teaching & Learning Guide for: The Ethics of Crashes with Self-Driving Cars: A Roadmap, I-II," *Philosophy Compass* 13(7), e12508.

Nyholm, Sven (2019), "Other Minds, Other Intelligences: The Problem of Attributing Agency to Machines," *Cambridge Quarterly of Healthcare Ethics* 28(4), 592–98.

Nyholm, Sven, and Frank, Lily (2017), "From Sex Robots to Love Robots: Is Mutual Love with a Robot Possible?", in Danaher and McArthur, *Robot Sex: Social and Ethical Implications*, Cambridge, MA: The MIT Press.

Nyholm, Sven, and Frank, Lily (2019), "It Loves Me, It Loves Me Not: Is It Morally Problematic to Design Sex Robots That Appear to 'Love' Their Owners?," *Techné: Research in Philosophy and Technology* 23(3): 402–24.

Nyholm, Sven, and Smids, Jilles (2016), "The Ethics of Accident-Algorithms for Self-Driving Cars: An Applied Trolley Problem?," *Ethical Theory and Moral Practice* 19(5), 1275–89.

Nyholm, Sven, and Smids, Jilles (in press), "Automated Cars Meet Human Drivers: Responsible Human-Robot Coordination and the Ethics of Mixed Traffic," *Ethics and Information Technology*, 1–10: https://link.springer.com/article/10.1007/s10676-018-9445-9.

Olson, Eric T. (2004), *What Are We? A Study in Personal Ontology*, Oxford: Oxford University Press.

Oppy, Graham, and Dowe, David (2019), "The Turing Test," *The Stanford Encyclopedia of Philosophy*, Edward N. Zalta (ed.), https://plato.stanford.edu/archives/spr2019/entries/turing-test/.

Parfit, Derek (2011), *On What Matters, Volume One*, Oxford: Oxford University Press.

Parfit, Derek (2012), "We Are Not Human Beings," *Philosophy* 87(1), 5–28.

Parke, Phoebe (2015), "Is It Cruel to Kick a Robot Dog?," *CNN Edition*, https://edition.cnn.com/2015/02/13/tech/spot-robot-dog-google/index.html (Accessed on July 18, 2019).

Parnell, Brid-Aine (2019), "Robot, Know Thyself: Engineers Build a Robotic Arm That Can Imagine Its Own Self-Image," *Forbes*, https://www.forbes.com/sites/bridaineparnell/2019/

01/31/robot-know-thyself-engineers-build-a-robotic-arm-that-can-imagine-its-own-self-image/#33a358274ee3 (Accessed on August 26, 2019).

Pariser, Eli (2011), *The Filter Bubble: How the New Personalized Web Is Changing What We Read and How We Think*, London: Penguin.

Penrose, Roger (1989), *The Emperor's New Mind: Concerning Computers, Minds and the Laws of Physics*, Oxford: Oxford University Press.

Persson, Ingmar, and Savulescu, Julian (2012), *Unfit for the Future*, Oxford: Oxford University Press.

Peterson, Andrew, and Bayne, Tim (2017), "A Taxonomy for Disorders of Consciousness That Takes Consciousness Seriously," *AJOB Neuroscience* 8(3), 153–55.

Peterson, Andrew, and Bayne, Tim (2018), "Post-Comatose Disorders of Consciousness," in Rocco J. Gennaro (ed.), *Routledge Handbook of Consciousness*, New York: Routledge, 351–65.

Peterson, Robert W. (2012), "New Technology—Old Law: Autonomous Vehicles and California's Insurance Framework," *Santa Clara Law Review* 52, 101–53.

Peterson, Steve (2007), "The Ethics of Robot Servitude," *Journal of Experimental and Theoretical Artificial Intelligence* 19(1), 43–54.

Peterson, Steve (2017), "Designing People to Serve," in Patrick Lin, Keith Abney, and Ryan Jenkins (eds.), *Robot Ethics 2.0: From Autonomous Cars to Artificial Intelligence*, Oxford: Oxford University Press, 283–98.

Peterson, Steve (2017), "Is It Good for Them Too? Ethical Concern for the Sexbots," in John Danaher and Neil McArthur (eds.), *Robot Sex: Social and Ethical Implications*, Cambridge, MA: The MIT Press, 155–72.

Pettigrew, Richard (2013), "Epistemic Utility and Norms for Credences," *Philosophy Compass*, 8(10), 897–908.

Pettit, Philip (1990), "The Reality of Rule-Following," *Mind, New Series* 99(393), 1–21.

Pettit, Philip (1997), *Republicanism: A Theory Government*, Oxford: Oxford University Press.

Pettit, Philip (2007), "Responsibility Incorporated," *Ethics*, 117(2), 171–201.

Pettit, Philip (2012), *On the People's Terms*, Cambridge: Cambridge University Press.

Pettit, Philip (2014), *Just Freedom: A Moral Compass for a Complex World*, New York: Norton.

Pettit, Philip (2015), *The Robust Demands of the Good: Ethics with Attachment, Virtue, and Respect*, Oxford: Oxford University Press.

Pinker, Steven (2002), *The Blank Slate: The Modern Denial of Human Nature*, New York: Viking.

Purves, Duncan, Jenkins, Ryan, and Strawser, B. J. (2015), "Autonomous Machines, Moral Judgment, and Acting for the Right Reasons," *Ethical Theory and Moral Practice* 18(4), 851–72.

Railton, Peter (2009), "Practical Competence and Fluent Agency," in David Sobel and Steven Wall (eds.), *Reasons for Action*, Cambridge: Cambridge University Press, 81–115.

Rani, Anita (2013), "The Japanese Men Who Prefer Virtual Girlfriends to Sex," *BBC News Magazine*, http://www.bbc.com/news/magazine-24614830 (Accessed on August 25, 2019).

Ravid, Orly (2014), "Don't Sue Me, I Was Just Lawfully Texting and Drunk When My Autonomous Car Crashed into You," *Southwest Law Review* 44(1), 175–207.

Richards, Norvin (2010), *The Ethics of Parenthood*, Oxford: Oxford University Press.

Richardson, Kathleen (2015), "The Asymmetrical 'Relationship': Parallels between Prostitution and the Development of Sex Robots," *SIGCAS Computers & Society* 45(3), 290–93.

Roeser, Sabine (2018), *Risk, Technology, and Moral Emotions*, London: Routledge.

Romero, Simon (2018), "Wielding Rocks and Knives, Arizonans Attack Self-Driving Cars," *New York Times*, https://www.nytimes.com/2018/12/31/us/waymo-self-driving-cars-arizona-attacks.html (Accessed on August 23, 2019).

Rosen, Michael (2012), *Dignity*, Cambridge, MA: Harvard University Press.

Roth, Andrew (2018), "'Hi-Tech Robot' at Russia Forum Turns Out to Be Man in Suit," *The Guardian*, https://www.theguardian.com/world/2018/dec/12/high-tech-robot-at-russia-forum-turns-out-to-be-man-in-robot-suit (Accessed on September 4, 2019).

Rousseau, Jean-Jacques (1997), *The Social Contract and Other Political Writings*, edited and translated by Victor Gourevitch, Cambridge: Cambridge University Press.

Royakkers, Lambèr, and van Est, Rinie (2015), *Just Ordinary Robots: Automation from Love to War*, Boca Raton, FL: CRC Press.

Rubel, Alan, Pham, Adam, and Castro, Clinton (2019), "Agency Laundering and Algorithmic Decision Systems," in Natalie Greene Taylor, Caitlin Christiam-Lamb, Michelle H. Martin, and Bonnie A. Nardi (eds.), *Information in Contemporary Society*, Dordrecht: Springer, 590–600.

Russell, Stuart, and Norvig, Peter (2009), *Artificial Intelligence: A Modern Approach, 3rd edition*, Saddle River, NJ: Prentice Hall.

Russell, Stuart (2016), "Should We Fear Supersmart Robots?," *Scientific American* 314, 58–59.

Santoni de Sio, Filippo, and Van den Hoven, Jeroen (2018), "Meaningful Human Control over Autonomous Systems: A Philosophical Account," *Frontiers in Robotics and AI*, https://www.frontiersin.org/articles/10.3389/frobt.2018.00015/full.

Sartre, Jean-Paul (2007), *Existentialism Is a Humanism*, translated by Carol Macomber, New Haven, CT: Yale University Press.

Scanlon, T. M. (1998), *What We Owe to Each Other*, Cambridge, MA: Harvard University Press.

Schlosser, Markus (2015), "Agency," *The Stanford Encyclopedia of Philosophy* (Fall 2015 Edition), Edward N. Zalta (ed.), https://plato.stanford.edu/archives/fall2015/entries/agency/ (Accessed on August 21, 2019).

Schoettle, B., and Sivak, M. (2015), "A Preliminary Analysis of Real-World Crashes Involving Self-Driving Vehicles" (No. UMTRI-2015-34), Ann Arbor: The University of Michigan Transportation Research Institute.

Schwitzgebel, Eric, and Garza, Mara (2015), "A Defense of the Rights of Artificial Intelligences," *Midwest Studies in Philosophy* 39(1), 98–119.

Searle, John (1990), "Is the Brain's Mind a Computer Program?," *Scientific American* 262(1), 26–31.

Sharkey, Noel (2018), "Mama Mia, It's Sophia: A Show Robot or Dangerous Platform to Mislead?," *Forbes*, https://www.forbes.com/sites/noelsharkey/2018/11/17/mama-mia-its-sophia-a-show-robot-or-dangerous-platform-to-mislead/#407e37877ac9 (Accessed on December 27, 2018).

Sharkey, Noel, and Sharkey, Amanda (2010), "The Crying Shame of Robot Nannies: An Ethical Appraisal," *Interaction Studies: Social Behaviour and Communication in Biological and Artificial Systems* 11(2), 161–90.

Shumaker, Robert W., Walkup, Kristina R., and Beck, Benjamin B. (2011), *Animal Tool Behavior: The Use and Manufacture of Tools by Animals*, Baltimore: Johns Hopkins University Press.

Simon, Herbert A. (1956), "Rational Choice and the Structure of the Environment," *Psychological Review* 63(2), 129–38.

Sivak, Michael, and Schoettle, Brandon (2015), "Road Safety with Self-Driving Vehicles: General Limitations and Road Sharing with Conventional Vehicles," *Deep Blue*, http://deepblue.lib.umich.edu/handle/2027.42/111735.

Skinner, Quentin (1997), *Liberty before Liberalism*, Cambridge: Cambridge University Press.

Smids, Jilles (2018), "The Moral Case for Intelligent Speed Adaptation," *Journal of Applied Philosophy* 35(2), 205–21.

Sparrow, Robert (2004), "The Turing Triage Test," *Ethics and Information Technology* 6(4), 203–13.

Sparrow, Robert (2007), "Killer Robots," *Journal of Applied Philosophy* 24(1), 62–77.

Sparrow, Robert (2011), "Can Machines Be People? Reflections on the Turing Triage Test," in Patrick Lin, Keith Abney, and G. A. Bekey (eds.), *Robot Ethics: The Ethical and Social Implications of Robotics*, Cambridge, MA: The MIT Press, 301–16.

Sparrow, Robert (2014), "Better Living Through Chemistry? A Reply to Savulescu and Persson on 'Moral Enhancement,'" *Journal of Applied Philosophy* 31(1), 23–32.

Sparrow, Robert, and Howard, Mark (2017), "When Human Beings Are Like Drunk Robots: Driverless Vehicles, Ethics, and the Future of Transport," *Transport Research Part C: Emerging Technologies* 80: 206–15.

Strange, Adario (2017), "Robot Performing Japanese Funeral Rites Shows No One's Job Is Safe," *Mashable*, https://mashable.com/2017/08/26/pepper-robot-funeral-ceremony-japan/?europe=true (Accessed on August 21, 2019).

Strohminger, Nina, Knobe, Joshua, and Newman, George (2017), "The True Self: A Psychological Concept Distinct from the Self," *Perspectives on Psychological Science* 12(4), 551–60.

Sung, Ja-Young, Guo, Lan, Grinter, Rebecca E., and Christensen, Henrik I. (2007), "'My Roomba Is Rambo': Intimate Home Appliances," in John Krumm, Gregory D. Abowd, Aruna Seneviratne, and Thomas Strang (eds.), *UbiComp 2007: Ubiquitous Computing*, Berlin: Springer, 145–62.

Talbot, Brian, Jenkins, Ryan, and Purves, Duncan (2017), "When Reasons Should Do the Wrong Thing," in Patrick Lin, Keith Abney, and Ryan Jenkins (eds.), *Robot Ethics 2.0: From Autonomous Cars to Artificial Intelligence*, Oxford: Oxford University Press, 258–73.

The Tesla Team, "A Tragic Loss," *Tesla Blog*, https://www.tesla.com/blog/tragic-loss (Accessed on August 22, 2019).

Tigard, Daniel (forthcoming), "Artificial Moral Responsibility: How We Can and Cannot Hold Machines Responsible," *Cambridge Quarterly in Healthcare Ethics*.

Turing, Alan M. (1950), "Computing Machinery and Intelligence," *Mind* 49: 433–60.

Turkle, Sherry (2011), *Alone Together: Why We Expect More from Technology and Less from Each Other*, New York: Basic Books.

Turner, Jacob (2019), *Robot Rules: Regulating Artificial Intelligence*, Cham: Palgrave Macmillan.

Uncredited (2015), "Court Upholds Ontario Truck Speed Limiter Law," *Today's Trucking*, https://www.todaystrucking.com/court-upholds-ontario-truck-speed-limiter-law/ (Accessed on August 23, 2019).

Uncredited (2017), "Saudi Arabia Is First Country in the World to Grant a Robot Citizenship," Press Release, October 26, 2017, https://cic.org.sa/2017/10/saudi-arabia-is-first-country-in-the-world-to-grant-a-robot-citizenship/ (Accessed on December 27, 2018).

Uncredited (2018), "Robot Turns Out to Be Man in Suit," *BBC News*, https://www.bbc.com/news/technology-46538126 (Accessed on September 4, 2019).

Uncredited (2018), "Amazon Alexa to Reward Kids Who Say: 'Please,'" BBC, https://www.bbc.com/news/technology-43897516 (Accessed on August 28, 2019).

Uncredited (2019), "Road Safety: UK Set to Adopt Vehicle Speed Limiters," BBC, https://www.bbc.com/news/business-47715415 (Accessed on August 23, 2019).

Uncredited (2019), "Meet ADAM, Malaysia's Own Version of Sophia the Humanoid Robot," *Malay Mail*, https://www.malaymail.com/news/malaysia/2019/07/19/meet-adam-malaysias-own-version-of-sophia-the-humanoid-robot/1772989 (Accessed on August 28, 2019).

US Department of Defense Science Board (2012). "The Role of Autonomy in DoD Systems," https://fas.org/irp/agency/dod/dsb/autonomy.pdf (Accessed on August 22, 2019).

Urmson, Chris (2015), "How a Self-Driving Car Sees the World," *Ted*, https://www.ted.com/talks/chris_urmson_how_a_driverless_car_sees_the_road/transcript (Accessed on August 22, 2019).

Van de Molengraft, René (2019), "Lazy Robotics," Keynote Presentation at *Robotics Technology Symposium 2019*, Eindhoven University of Technology, January 24, 2019.

Van Gaal, Judith (2013), "RoboCup, Máxima onder de indruk von robotica," *Cursor*, https://www.cursor.tue.nl/nieuws/2013/juni/robocup-maxima-onder-de-indruk-van-robotica/ (Accessed on August 21, 2019).

Van Loon, Roald J., and Martens, Marieke H. (2015), "Automated Driving and Its Effect on the Safety Ecosystem: How Do Compatibility Issues Affect the Transition Period?," *Procedia Manufacturing* 3, 3280–85.

Van Wynsberghe, Aimee, and Robbins, Scott (2018), "Critiquing the Reasons for Making Artificial Moral Agents," *Science and Engineering Ethics* 25(3), 719–35.

Verbeek, Peter-Paul (2011), *Moralizing Technology: Understanding and Designing the Morality of Things*, Chicago: University of Chicago Press.

Vincent, James (2017), "Pretending to Give a Robot Citizenship Helps No One," *The Verve*, https://www.theverge.com/2017/10/30/16552006/robot-rights-citizenship-saudi-arabia-sophia (Accessed on December 27, 2018).

Wachenfeld, Walther et al. (2015), "Use Cases for Autonomous Driving," in Markus Maurer, J. Christian Gerdes, Barbara Lenz, and Hermann Winner (eds.), *Autonomous Driving: Technical, Legal and Social Aspects*, Berlin: Springer.

Wagter, Herman (2016), "Naughty Software," presentation at *Ethics: Responsible Driving Automation*, at Connekt, Delft.

Wakabayashi, Daisuke, and Conger, Kate (2018), "Uber's Self-Driving Cars Are Set to Return in a Downsized Test," *New York Times*, https://www.nytimes.com/2018/12/05/technology/uber-self-driving-cars.html (Accessed on August 22, 2019).

Wakefield, Jane (2018), "Robot 'Talks' to MPs about Future of AI in the Classroom," BBC, https://www.bbc.com/news/technology-45879961 (Accessed on August 21, 2019).

Waldron, Jeremy (2012), *Dignity, Rank, and Rights*, Oxford: Oxford University Press.

Wallach, Wendell, and Allen, Colin, *Moral Machines: Teaching Robots Right from Wrong*, Oxford: Oxford University Press, 14.

Weaver, John Frank (2013), *Robots Are People Too: How Siri, Google Car, and Artificial Intelligence Will Force Us to Change Our Laws*, Santa Barbara, CA: Praeger.

Wiegman, Isaac (2017), "The Evolution of Retribution: Intuitions Undermined," *Pacific Philosophical Quarterly* 98, 193–218.

Williams, Bernard (1982), *Moral Luck*, Cambridge: Cambridge University Press.

Winch, Peter (1981), "Eine Einstellung zur Seele," *Proceedings of the Aristotelian Society* 81(1), 1–16.

Winfield, Alan (2012), *Robotics, A Very Short Introduction*, Oxford: Oxford University Press.

Wittgenstein, Ludwig (2009), *Philosophical Investigations*, Oxford: Wiley Blackwell.

Wolf, Ingo (2016), "The Interaction between Humans and Autonomous Agents," in Markus Maurer, J. Christian Gerdes, Barbara Lenz, and Hermann Winner, (eds.), *Autonomous Driving: Technical, Legal and Social Aspects*, Berlin: Springer.

Wollstonecraft, Mary (2009), *A Vindication of the Rights of Woman*, New York: Norton & Company.

Wood, Luke J. et al. (2017), "The Iterative Development of the Humanoid Robot Kaspar: An Assistive Robot for Children with Autism," in Abderrahmane Kheddar, Eiichi Yoshida, Shuzhi Sam Ge, Kenji Suzuki, John-John Cabibihan, Friederike Eyssel, and Hongsheng He (eds.), *International Conference on Robotics*, Berlin: Springer, 53–63.

Yampolskiy, Roman (2017), "Detecting Qualia in Natural and Artificial Agents," available at https://arxiv.org/abs/1712.04020 (Accessed on September 6, 2019).

Yeung, Karen (2011), "Can We Employ Design-Based Regulation While Avoiding Brave New World?," *Law Innovation and Technology* 3(1), 1–29.

Yuan, Quan, Gao, Yan, and Li, Yibing (2016), "Suppose Future Traffic Accidents Based on Development of Self-Driving Vehicles," in Shengzhao Long and Balbir S. Dhillon (eds.), *Man-Machine-Environment System Engineering*, New York: Springer.

Žižek, Slavoj (2002), *For They Know Not What They Do: Enjoyment as a Political Factor*, London: Verso.

INDEX

ABOUT THE AUTHOR

Sven Nyholm's 2012 dissertation (from the University of Michigan) won the Proquest Distinguished Dissertation Award, and was published in book form by De Gruyter. Nyholm's articles have appeared in general philosophy journals, ethics journals, philosophy of technology journals, and bioethics journals. He writes about ethical theory, human self-understanding, and emerging technologies. He is currently Assistant Professor of Philosophical Ethics at Utrecht University.